Narrative Justice

Narrative Justice

Rafe McGregor

ROWMAN &
LITTLEFIELD
INTERNATIONAL

Lanham • Boulder • New York • London

Published by Rowman & Littlefield International Ltd
Unit A, Whitacre Mews, 26-34 Stannary Street, London SE11 4AB
www.rowmaninternational.com

Rowman & Littlefield International Ltd. is an affiliate of Rowman & Littlefield
4501 Forbes Boulevard, Suite 200, Lanham, Maryland 20706, USA
With additional offices in Boulder, New York, Toronto (Canada), and Plymouth (UK)
www.rowman.com

British Library Cataloguing in Publication Data
A catalogue record for this book is available from the British Library

ISBN: HB 978-1-7866-0633-4

Library of Congress Cataloging-in-Publication Data

Names: McGregor, Rafe, author.
Title: Narrative justice / Rafe McGregor.
Description: London ; New York : Rowman & Littlefield International, Ltd.,
  [2018] | Includes bibliographical references and index.
Identifiers: LCCN 2018019855 (print) | LCCN 2018032254 (ebook) | ISBN
  9781786606341 (Electronic) | ISBN 9781786606334 (hb : alk. paper)
Subjects: LCSH: Criminology. | Criminal behavior. | Narrative inquiry
  (Research method) | Justice, Administration of—Moral and ethical aspects.
Classification: LCC HV6025 (ebook) | LCC HV6025 .M3755 2018 (print) | DDC
  364.01—dc23
LC record available at https://lccn.loc.gov/2018019855

Printed in the United States of America

Contents

Preface

Watching Ridley Scott's *Blade Runner* at the drive-in—probably in late 1982, the year of its release—is one of my first memories of the big screen. At the time, my main interest on the small screen was cop shows rather than sci-fi, and my parents had told me that *Blade Runner* was a cop movie set in the future in order to pique my interest. I understood that "cop movie" referred to a particular type of story, that "sci-fi" referred to a particular type of setting, and that *Blade Runner* could in consequence be accurately categorised as either. What I did not understand—and would only come to understand once I had seen a different version of the film and grasped some of the complexities of philosophical value theory—was that *Blade Runner* was also telling me something about the difference between biological and evaluative humanity and that it was providing this knowledge in a very special way. It is that special way I want to articulate here, in anticipation of the chapters to follow, which take what we can do with the knowledge provided in a special way as their central subject. I say a *special* way because I believe the way in which *Blade Runner* provides knowledge is rare, albeit not unique to the film (or unique to cinematic representation more generally). To make an obvious comparison, Denis Villeneuve's sequel—*Blade Runner 2049*—is striking in its visual beauty, profound in its thematic complexity, and performs an erudite deconstruction that both reproduces and revokes the constituents of Scott's narrative framework. What it does not do, however, is provide knowledge in the same way as its predecessor.

What may, at least in part, have accounted for the sustained interest between the release of the original in 1982 and the sequel in 2017 is the existence of so many versions of *Blade Runner*. Excluding those edited for television and minor alterations in the Swedish release, there are six: the *Workprint* (1982), the *San Diego Sneak Preview* (1982), the *US Theatrical*

Cut (1982), the *International Cut* (1982), the *Director's Cut* (1992), and the *Final Cut* (2007).[1] The first four and last two are sufficiently similar to justify reducing the list to two, and I shall compare:

(IC)   the *International Cut* of 113 minutes; and
(FC)   the *Final Cut* of 113 minutes.[2]

There are four significant changes from *IC* to *FC*:

(a) the removal of Deckard's voiceover narration;
(b) the alteration of Batty's demand of Tyrell, from "I want more life, *fucker*" to "I want more life, *father*";
(c) the insertion of the unicorn sequence; and
(d) the removal of the happy ending.

(a), (c), and (d) combine to alter the viewer's perception of whether Deckard is a human being or a replicant (an android that is almost identical to a human being). Interpretations of both versions vary, with evidence advanced for Deckard as definitely one or the other, as well as ambiguity, as crucial to both works. For my purposes I shall take Deckard to be a human being in *IC* and a replicant who thinks he is a human being in *FC*. The revelation that Deckard is a replicant in the latter occurs in the final scene of the film, when he discovers an origami unicorn outside his apartment. In *IC*, the unicorn serves only to indicate that Gaff, a police officer, has spared Rachael's life and is allowing Deckard to escape with her. The insertion of the unicorn sequence in the forty-first minute of *FC* produces a second and more important layer of meaning: that Gaff has access to Deckard's thoughts, which—in the context of the work—can only mean that Deckard is a replicant who thinks he is a human being due to memory implants.

In *FC*, the twist in the tale is Deckard's realisation that he is a replicant and is represented as follows (film time in minutes and seconds):

106:49: Deckard opens the door of his apartment, gun in hand, and checks the corridor. When he is satisfied that it is empty, he beckons Rachael to move to the lift.
107:14: En route to the lift, one of her heels clips a silver origami figure, which catches Deckard's attention.
107:23: He picks it up and it is revealed to be a unicorn. He holds it in front of his face, contemplating it.
107:34: He smiles, and Gaff's words are repeated in a voiceover: "It's too bad she won't live, but then again who does?"
107:39: Deckard nods, crumples the unicorn, and enters the lift.

107:44: Before he can turn around, the lift door closes and the screen is black for three seconds.

107:48: The credits roll.

Deckard's discovery is a simultaneous *anagnorisis* (recognition) and *peripeteia* (reversal of fortune) because the change from ignorance to knowledge is accompanied by the change from one state of affairs (Deckard qua human being) to its opposite (Deckard qua replicant). Aristotle maintained that this combination was "the most effective form of discovery," and the peripeteia in *FC* is exceptionally effective.[3] I shall argue that *FC* provides knowledge that *there is no necessary relation between human beings and humanity*, which draws on Berys Gaut's distinction between the film's twofold representation of biological humanity and evaluative humanity.[4]

There are four features of the peripeteia in *FC* that are relevant to the way in which *FC* provides this knowledge:

(i) it is unexpected;
(ii) it has retrospective significance (i.e., it casts the whole narrative up to this point in a fresh light by introducing new layers of meaning);
(iii) it occurs quickly; and
(iv) it occurs in the final few seconds of the film.

The effect in *FC* is best examined by comparison with two other films in which the peripeteia shares features (i) and (ii): M. Night Shyamalan's *Unbreakable* and Roger Donaldson's *No Way Out*. In *Unbreakable*, reluctant superhero David Dunn realises that Elijah Price is not in fact his friend and mentor but an arch-villain. As in *FC*, this revelation casts a fresh light on the whole narrative, although it is followed by approximately three minutes of flashbacks as well as an explicit explanation by Price, and thus lacks (iii) and (iv). The peripeteia in *No Way Out* has a reversal that shares (i) to (iii) with *FC*: at the end of a tragic series of events in which he appears to have played an unwitting role, Lieutenant Commander Farrell is revealed to be Evgeny Segevich, a KGB agent. The revelation is confirmed when Schiller, the manager of his apartment block, emerges as his handler. This occurs approximately one and a half minutes before the credits roll, but nonetheless lacks (iv).

The earliest point at which a viewer has justification for believing that Deckard is a replicant in *FC* is when he picks up the unicorn and the camera focuses on the figure, twenty-one seconds before the screen turns black (the first sight of the unicorn, nine seconds before Deckard picks it up, is too brief for the audience to be able to determine with certainty what the figure is). Cinematic depiction produces detailed and lifelike representations that audiences are able to understand with relative ease.[5] In *FC*, one can immediately perceive that there is no physical feature that distinguishes replicants from human beings and that the behavioural differences are only revealed in specific circumstances, such as empathy tests and combat. Furthermore, when Rachael is introduced as a human being and subsequently revealed to be a replicant, no physical or behavioural changes occur. Cinematic depiction thus reinforces the superficial similarity between humans and replicants in a way that the novel upon which the film is based, Philip K. Dick's *Do Androids Dream of Electric Sheep?*, could not. Deckard first appears on-screen in the eighth minute of the film, and the standard mode of engagement with the representation involves accepting that he is a human being. As the narrative progresses the audience is invited to approve of his growing humanity, revealed in both his reluctance to execute the fugitive replicants and his romantic relationship with Rachael. The audience thus attributes both biological and evaluative humanity to Deckard for approximately one hundred minutes before the two senses of the term are severed in a matter of seconds.

The crucial difference between the peripeteia in *FC* and *No Way Out* is the lack of time the audience is afforded to process the radical change of perspective in the former. Once Farrell/Segevich speaks to Schiller in Russian, there can be no doubt that he is a Soviet agent, and although there is precious little of the film left, there is some explanation. Farrell/Segevich confirms previous suspicion that the KGB agent is a sleeper and there is a very brief exposition of an earlier incident where his bag was stolen. This is followed by a similarly brief dialogue in which Farrell/Segevich refuses to return to the Soviet Union, and the film ends with an aerial shot of him driving away, which continues as the credits roll. Where *No Way Out* provides viewers with seventy-odd seconds in which to consider the implications of the peripeteia with the assistance of a short explanation, *FC* provides a maximum of twenty-one seconds unassisted in which to consider implications that are much more far-reaching and subtle. Deckard does not comment on what it means to be human (or, more accurately, what it means to be a replicant)—he simply gives a stoical nod and makes good his escape.

The combination of anagnorisis and peripeteia produces an anagnorisis in the audience whereby the viewer recognises not only that Deckard is a replicant, but that he or she has shared Deckard's experience of thinking he was a human being and then realising he is a replicant. Deckard's experience is reproduced rather than replicated because the audience does not realise that they are replicants, but that the protagonist of the narrative they have been watching is a replicant. This experience of *audience-anagnorisis* conveys a particular type of knowledge, which is characteristically specifiable and verifiable, in the following manner. The audience is invited to imagine Deckard as a human being and to admire his growing humanity as the narrative unfolds.

Then, in the final few seconds of the film, Deckard's experience of the sudden and abrupt severance of the biological and evaluative senses of "human" is reproduced in the audience. Due to the combination of features (i) to (iv) of the peripeteia, there is little time in which to consider the implications of the reversal and no time in which to reorientate one's attitude toward Deckard; there is also no further character or plot development. In *No Way Out* one has a single opportunity to judge Farrell/Segevich qua spy (his refusal to return to the Soviet Union), but there is no further story in which to judge Deckard qua replicant. One's positive judgement of Deckard remains the same despite his loss of biological humanity, and one therefore experiences the irrelevance of biological humanity to the judgement of evaluative humanity (i.e., one realises that *there is no necessary relation between human beings and humanity*).

The knowledge provided by the representation is conveyed by the combination of the reproduction of Deckard's experience in the audience and audience-anagnorisis. As such, the film provides knowledge about humanity in virtue of its narrativity (i.e., it has cognitive value that is provided by its status as a narrative representation rather than its status as documentary or fiction). What is true of humanity is also true of inhumanity: in showing that there is no necessary relation between biological humanity and evaluative humanity, *Blade Runner* also shows that there is no necessary relation between replicants and inhumanity either. Both human beings and replicants are capable of inhumanity, and both humanity and inhumanity can be instantiated in the same individual. This is most dramatically illustrated in the scene immediately prior to the peripeteia, where Batty first defends himself from Deckard, then tortures him, and finally saves his life. *Narrative Justice* begins with the way in which stories provide genuine knowledge, regardless of whether they are true or false, and examines the influence of stories on a particular type of inhumanity: serious crimes committed by a state or nonstate actor against a civilian population, government, or public for ideological reasons. My thesis is that criminal inhumanity can be reduced by the cultivation of narrative sensibility (i.e., the cultivation of narrative sensibility reduces criminal inhumanity). Or, in colloquial terms, stories can reduce ideologically motivated crime.

NOTES

1. Internet Movie Database (IMDb), "*Blade Runner* (1982)—Alternate Versions." Available at: http://www.imdb.com/title/tt0083658/alternateversions.

2. Both of these running times are taken from *Blade Runner: The Final Cut (5-Disc Ultimate Collectors' Edition)*, released on 3 December 2007.

3. Aristotle, *Poetics*, trans. P. Murray and T. S. Dorsch, in *Classical Literary Criticism*, ed. P. Murray (London: Penguin, 2004), 57–97, 1452a.

4. Berys Gaut, "Elegy in L.A.: *Blade Runner*, Empathy and Death," in *Blade Runner (Philosophers on Film)*, ed. A. Coplan and D. Davies (New York: Routledge, 2015), 31–45, 35–36.

5. For a detailed discussion of cinematic depiction, see: Rafe McGregor, "The Problem of Cinematic Imagination," *Contemporary Aesthetics 10* (2012). Available at: http://www.contempaesthetics.org/newvolume/pages/article.php?articleID=629.

Acknowledgments

I am grateful to Sarah Campbell for her enthusiasm and advice, to three anonymous referees at Rowman & Littlefield International for making this a better book, and to Nicola Harding, Miriam Sang-Ah Park, Vladimir Rizov, and Dominic Willmott for making me a more critical reader of my work-in-progress.

The preface and four chapters (3, 4, 7, and 8) draw on five previously published papers, cited below. I am grateful to the publishers for permission to reproduce them here.

1. "The Silence of the Night: Collaboration, Deceit, and Remorselessness," *Orbis Litterarum* 71 (2016): 163–84.
2. "Narrative Representation and Phenomenological Knowledge," *Australasian Journal of Philosophy* 94 (2016): 327–42.
3. "The Cognitive Value of Blade Runner," *Aesthetic Investigations* 1 (2016): 328–35.
4. "The Ethical Value of Narrative Representation," *Journal of Aesthetics and Phenomenology* 4 (2017): 57–74.
5. "The Person of the Torturer: Secret Policemen in Fiction and Non-Fiction," *Journal of Aesthetic Education* 51 (2017): 44–59.

Chapter One

Narrative Representation

The purpose of this chapter is to situate my thesis of narrative justice in two contexts: first, as belonging to the philosophical tradition of aesthetic education; and second, as part of the contemporary narrative turn in the human sciences, specifically the emergent tradition of narrative criminology. I distinguish narrative representation from non-narrative representation in section 1, defining both *minimal* and *exemplary* narratives. Section 2 introduces philosophical value theory, isolates the various values associated with narrative representation, and identifies my concerns as being cognitive value, moral value, and political value. In section 3, I summarise the tradition of aesthetic education, which was popularised by Friedrich Schiller, who argued that political harmony could only be achieved by the cultivation of aesthetic sensibility. I define *criminal inhumanity*, a category that includes both crimes against humanity and terrorism, in terms of political crime in section 4. I present, in section 5, a summary of the emergent tradition of narrative criminology, understood as a late development within the narrative turn in social science research. I conclude with a delineation of narrative justice: the cultivation of narrative sensibility can reduce criminal inhumanity.

1. NARRATIVE REPRESENTATION AND NON-NARRATIVE REPRESENTATION

Here are four characterisations of narrative representation by philosophers working in the analytic tradition. (a) Peter Lamarque begins with "the intuitive notion of a story. What is that notion? Minimally, just this: the representation of two or more events, real or imaginary, from a point of view, with some degree of structure and connectedness."[1] (b) Noël Carroll defines

1

narrative at its most basic as "the mere recounting or representation of any event and/or state of affairs through some interval of time."[2] He moves on to prototypical narratives: "most narratives involve at least two, but generally more, events and/or states of affairs which are related or arranged temporally and causally (where the causation in question may include mental states such as desires, intentions, and motives)."[3] He divides narratives into two broad categories, episodic and unified. Episodic narratives consist of smaller stories where causal linkage is weak and frequently achieved by means of a recurring protagonist. Unified narratives are those that have a smooth transition from beginning to middle to end and where the end "secures the feeling of closure in an audience."[4] (c) Gregory Currie initiates his discussion of narrativity by noting that all representations are created rather than found and are therefore the product of a process of intentional shaping.[5] He claims that narratives "are distinguished from other representations by what they represent: sustained temporal-causal relations between particulars, especially agents."[6] (d) Peter Goldie provides the following definition:

> A narrative or story is something that can be told or narrated, or just thought through in narrative thinking. It is more than just a bare annal or chronicle or list of a sequence of events, but a representation of those events which is shaped, organized, and coloured, presenting those events, and the people involved in them, from a certain perspective or perspectives, and thereby giving narrative structure—coherence, meaningfulness, and evaluative and emotional import— to what is related.[7]

He differentiates stories from lists, annals, chronicles, and subsequently many—if not most—diaries.[8] Of the four philosophers, Currie is the only one to distinguish a story from a narrative, and my starting point is to take the two terms as synonymous.[9]

Here is what four critics working in the theoretical tradition have to say about the relation between narrative form and narrative content. (e) Tzvetan Todorov draws on the work of the Russian Formalists to differentiate *fabula*, real or fictional events, from *sjužet*, the way in which those events are presented.[10] (f) Gérard Genette employs *histoire* and *récit* to identify a similar distinction, where the latter term is also called *discourse*.[11] (g) Peter Brooks notes that the translation of *fabula/histoire* as "story" and *sjužet/récit* as "plot" has been subject to much criticism, and it does indeed misrepresent both his and Todorov's discussions.[12] The distinction with which they are concerned is between a real or fictional *sequence of events* and the *story* of those real or fictional events.[13] This distinction is crucial because whichever characterisation of narrative one prefers, narratives are representations of events, not the events themselves.[14] Representations of sequences of events are *selective*, as (h) Hayden White demonstrates in his translation of the *Annals of Saint Gaul*:

709.   Hard winter. Duke Gottfried died.
710.   Hard year and deficient in crops.
711.
712.   Flood everywhere.
713.
714.   Pippin, Mayor of the Palace, died.[15]

Many more events occurred in 709 than the two described, and a representation of a historical sequence of events will necessarily exclude some—or, more likely, many—of the events that occurred.[16]

Representations of real and fictional sequences of events can be communicated by a variety of means, including the written and spoken word and still and moving images.[17] In what follows, I shall distinguish between narrative and non-narrative representations, but not between narratives that represent real and fictional events or between linguistic and visual (or descriptive or depictive) narratives. With this in mind, an uncontroversial definition of narrative representation can be derived from (a) to (h) above:

> *Minimal narrative*: the product of an agent that represents (i) one or more agents[18] and (ii) two or more events which are (iii) connected.

Lamarque, Currie, Goldie, and White are all in agreement that narrative representation is gradational rather than categorical (i.e., that narrativity admits of degrees). Paul Ricouer defines *narrativity* as "the language structure that has temporality as its ultimate referent," but this is both too restrictive and overly inclusive.[19] There are some representations of sequences of events that do not employ language and some representations of sequences of events that appear to lack the features typically associated with narratives. The manner in which (i) and (ii) above contribute to narrativity is straightforward, but (iii) has been subject to much debate. Lamarque takes the broadest view of the requisite connection, claiming that:

> there must be some more or less loose, albeit non-logical, relation between the events. Crucially, there is a temporal dimension in narrative, not just in the sense that component sentences are tensed but also in that there must be a temporal relation between the events, even if just that of simultaneity.[20]

As such, the utterance "Katy kicked the stone and missed her bus" meets the criteria for a minimal narrative. In consequence, Currie is correct to claim that it is not the concept *narrative* that is philosophically interesting but "the concept *thing high in narrativity*."[21]

Carroll, like Currie, favours a stronger connection: "the earlier events in the sequence are at least causally necessary conditions for the causation of later events and/or states of affairs (or are contributions thereto)."[22] I shall accept the weaker, temporal connection between events for minimal narratives while acknowledging that non-minimal narratives have a causal connection between events and that exemplary narratives[23] have a causal connection which is so strong as to contribute to the thematic unity of the narrative. Currie defines thematic unity as follows:

> unity is provided by a focus on some common thread in the activity of particular persons in particular connected circumstances, though narratives often do have, in addition, general thematic unity in that we are invited to generalize from the case in question.[24]

The significance of thematic unity restricts exemplary narratives to the type Carroll categorises as unified.

There is a further feature of narrativity that emerges from thematic unity: *closure*. White employs Richerus of Reims's *History of France* as an example of a chronicle, noting that the text has a central subject, a geographical and social focus, a demarcated beginning, and a narrative voice.[25] What is absent, however, is a conclusion, and the representation merely terminates *in medias res*, leaving the reader to connect the end of the sequence of events with its beginning.[26] Within White's taxonomy of historical representations, it is this absence of closure that characterises the text as a chronicle rather than a narrative. In the taxonomy I am establishing, chronicles meet the criteria for minimal narratives but not exemplary narratives. White's insistence on the significance of closure might be considered overly demanding, and Carroll claims that soap operas and national histories are examples of narrative representations without closure.[27] Soap operas are indeed high in narrativity, but they lack thematic unity and are episodic in nature. Every soap opera has several stories running parallel, usually involving characters who live in the same place, and the narrativity within these sub-narratives may be high despite the absence of an overarching, thematic connection. National histories are similar in that they take a place as their primary focus, involve a large number of characters and sub-narratives, and are typically lacking in an overarching theme. On the basis that they are at best borderline cases, I shall exclude both soap operas and national histories from the category of exemplary narratives. White maintains that closure is linked to meaning, which can be shifted by narrative representation as form is imposed upon a sequence of events and has a specific type of closure in mind (to which I shall return in chapter 3).[28] My conception of closure as a criterion for an exemplary narrative is general: "the almost palpable sensation that the story has finished-up at exactly the right spot," as described by Carroll.[29]

Taking the above advances on minimal narratives into consideration, an uncontroversial definition of exemplary narrative representation can be derived as follows:

> *Exemplary narrative*: the product of an agent that is high in narrativity in virtue of representing (i) one or more agents and (ii) two or more events which are (iii) causally connected, (iv) thematically unified, and (v) conclude.

As such, the following are all examples of exemplary narratives: the *Bayeux Tapestry*, William H. Prescott's *History of the Conquest of Peru*, Joseph Conrad's *Heart of Darkness*, Leni Riefenstahl's *Triumph of the Will*, Orson Welles' *Citizen Kane*, and Art Spiegelman's *Maus*.

2. VALUES OF NARRATIVE

To attribute value to an entity is to judge that the entity counts in some way, that it is worth something. The most basic distinction in value is between instrumental values and non-instrumental values. Money is typically valued for its purchasing power rather than for the values of the metal coins or paper notes themselves and is therefore instrumentally valuable (i.e., valuable as an instrument for purchasing goods and services). Analgesic pills are similarly typically valued as instruments for relieving pain rather than for their taste. Instrumental value is often called extrinsic value because the value attributed to the entity (currency note, pill) is attributed in virtue of something (purchasing power, pain relief) to which the entity is related as opposed to the entity itself. Another way to characterise instrumental value is that it is derivative, because the values of currency notes and analgesic pills to which I have alluded are derived from their value in purchasing and pain-relieving, respectively. For obvious reasons, instrumental value is further characterised as the entity having value "for the sake of" (something else) and being valuable as a means (rather than an end).

If the above values are derivative, then there is a category of values—or perhaps just one value—that is not derivative. In the case of money, the chain between the currency note and non-derivative value may be long and complex, but in the case of the analgesic pill it might be short: a derivative value of the pill is its value in reducing pain, and if the reduction of pain is considered pleasurable, then the pleasure produced by the pill could be considered non-derivatively valuable. One does not appear to have to seek something else from which pleasure derives its value, to ask why pleasure is good or desirable; the goodness and desirability are self-evident, part of the meaning of the concept itself. Non-derivative, non-instrumental value is also called intrinsic value because the value of, for example, pleasure with which I am concerned is not related to something outside it, but to the pleasure itself, the experience of pleasure by an individual. The view that the most obvious intrinsic good is pleasure (and the most obvious intrinsic evil is pain) is widely held. Pleasure is also characterised as having value "for its own sake" or being valuable (as an end) in itself.

There are thus at least two categories of value:

(a) instrumental, derivative, or extrinsic value; value for the sake of (something else) or as a means (to an end); and
(b) non-instrumental, non-derivative, or intrinsic value; value for its own sake or (as an end) in itself.

A narrative representation may be valuable instrumentally, non-instrumentally, or both, and it may be valuable instrumentally and non-instrumentally simultaneously. For example, the experience afforded by watching the first half hour of Steven Spielberg's *Saving Private Ryan* may be both: (i) pleasurable in its simultaneous and interactive activation of the sensory, imaginative, affective, and intellective capacities of the audience (i.e., unequivocally non-instrumentally valuable), and (ii) educational in producing true, justified beliefs about Omaha Beach on D-Day in its audience (i.e., apparently instrumentally valuable). The pleasure of experiencing an exemplary narrative such as *Saving Private Ryan* is often regarded as identical with or constitutive of the aesthetic value of a representation. The standard usage of "aesthetic value" in philosophical aesthetics is the value of either a representation qua representation or a work of art qua art (i.e., its characteristic value, whether that character is understood in terms of being a narrative representation or a work of cinematic art). Similarly, artistic value is either taken to be identical with aesthetic value or to be partly constituted by aesthetic value. In the latter case, artistic value usually includes a set of values that may be regarded as either instrumental or non-instrumental, which I discuss below. I shall accept the standard view that there is a strong relation between aesthetic value and artistic value (i.e., that aesthetic value is at the very least a significant component of artistic value), but shall have very little to say about the former and nothing at all to say about the latter.

I noted that pleasure or satisfaction was an unequivocal candidate for the non-instrumental value of the experience of watching *Saving Private Ryan*. The instrumental values of the experience can be divided into two categories. First, there are the adventitious values of a narrative representation, such as its value in distracting me from the worries of everyday life or its value in passing the time while I wait for a friend to finish his shopping. It is not clear that either of these values has a necessary relation to the narrative representation itself, as they involve my contingent choice to select that particular film as a means to the end of distracting me or passing the time. I am not concerned with the adventitious instrumental values of narrative representations. The second category is the family of values with which I am concerned—cognitive, religious, moral, and political values—all of which may be regarded as either instrumentally or non-instrumentally valuable (or as both). In the former case, these values are regarded as being an end (or ends) toward which a narrative representation is a means (for example, *Saving Private Ryan* as a means to an educational end). In the latter case, cognitive, religious, moral, or political values (or any combination thereof) are regarded as part and parcel of either aesthetic or artistic value. I shall focus on the cognitive, moral, and political value of narrative representations.

John Gibson introduces the first in terms of literature as follows: "Whatever 'cognitive' may mean in its various technical uses, as I will use the term here (and as it is generally used in the literature on aesthetics), it has the sense of asking whether literature can be seen as in some significant respect *informative* of extra-textual reality."[30] The cognitive value of literature is often understood in terms of propositional knowledge, a theory that has recently been defended by Richard Gaskin: "literary works [. . .] may have a cognitive value which is part and parcel of their aesthetic value, and [. . .] their cognitive value and aesthetic value, if they do have it, depends essentially on their referring to, and making true statements about, the world."[31] Catherine Wilson is highly critical of propositional theorists, arguing instead that literature is a source of knowledge by means of "a modification of a person's concepts."[32] She is nonetheless concerned with modification that enables rather than disables learning (i.e., with truth value, albeit in a less explicit manner than Gaskin). If one accepts that knowledge is "justified true belief" (or "justified true belief plus something"), then the cognitive value of a narrative representation can be understood in terms of its capacity to provide knowledge of the world.

The second of the values of narrative I shall discuss is moral value. Where the concept of narratives having cognitive value is relatively straightforward—whether representations can inform readers about the world—the case is more complex for moral value. There seem to be several answers to the question of how moral value can be attributed to representations. The emphasis in philosophical aesthetics and art criticism has tended to focus on immorality in art, and A. W. Eaton identifies five ways in which a work of art can be morally defective:

(A) the subject matter represented,
(B) the character of the artist,
(C) the methods of production,
(D) the behavioural consequences, and
(E) the vision or perspective embodied by the work.[33]

Setting aside the question of defects in particular, Eaton's list specifies five potential sources of moral valence in narrative representation. (A) is based on the naïve view that some subjects—for example, human nudity or lifestyles that are immoral—should not be represented. I call this view naïve because it fails to acknowledge the significance of (E). Representations can embody radically different perspectives on the same subject, and where that subject is immoral—such as rape—the work can embody a "pro-" or "anti-" attitude, as Eaton's discussion of the contrasting depictions of rape in Titian's *Rape of Europa* and Nicolas Poussin's *The Rape of the Sabine Women* demonstrates. I shall therefore have nothing further to say about (A). The relevance of genetic features—(B) and (C) above—to the value of representations is a much-disputed debate that is beyond the scope of my inquiry, so I shall ignore morally relevant genetic facts about works of art. Finally, Wilson is one of several who warns against questions about "the mechanics of the influence of literary works," and I shall discuss the problems in attempting to quantify this influence in chapter 6.[34] I shall therefore follow Eaton in excluding (D) and restricting my interest to (E), such that the moral value of a narrative representation is the moral value of the perspective embodied by the narrative representation. I discuss the moral value of narrative representation in detail in chapter 3 and the cognitive value of narrative representation in detail in chapter 4.

Carroll identifies two distinct relationships between art and politics—support and opposition—while noting that opposition to one ideology can readily be conceived as support for another. The two relationships are set out as follows:

(I) Art presupposes many of the beliefs and values of the society from which it emerges, and readers, listeners, and viewers must fill in these presuppositions in the process of assimilating the artworks in question. In this way, artworks may come not only to reflect but also to reinforce the beliefs and values of the larger culture.[35]

(II) Art as social criticism may be explicit or implicit, and it may be targeted broadly or narrowly. Social criticism is narrowly targeted where its domain of concern comprises formally individuated entities like states and political parties. It is broadly targeted where it is directed at society or culture at large (or, at least, at substantial portions thereof, such as bourgeoisie culture or patriarchal ideology).[36]

Political value is usually regarded as closely related to, or supervenient upon, moral value, such that there cannot be a change in the former without a change in the latter. If moral value is evaluation in terms of right and wrong or virtue and vice, political value is evaluation in terms of the organisation and administration of the state or of society. The link between the two forms of value is that political leaders (whether monarchs, dictators, parties, or representatives) typically seek to establish some form of legitimacy for the power they exert in organisation and administration (whether that be the divine right of kings, patrilineal succession, a social contract, or election by the citizenry). The answer to the question of how political value can be attributed to representations appears more straightforward than the question of moral value and is usually restricted to (D) or (E) in Eaton's list. For the same reasons noted above, I shall employ (E) such that the political value of a narrative representation is the political value of the perspective embodied by the narrative representation.

3. AESTHETIC EDUCATION

Aesthetic education is a thesis about the relationship between aesthetic or artistic value on the one hand and moral and political value on the other hand. In consequence of the relationship identified in section 2, historical and contemporary theses of aesthetic education make claims about political value in addition to or in virtue of an initial claim about moral value. The essence of the aesthetic education thesis is thus that there is some kind of causal relation between aesthetic or artistic experiences and moral—and political—development. The term is ambiguous because aesthetic education is not an education *in* aesthetics but education *by* aesthetics, specifically a *moral education* by aesthetic means, which is in turn a means to the end of political education. This is how the thesis was initially established by J. C. Friedrich von Schiller in his *Ueber die ästhetische Erziehung des Menschen in einer Reihe von Briefen* (*Letters on the Aesthetic Education of Man*).[37] Schiller was a philosopher and a poet who drew on two distinct sets of predecessors.[38] With respect to poetry and criticism, he was influenced by both Johann Gottfried Herder and Johann Wolfgang von Goethe, specifically the *Bildung* tradition, which was concerned with the role of poetry and literature in the education of the public. With respect to philosophy, Schiller's most obvious influences are Immanuel Kant and Jean-Jacques Rousseau, and *On the Aesthetic Education*

of Man is both a development of Kant's *Third Critique* and a response to
Rousseau's *Of the Social Contract, or Principles of Political Law*.

Like so much else in value theory, however, the prototypical aesthetic education thesis appears to have been the work of Anthony Ashley-Cooper, the
Third Earl of Shaftesbury. His philosophy was highly original but notoriously
unsystematic, and the precise nature of the close relationships among beauty,
virtue, truth, and divinity envisaged by him is unclear.[39] Shaftesbury's historical perspective of the progress of civilization from absolutism to democracy
emphasised the importance of persuasion and proposed the development of
rhetoric and poetry as causally related to the process of democratization.[40]
Those in government promoted the arts to which they owed their position, and
the development of art facilitated the development of science and ingenuity.
Science and philosophy could not flourish without being preceded by art,
and critics thus had an essential role to play in assisting in the refinement of
a society's taste.[41] Taste, natural genius, the judgement of taste, and the sense
of beauty were all used by Shaftesbury to denote *aesthetic sensibility* (i.e.,
awareness of and sensitivity to aesthetic value). Shaftesbury was adamant
that unlike the standard five senses, the sense of beauty required a great deal
of effort and attention before it could function properly.[42] Taste in beauty not
only shared this requirement for development with taste in character (moral
sensibility) but contributed to moral education:

> A LITTLE better Taste (were it a very *little*) in the Affair of *Life it-self* wou'd, if
> I mistake not, mend the Manners, and secure the Happiness of some of our *noble
> Countrymen*, who come with high Advantage and a worthy *Character* into the
> Publick. But ere they have long engag'd in it, their Worth unhappily becomes
> venal. *Equipages, Titles, Precedencys, Staffs, Ribbons,* and other such glittering
> *Ware,* are taken in exchange for *inward* Merit, Honour, and a Character.[43]

Neither the causal relation between art and science nor the causal relation
between beauty and virtue are, however, explored in detail or analysed with
rigour. The result is, somewhat typically of Shaftesbury's work, the sketch of
a thesis that is rich in potential but requires significant elaboration before a
comprehensive theory can be proposed.

Kant's *Third Critique* plays a crucial role in his transcendental idealism,
reconciling subject with object, freedom with nature, and human beings
with the world in which they live. He identifies two independent realms,
supersensible freedom and sensible nature, and claims that the power of
judgement mediates between the two by means of "the concept of a *purposiveness* of nature."[44] Kant establishes a complex taxonomy of powers
of judgement, which begins by distinguishing the judgement of beauty
(which he called the *judgement of taste* and I shall abbreviate as *aesthetic*

judgement) from the judgement of virtue (and agreeability) in terms of the former's disinterest and the latter's interest.[45] Aesthetic judgement placed the cognitive faculties of imagination and understanding in harmonious "free play."[46] This cognitive harmony was experienced as disinterested pleasure, which is contrasted with the pleasure associated with moral judgement, which is the interested pleasure experienced when the need created by the moral law is satisfied.[47] Beauty is defined as "the form of the *purposiveness* of an object, insofar as it is perceived in it *without represen-tation of an end*."[48] The relation between aesthetic judgement and the form of purposiveness draws attention to the significance of the power of aesthetic judgement as the bridge between human freedom and natural law, because human beings perceive purpose in nature. The relation between aesthetic judgement and disinterested pleasure draws attention to humanity belonging to and being at home in the world, in whose beauty human beings take pleasure.

Having initially separated aesthetic and moral judgement, Kant then states that "the beautiful is the symbol of the morally good."[49] The cultivation of aesthetic judgement facilitates and encourages the development of morality (i.e., the aesthetic realises the moral). Humanity is not only at home in the world in consequence of human beings taking pleasure in beauty, but in consequence of beauty having a function beyond the experience of pleasure it affords: "Taste as it were makes possible the transition from sensible charm to habitual moral interest without too violent a leap."[50] The realisation of the moral by the aesthetic and the relationship among the aesthetic, the moral, and the sensible is made more explicit in the claim that "taste is at bottom a faculty for the judging of the sensible rendering of moral ideas."[51] This proposition follows a brief discussion by Kant on the significance of the cultivation of shared standards of taste in the drive toward "*lawful* sociability," which refers to the maintenance of social order by consent rather than coercion.[52] The claim both recalls Shaftesbury's notion of the existence of a causal relation between art and civilisation and preempts Schiller's argument for a causal relation between aesthetic sensibility and political harmony.

Schiller's *Letters* were published in 1794 and are described by Frederick Beiser as "a defense of the aesthetic dimension of human life."[53] They were written during the Reign of Terror that followed the French Revolution of 1789 and reflect Schiller's disappointment and distress at the practical effects of the republican ideals advocated by Rousseau and others. Schiller believed that the Terror was a consequence of the tyranny of reason, the complete domination of one part of human nature over the other. He regarded human nature as an essentially dualist combination of the divine (reason and morality) with the animal (desire and the senses). The two separate aspects of human nature were understood in terms of drives: (a) the *form drive*, toward reason, universality, and unity; and (b) the *sense drive*, toward sense, individuality, and variety.[54] Schiller saw Kant as having provided a solution to the reconciliation between these drives by means of aesthetic judgement because the appreciation of beauty facilitated the transition from the sensible to the supersensible, uniting the two aspects of humanity and allowing human beings to become fully human. Recall that for Kant aesthetic judgement places imagination and understanding in free play, a cognitive harmony experienced as a particular type of pleasure. Similarly, the form and sense drive are synthesised by the *play drive*, which produces harmony in the character of the individual.[55] The object of the play drive is "living form: a concept serving to designate all the aesthetic qualities of phenomena and, in a word, what in the widest sense of the term we call beauty."[56] Like Kant, Schiller considered beauty as both finally valuable (i.e., an end in itself) and instrumentally valuable (as the means to a moral end). Unlike Kant, whose commentary on beauty as a symbol of morality is fragmentary, Schiller established an explicit connection between the two by means of the play drive: freedom constitutes the full realisation of the sense and form drives; the full realisation of the sense and form drives constitutes beauty; therefore freedom constitutes beauty.[57] The result of this close relationship was that the harmony of character achieved by the play drive was characterised by: (i) the internalisation of moral principles, and (ii) pleasure in acting in accordance with moral principles.[58]

The actual mechanism by which aesthetic—as opposed to physical or moral (sensory or rational)—education operates is indirect rather than direct. Neither aesthetic experiences nor aesthetic sensibility produce moral thought or moral behaviour, but an aesthetic experience is an experience of play (the synthesis of the form and sense drives) and thus an experience of freedom, which is a necessary condition for moral action. This freedom is not just freedom to act in accordance with moral principles (the form drive), but freedom to act in accordance with fully realised human nature (the play drive). The synthesis of the form and sense drives in fully realised human beings provides the aesthetic with its political relevance, and "if man is ever to solve that problem of politics in practice he will have to approach it through the problem of the aesthetic."[59] For Schiller, aesthetic education was the only means of achieving harmony of character in the individual, and harmony in the individual was required in order to achieve political harmony. In an analogy of the form and sense drives in individual human beings, Schiller proposed an ethical and dynamic state. The former state treats its citizens as purely rational beings and subsumes the individual will under the moral law; the latter state treats its citizens as purely sensuous beings and manages their conflicting desires by coercive power.[60] Neither state is satisfactory for Schiller, for whom:

Taste alone brings harmony into society, because it fosters harmony in the individual. All other forms of perception divide man, because they are founded exclusively either upon the sensuous or upon the spiritual part of his being; only the aesthetic mode of perception makes him a whole, because both his natures must be in harmony if he is to achieve it.[61]

Political harmony is achieved by (A) harmony of character within individual citizens, and (B) providing those citizens with the freedom to act in accordance with the harmony they have achieved. The aesthetic state is thus a state in which citizens are free to act in accordance with their fully realised human nature (rather than being subjected to the moral law or coercive power) and where the programme of education facilitates this achievement by individual citizens. In other words, the aesthetic state promotes moral harmony achieved by aesthetic means and achieves political harmony by recognising the moral harmony of its citizenry. The role of art, aesthetic experience, and aesthetic sensibility is crucial to moral harmony, and moral harmony in the individual is crucial to political harmony in the state. Schiller concludes the *Letters* on a somewhat wistful note, which reinforces Beiser's claim that they are intended as a defence of aesthetics, an ideal to which human beings should aspire:

But does such a State of Aesthetic Semblance really exist? And if so, where is it to be found? As a need, it exists in every finely attuned soul; as a realized fact, we are likely to find it, like the pure Church and the pure Republic, only in some few chosen circles.[62]

Schiller's inaugural thesis of aesthetic education can thus be defined as follows:

Aesthetic education (1): political harmony can only be achieved by the cultivation of aesthetic sensibility (i.e., aesthetic sensibility is a necessary and sufficient condition of political harmony).

Schiller was, as I have noted, both a poet and a philosopher, and it should therefore come as no surprise that the tradition of aesthetic education has been sustained by a combination of poets and philosophers across the nineteenth and twentieth centuries. Walt Whitman and Matthew Arnold were particularly influential successors to Schiller and developed the tradition by achieving fame as cultural critics as well as poets. The former is famous for what Jason Frank calls his *aesthetic democracy* and the latter for his claim that poetry was in the process of replacing religion.[63] The transition from philosophy to cultural criticism reached its apotheosis in the twentieth century, with *Négritude*. The three pillars of this literary and philosophical movement were all born in French colonies, achieved critical recognition for their poetry,

and held prominent political positions: Léopold Sédar Senghor was president
of Senegal from 1960 to 1980; Léon-Gontran Damas was a Guianan deputy
in the French National Assembly from 1948 to 1951; and Aimé Césaire was
president of the Regional Council of Martinique from 1983 to 1988.[64] The
mid-twentieth century also saw the emergence of a strand of aesthetic education rooted first in Marxism and then Critical Theory, driven by György
Lukács, Walter Benjamin, Bertolt Brecht, Theodor Adorno, Jacques Rancière,
and Terry Eagleton.

At the end of the twentieth century, aesthetic education became associated
with the ethical turn in criticism, described by Patrick Fessenbecker as
involving a confluence of three traditions: the neo-Aristotelian, exemplified
by Martha Nussbaum; the challenge to scientistic epistemology, exemplified
by Richard Rorty; and Levinasian poststructuralism, exemplified by Jacques
Derrida.[65] I discussed Nussbaum's thesis of aesthetic education in detail in
The Value of Literature, arguing that she failed to demonstrate the relationship
between literary form and moral content required by her theory.[66] Rorty sets
out a subtle and complex thesis of aesthetic education in *Contingency, Irony,
and Solidarity*, but it is beyond the scope of my inquiry as it requires engagement with both his philosophy of art criticism and the idiosyncratic version
of philosophical pragmatism within which his art criticism is embedded.[67]
While Derrida's contribution to the ethical turn is similarly nuanced and
intricate, I shall examine the work of Gayatri Chakravorty Spivak instead, as
she establishes an explicit theory of aesthetic education from a poststructural
perspective. I summarise the aesthetic education of both Spivak and Sarah
E. Worth (who draws on, and improves upon, Nussbaum's work) in chapter 2.
Broadly, the contemporary use of the term can be defined as:

> *Aesthetic education (II)*: political harmony can be achieved by the cultivation
> of aesthetic sensibility (i.e., the cultivation of aesthetic sensibility develops pol-
> itical harmony).

4. CRIMINAL INHUMANITY

The first recorded use of the phrase *crimes against humanity* was in 1890,
in a letter from George Washington Williams to the US secretary of state
protesting the conditions prevalent in the Congo Free State.[68] The phrase
was first employed in the context of international law in May 1915, when
the members of the Triple Entente protested the massacre and deportation
of Armenians in the Ottoman Empire.[69] The Armenian holocaust of 1915 to
1923 is one of the early genocides of the twentieth century, although *genocide* was not coined until 1944, by Raphael Lemkin in *Axis Rule in Occupied*

Europe: Laws of Occupation, Analysis of Government, Proposals for Redress.
Lemkin defined his neologism as "the destruction of a nation or of an ethnic
group," and there is a close relation between genocide and crimes against
humanity.[70] By the end of the First World War the concept of crimes against
humanity had gained political currency, but it was not recognised in international law until the Charter of the International Military Tribunal (known
as the London Charter), established in August 1945 to determine the conduct
of the Nuremberg Trials (November 1945 to October 1946). The initial definition contains what Norman Geras calls a *war nexus*, which stipulated that the
crimes must have occurred either during or before the Second World War.[71]

The London Charter identified three distinct types of crime within the jur-
isdiction of the Nuremburg Trials: crimes against humanity, crimes against
peace, and war crimes. Crimes against peace were concerned with the waging
of war in violation of international treaties and with the waging of wars of
aggression. War crimes were simply "violations of the laws or customs of
war."[72] The concept of war crimes originated with The Hague Conventions
(1899 and 1907) and their annexes, and the Geneva Conventions (1864, 1907,
1929, and 1949) and their additional protocols and commentaries. The Hague
Conventions were concerned with establishing standards of international
law for the customs of war, and the Geneva Conventions with establishing
standards of international law for humanitarian treatment in war. Article 2 of
the Geneva Convention (I) 1949 establishes the scope of its code of conduct
as follows:

> the present Convention shall apply to all cases of declared war or of any other
> armed conflict which may arise between two or more of the High Contracting
> Parties, even if the state of war is not recognized by one of them.[73]

The next article prohibits certain acts in the case of an armed conflict that is
not international (i.e., that occurs within the borders of one of the contracting
nations). In contemporary terms, therefore, war crimes are acts that are in
breach of the Geneva Conventions of 1949.

The war nexus of crimes against humanity was reproduced in implicit
form for genocide in the Convention on the Prevention and Punishment of
the Crime of Genocide, which was adopted by the United Nations General
Assembly in 1948. The definition of genocide appears in Article II:

> In the present Convention, genocide means any of the following acts committed
> with intent to destroy, in whole or in part, a national, ethnical, racial or religious
> group, as such:
>
> (a) Killing members of the group;
> (b) Causing serious bodily or mental harm to members of the group; and

(c) Deliberately inflicting on the group conditions of life calculated to bring about its physical destruction in whole or in part;
(d) Imposing measures intended to prevent births within the group;
(e) Forcibly transferring children of the group to another group.[74]

Nicole Rafter notes that this excludes the recently developed concept of cultural genocide, the "destruction of a group by depriving it of access to its land, traditions, history, and values, not necessarily through physical violence but more slowly."[75] Although genocide and war are often linked, there is no necessary relation between the two, and Rafter therefore prefers Daniel Feierstein's more inclusive definition of genocide as ' "the execution of a large-scale and systematic plan with the intention of destroying a human group as such in whole or in part." '[76]

The United Nations established crimes against humanity in international law with Principle VI(c) of the resolution of the General Assembly in 1950, which retained the war nexus albeit not with the Second World War.[77] In 1973, however, the General Assembly declared that apartheid was a crime against humanity.[78] The requirement that, like apartheid in South Africa, discriminatory intent on the basis of group characteristics is a necessary condition for the crime was laid down by the Statute of the International Criminal Tribunal for Rwanda in 1994, but was—like the war nexus—controversial.[79] Christopher Macleod notes that the difficulty of defining crimes against humanity has been exacerbated by the ambiguity associated with "humanity," which can refer to either the human species or the quality of humane-ness valued by the species.[80] The current definition in use is from the Rome Statute of the International Criminal Court, from Article 7 (1). The Rome Statute is considered authoritative because the definition is neither created for a specific historical case nor an example of victors' justice:

> For the purpose of this Statute, "crime against humanity" means any of the following acts when committed as part of a widespread or systematic attack directed against any civilian population, with knowledge of the attack.[81]

The statute then lists eleven crimes, (a) to (k), including murder, enslavement, torture, rape, persecution on impermissible grounds, and apartheid. Massimo Renzo provides a useful summary of crimes against humanity as defined in the Rome Statute:

(1) they constitute *particularly odious offences*. These crimes are so barbarous as to violate the human dignity of the victims;
(2) they are *international crimes*. These crimes concern the international community, rather than just the domestic political community, and

therefore trigger international intervention. It is permissible for the international community to trump state sovereignty in order to punish them;

(3) they have a *policy element*: they are committed, instigated, or at least tolerated, by a state, a de facto authority or a politically organized group.

(4) they have a *collective element*: they target victims qua members of a group.[82]

Geras offers a more concise account of the criteria:

> From the London Charter of the Nuremberg Tribunal to the Rome Statute of the ICC it has been taken to be embodied in the requirement that, in order to fall within the category of crimes against humanity, the violations listed in those two instruments must be directed "against a civilian population." They must be part of a "widespread" or "systematic" attack.[83]

For my purposes, war crimes, genocide, and crimes against humanity can be subsumed under the category of *political crime*, understood as crimes committed with an ideological inspiration, motivation, or intention.[84] More specifically, the three can be identified as the subcategory of political crime that are committed by (or in service of) the state and defined as follows:

> *War crimes*: acts that are in breach of the Geneva Conventions of 1949.
> *Genocide*: the execution of a large-scale and systematic plan with the intention of destroying a human group as such in whole or in part.
> *Crimes against humanity (I)*: the execution of a widespread and systematic attack against a civilian population.

War crimes as a separate category are beyond the scope of my inquiry, and my interest in genocide is restricted to its identity as a subcategory of crimes against humanity.

There is no universally accepted definition of terrorism, which is likely a consequence of two features of the phenomenon. First, the combination of the pejorative denotation and connotations of the term with its standard use in describing the actions of non-state actors is controversial. The idea is that the term endorses a bias in favour of state actors and may legitimise their actions even when they are identical to, or more reprehensible than, those undertaken by non-state actors. Second, the counterterror approaches of nation-states, as enshrined in their respective legislations, is both varied and continually evolving, making international consensus highly unlikely. These and other complexities are reflected in the failure of the United Nations' Ad Hoc Committee established by General Assembly resolution 51/210 of 17 December 1996 to agree on a comprehensive convention on international terrorism to date.[85]

The European Union's (EU's) conception of terrorism is set out in two documents: the Council Common Position 2001/931/CFSP and the Council Framework Decision 2002/475/JHA. Neither offers a straightforward definition of terrorism, but Patryk Pawlak summarises the EU's approach to terrorist offences as:

> acts committed with the aim of "seriously intimidating a population," "unduly compelling a government or international organisation to perform or abstain from performing any act," or "seriously destabilising or destroying the fundamental political, constitutional, economic or social structures of a country or an international organisation."[86]

In the United States, 22 U.S. Code § 2656f defines terrorism as "premeditated, politically motivated violence perpetrated against noncombatant targets by subnational groups or clandestine agents."[87] The 18 U.S. Code § 2331 describes international terrorism in more detail, including the intention behind the violent or dangerous acts, which:

(B) appear to be intended—
    (i)   to intimidate or coerce a civilian population;
    (ii) to influence the policy of a government by intimidation or coercion; or
    (iii) to affect the conduct of a government by mass destruction, assassination, or kidnapping.[88]

In the United Kingdom, terrorism is defined in the Terrorism Act 2000, the first two subsections of which state:

(1) In this Act "terrorism" means the use or threat of action where—
    (a) the action falls within subsection (2);
    (b) the use or threat is designed to influence the government or an international governmental organisation or to intimidate the public or a section of the public; and
    (c) the use or threat is made for the purpose of advancing a political, religious, racial, or ideological cause.

(2) Action falls within this subsection if it—
    (a) involves serious violence against a person,
    (b) involves serious damage to property,
    (c) endangers a person's life, other than that of the person committing the action,

(d) creates a serious risk to the health or safety of the public or a section of the public, or

(e) is designed seriously to interfere with or seriously to disrupt an electronic system.[89]

The core components of the definition are: (I) serious violence against a person, or serious risk to public health or safety, or serious damage to property, or serious disruption of an electronic system in order to (II) influence the government or intimidate the public (III) for the purpose of advancing a political, religious, racial, or ideological cause.

The one point common to the definitions of terrorism in the EU, US, and UK is that the acts are intended to intimidate a government or public. The US and UK definitions also specify that the motive for the act is ideological—referred to variously as political, social, religious, or racial—rather than financial or material gain. The EU definition's reference to compelling a government or destroying structures within a country implies that the motive will not be financial or material gain, although it does not exclude, for example, hostage-taking for financial rather than ideological reasons. Nonetheless, an uncontroversial definition of terrorism is: serious violence, damage, or disruption motivated by ideological reasons and aimed at the intimidation of a government or public. Of the definitions quoted above, only 22 U.S. Code § 2656f makes explicit reference to the kind of organisations that can commit terrorist acts, but the inclusion of clandestine agents in addition to subnational groups implies that terrorist acts can be committed by both non-state (subnational) actors and state (clandestine) actors. The question of whether or not to restrict terrorism to non-state actors is, as noted, one of the controversies that has impeded the definition of terrorism. As my intent is to include political crime committed by both state and non-state actors, I can avoid this controversy by revising my definition of crimes against humanity in the context of both terrorism and the concept of criminal inhumanity. *Criminal inhumanity* is an umbrella term that includes not only serious political crime, but all ideologically motivated serious crime, regardless of whether that ideology is grounded in political, social, religious, or racial values. I shall thus employ the following terminology henceforth:

Crimes against humanity (II): the execution of a widespread and systematic attack by a state actor against a civilian population for ideological reasons.

Terrorism: serious violence, damage, or disruption by a non-state actor aimed at the intimidation of a government or public for ideological reasons.

Criminal inhumanity: serious crimes committed by a state or non-state actor against a civilian population, government, or public for ideological reasons.

My thesis, narrative justice, is applicable to criminal humanity in general but focuses on the following three crimes: collaboration with an occupying power, extrajudicial killing, and terrorist recruitment.

5. NARRATIVE CRIMINOLOGY

The ethical turn in literary criticism mentioned in section 3 was partly a response to what has been called the narrative turn in the discipline, which began with Russian structuralism in the interwar years, was popularised by French poststructuralism, and spread from literary studies to the humanities in the form of the linguistic turn of the second half of the twentieth century. As such, the ethical turn was a divergence within literary criticism rather than a disciplinary change of direction. The linguistic turn in the humanities was matched by a postwar increase in humanistic approaches to the social sciences. Qualitative research methods, which sought to privilege rather than eliminate subjectivity, became both more prolific and more respected. Although the structuralist and humanist traditions were at odds in several significant ways, they were sufficiently similar to facilitate a narrative turn in the human sciences as a whole.[90] Matti Hyvärinen identifies four distinct stages within this turn, beginning with literary studies in the 1960s, moving to historiography in the 1970s, social research in the 1980s, and culture itself in the 1990s.[91] Catherine Kohler Riessman explores the turn in more detail, noting the influence of narrative beyond the disciplines of anthropology, psychology, sociolinguistics, and sociology to the professions of law, medicine, nursing, occupational therapy, and social work in the last two decades of the century.[92] As the century changed, the concept of narrative identity—of personality as reducible to or dependent upon autobiographical narrative representation or narrative thinking—was adopted within the cultural turn. Writing in 2013, psychologist Mark Freeman provides an informed commentary:

> Indeed, as a colleague of mine insisted a while back, it's just the latest intellectual fad and, as with most fads, will fade away in due time. But that was nearly thirty years ago, and here we are, still, seeing in the idea of narrative a central organizing principle for understanding and predicting some significant dimensions of the human condition.[93]

As a social science, criminology has not been immune to the narrative turn, but it has been slow to embrace narrative as a tool for understanding, explaining, and reducing crime. There were only two book-length applications of narrative to crime in the previous century: D. Lawrence Wieder's *Language and Social Reality: The Case of Telling the Convict Code* and

David Canter's *Criminal Shadows: Inside the Mind of the Serial Killer*, published twenty years apart, in 1974 and 1994, respectively.[94] The narrative turn in criminology is a phenomenon of the new century, with four books published in little more than a decade: Shadd Maruna's *Making Good: How Ex-Convicts Reform and Rebuild Their Lives* (2001), Lois Presser's *Been a Heavy Life: Stories of Violent Men* (2008), Sveinung Sandberg and Willy Pedersen's *Street Capital: Black Cannabis Dealers in a White Welfare State* (2009), and Presser's *Why We Harm* (2013). The term *narrative criminology* was first coined by Presser in 2009, in an article titled "The Narratives of Offenders," and Presser and Sandberg collaborated to edit *Narrative Criminology: Understanding Stories of Crime* (2015), the definitive work on the narrative turn in criminology.[95] In a parallel with Hyvärinen on the narrative turn in the human sciences, Presser and Sandberg identify four theoretical traditions from which narrative criminology has developed: narrative psychology, ethnomethodology, cultural structuralism, and postmodernism.

> These four theoretical traditions bring important insights to bear on narrative criminology. Narrative psychology reminds us that a speaker is an agent who seeks coherence, ethnomethodology that speakers use narratives as devices in particular social contexts, cultural structuralism that narration is essentially reproductive, and postmodernism that narratives are often fragmented and hybrid.[96]

Narrative criminology is a new approach within criminology, related to constitutive criminology and cultural criminology, and involving the mapping of narrative patterns onto criminal behaviour. Most of the studies in the collection are focused on the development of moral character and psychological well-being in offenders, but Presser and Sandberg define narrative criminology more broadly as "any inquiry based on the view of stories as instigating, sustaining, or effecting desistance from harmful action."[97]

This broad definition facilitates the inclusion of a small but growing body of work on the role of narratives in recruitment by terrorist organisations and of the use of narrative as a counterterror strategy as a distinct strand within narrative criminology. This is also recent and is, in consequence, focused primarily on violent Muslim extremism. Although this research has for the most part been disseminated by government and non-government organisations in strategic or policy documents, four books have been published thus far: Richard Jackson's *Writing the War on Terrorism: Language, Politics and Counter-Terrorism* (2005), Jeffry Halverson, H. L. Goodall, and Steven Corman's *Master Narratives of Islamist Extremism* (2011), Ajit Maan's *Counter-Terrorism: Narrative Strategies* (2015), and Thomas H. Johnson's *Taliban Narratives: The Use and Power of Stories in the Afghanistan Conflict*

(2017). I engage with this strand of narrative criminology, as applied to both Muslim fundamentalism and white supremacism, in detail in chapter 9.

This chapter has situated my approach within both the aesthetic education and narrative criminology traditions. My thesis is an instantiation of aesthetic education in that I shall be arguing for a version of the claim that the cultivation of aesthetic sensibility develops political harmony. My thesis is also an example of narrative criminology, as I shall be arguing that stories can instigate and sustain the prevention of and desistance from harmful action. Narrative justice is the thesis that the cultivation of narrative sensibility develops political harmony by reducing criminal inhumanity (i.e., that exemplary narratives reduce criminal inhumanity). Or, in colloquial terms, stories reduce ideologically motivated crime. In the chapters that follow, I shall demonstrate that exemplary narratives can be employed as a tool to reduce criminal inhumanity by three means: (a) evaluating responsibility for inhumanity, (b) understanding the psychology of inhumanity, and (c) undermining inhumanity. My intention is that by working within the philosophical and criminological traditions simultaneously, I shall be able to combine the theoretical rigour of the former with the focus on practice of the latter so that the thesis of narrative justice that emerges in chapter 5 is not merely compelling but has the potential for a significant impact on criminal inhumanity. Before I begin to construct narrative justice in chapter 3, I shall pick up contemporary aesthetic education where I left it in section 3, with its two most convincing proponents, Spivak and Worth.

NOTES

1. Peter Lamarque, *The Opacity of Narrative* (London: Rowman & Littlefield International, 2014), 1.

2. Noël Carroll, *Minerva's Night Out: Philosophy, Pop Culture, and Moving Pictures* (Malden, MA: Wiley-Blackwell, 2013), 122.

3. Carroll, *Minerva's Night Out*, 122.

4. Carroll, *Minerva's Night Out*, 123.

5. Gregory Currie, *Narratives & Narrators: A Philosophy of Stories* (Oxford: Oxford University Press, 2010), 2.

6. Currie, *Narratives & Narrators*, 27.

7. Peter Goldie, *The Mess Inside: Narrative, Emotion, and the Mind* (Oxford: Oxford University Press, 2012), 2.

8. Goldie, *The Mess Inside*, 8.

9. Currie employs the story/narrative distinction in a similar manner to *fabula/sjužet*, discussed below, which he then links to the internal/external perspective, which I discuss in chapter 3. See: *Narratives & Narrators*, 27, 49 fn. 1.

10. Tzvetan Todorov, *The Poetics of Prose*, trans. Richard Howard (Oxford: Blackwell, 1977), 45.

11. Gérard Genette, *Narrative Discourse: An Essay in Method*, trans. Jane E. Lewin (Ithaca, NY: Cornell University Press, 1980 [1972]), 25–27.

12. Peter Brooks, *Reading for the Plot: Design and Intention in Narrative* (Cambridge, MA: Harvard University Press, 1992 [1984]), 326. Due to the potential for confusion, I shall not characterise narrative representation in terms of "plot." I return to the concept in my discussion of the ethics of narrative representation in chapter 3.

13. Carroll endorses precisely this view of the distinction (*Minerva's Night Out*, 129).

14. This is true of Goldie's *narrative thinking* as well: "Narrative thinking involves not text or discourse, but another kind of representation: thoughts" (*The Mess Inside*, 3). I shall not discuss narrative thinking in this monograph.

15. Hayden White, "The Value of Narrativity in the Representation of Reality," *Critical Inquiry* 7 (1980): 11.

16. White explains this point with regard to historical representation: "if history consisted of all the human events that ever happened, it would make as little sense, be as little cognizable, as a nature conceived to consist of all of the natural events that ever happened" ("The Problem of Style in Realistic Representation: Marx and Flaubert," in *The Concept of Style*, ed. B. Lang [Ithaca: Cornell University Press, 1987], 280). Carroll maintains that this is true of all narrative representation; see: "Art, Narrative, and Moral Understanding," in *Aesthetics and Ethics: Essays at the Intersection*, ed. J. Levinson (Cambridge: Cambridge University Press, 1998), 139.

17. My preference is to distinguish representations of real sequences of events from representations of fictional sequences of events in terms of the different role played by the imagination in the respective engagement with each, a view which is endorsed by Lamarque and Currie. Derek Matravers recently questioned this distinction, first claiming that there is no relevant difference between the employment of the imagination in factual and fictional representations and then questioning the role of the imagination in engaging with representations at all. See: *Fiction and Narrative* (Oxford: Oxford University Press, 2014). My purpose here is to delineate an uncontroversial characterisation of narrative so I shall neither contribute to this debate nor employ the imagination in my elucidation of narrative representation.

18. Goldie (*The Mess Inside*, 19 fn. 20) notes the possibility of narratives with no human characters but excludes these from his discussion. I shall not stipulate that the agents must be human, merely that they are capable of intentional action, such as the anthropomorphised rabbits in Richard Adams's *Watership Down* and the false Maria robot in Fritz Lang's *Metropolis*.

19. Paul Ricoeur, "Narrative Time," *Critical Inquiry* 7 (1980): 169.

20. Lamarque, *Opacity of Narrative*, 52.

21. Currie, *Narratives & Narrators*, 34.

22. Noël Carroll, "On the Narrative Connection," in *Beyond Aesthetics: Philosophical Essays* (New York: Cambridge University Press, 2001), 126.

23. The term is from Currie (*Narratives and Narrators*, 35).

24. Currie, *Narratives & Narrators*, 39.

25. White, "Value of Narrativity," 20–21.

26. White, "Value of Narrativity," 21.

27. Noël Carroll, *Art in Three Dimensions* (Oxford: Oxford University Press, 2012 [2010]), 355–56.

28. White, "Value of Narrativity," 23.

29. Carroll, *Minerva's Night Out*, 123.

30. John Gibson, *Fiction and the Weave of Life* (Oxford: Oxford University Press, 2007), 82.

31. Richard Gaskin, *Language, Truth, and Literature: A Defence of Literary Humanism* (Oxford: Oxford University Press, 2013), vii.

32. Catherine Wilson, "Literature and Knowledge," *Philosophy* 58 (1983): 495.

33. A. W. Eaton, "Where Ethics and Aesthetics Meet: Titian's *Rape of Europa*," *Hypatia* 18 (2003): 164–66.

34. Wilson, "Literature and Knowledge," 495.

35. Carroll, *Art in Three Dimensions*, 273.

36. Carroll, *Art in Three Dimensions*, 275.

37. Friedrich Schiller, *On the Aesthetic Education of Man: In a Series of Letters*, trans. Elizabeth M. Wilkinson and L. A. Willoughby (London: Oxford University Press, 1967 [1794]).

38. Frederick Beiser, *Schiller as Philosopher: A Re-Examination* (New York: Syracuse University, 2005), 119–20.

39. John Andrew Bernstein, "Shaftesbury's Identification of the Good with the Beautiful," *Eighteenth-Century Studies 10* (1977), 308–14.

40. Third Earl of Shaftesbury (Anthony Ashley-Cooper), *Characteristicks of Men, Manners, Opinions, Times, Volume I* (Indianapolis, IN: Liberty Fund, 2001 [1714]), Treatise III, 2.ii, 236–43.

41. Third Earl of Shaftesbury (Anthony Ashley-Cooper), *Characteristicks of Men, Manners, Opinions, Times, Volume III* (Indianapolis, IN: Liberty Fund, 2001 [1714]), Miscellany III, 1, 136–42.

42. Third Earl of Shaftesbury (Anthony Ashley-Cooper), *Characteristicks of Men, Manners, Opinions, Times, Volume II* (Indianapolis, IN: Liberty Fund, 2001 [1714]), Treatise V, 3.ii, 401–2; Shaftesbury, *Characteristicks Vol. III*, Miscellany III, 2, 164–65.

43. Shaftesbury, *Characteristicks Vol. III*, Miscellany III, 2, 168–69.

44. Immanuel Kant, *Critique of the Power of Judgment*, trans. P. Guyer and E. Matthews (Cambridge: Cambridge University Press, 2001 [1790]), Introduction, 196.

45. Kant, *Critique of Judgment*, §§1–5: 203–11.

46. Kant, *Critique of Judgment*, §9: 217.

47. Kant, *Critique of Judgment*, §5: 210.

48. Kant, *Critique of Judgment*, §17: 236.

49. Kant, *Critique of Judgment*, §59: 353. For detailed and informed discussions of the relationship between aesthetic value and moral value in the *Third Critique*, see: Ted Cohen, "Why Beauty Is a Symbol of Morality," in *Essays in Kant's Aesthetics*, ed T. Cohen and P. Guyer (Chicago: University of Chicago Press, 1982),

221–36; Paul Guyer, "Feeling and Freedom: Kant on Aesthetics and Morality," *The Journal of Aesthetics and Art Criticism* 48 (1990): 137–46; Zvi Tauber, "Aesthetic Education for Morality: Schiller and Kant," *The Journal of Aesthetic Education* 40 (2006): 22–47.

50. Kant, *Critique of Judgment*, §59: 354.
51. Kant, *Critique of Judgment*, §60: 356.
52. Kant, *Critique of Judgment*, §60: 355.
53. Beiser, *Schiller as Philosopher*, 123.
54. Schiller, *Aesthetic Education*, XII: 79–81.
55. Schiller, *Aesthetic Education*, XIV: 97.
56. Schiller, *Aesthetic Education*, XV: 101.
57. Beiser, *Schiller as Philosopher*, 153.
58. Beiser, *Schiller as Philosopher*, 142.
59. Schiller, *Aesthetic Education*, II: 9.
60. Beiser, *Schiller as Philosopher*, 162–63.
61. Schiller, *Aesthetic Education*, XXVII: 215.
62. Schiller, *Aesthetic Education*, XVII: 219.
63. See: Jason Frank, "Walt Whitman: Aesthetic Democracy and the Poetry of the People," *The Review of Politics* 69 (2007): 402–30; Matthew Arnold, "The Study of Poetry," in *Essays in Criticism: Second Series* (London: Macmillan, 1925 [1880], 1–55.
64. For a historical and philosophical overview of *Négritude*, see: Reiland Rabaka, *The Negritude Movement: W. E. B. Du Bois, Leon Damas, Aime Cesaire, Leopold Senghor, Frantz Fanon, and the Evolution of an Insurgent Idea* (Lanham, MD: Rowman & Littlefield, 2016).
65. See: Patrick Fessenbecker, "In Defense of Paraphrase," *New Literary History* 44 (2013): 117–39.
66. See: Rafe McGregor, *The Value of Literature* (London: Rowman & Littlefield International, 2016), especially chapters 2 and 7.
67. Richard Rorty, *Contingency, Irony, and Solidarity* (New York: Cambridge University Press, 1989).
68. Norman Geras, *Crimes Against Humanity: Birth of a Concept* (Manchester: Manchester University Press, 2015), 4.
69. Geras, *Crimes Against Humanity*, 7.
70. Raphael Lemkin, *Axis Rule in Occupied Europe: Laws of Occupation, Analysis of Government, Proposals for Redress* (Washington, DC: Carnegie Endowment for International Peace, 1944), 79.
71. Geras, *Crimes Against Humanity*, 22.
72. *Nuremberg Trial Proceedings, Vol. 1: Charter of the International Military Tribunal*, Section II, article 6(b). Yale Law School, the Avalon Project. Available at: http://avalon.law.yale.edu/imt/imtconst.asp.
73. Convention (I) for the Amelioration of the Condition of the Wounded and Sick in Armed Forces in the Field, Geneva, 12 August 1949: article 2. Available at: https://ihl-databases.icrc.org/applic/ihl/ihl.nsf/ART/365-570005?OpenDocument.

74. United Nations, General Assembly Resolution 260, 9 December 1948. United Nations 1948: article 2. Available at: http://www.ohchr.org/EN/ProfessionalInterest/Pages/CrimeOfGenocide.aspx.

75. Nicole Rafter, *The Crime of All Crimes: Toward a Criminology of Genocide* (New York: New York University Press, 2016), 15.

76. Feierstein quoted in Rafter, *Crime of All Crimes*, 28.

77. Geras, *Crimes Against Humanity*, 21.

78. Geras, *Crimes Against Humanity*, 24.

79. Geras, *Crimes Against Humanity*, 28.

80. Christopher Macleod, "Towards a Philosophical Account of Crimes Against Humanity," *The European Journal of International Law* 21 (2010): 283. The ambiguity noted by Macleod is precisely that explored by Ridley Scott in *Blade Runner*, as discussed in the preface.

81. Rome Statute of the International Criminal Court (1998): article 7. Available at: http://legal.un.org/icc/statute/99_corr/cstatute.htm.

82. Massimo Renzo, "Crimes Against Humanity and the Limits of International Criminal Law," *Law and Philosophy* 31 (2012): 444.

83. Geras, *Crimes Against Humanity*, 92.

84. For discussions of the concept of political crime and its neglect in criminology, see: W. William Minor, "Political Crime, Political Justice, and Political Prisoners," *Criminology* 12 (1975): 385–98; Kenneth D. Tunnell, "Political Crime and Pedagogy: A Content Analysis of Criminology and Criminal Justice Texts," *Journal of Criminal Justice Education* 4 (1993): 101–14; Russell Hogg, "Criminology, Crime and Politics Before and After 9/11," *The Australian and New Zealand Journal of Criminology* 40 (2007): 83–105; Jeffrey Ian Ross, "Political Crime," in *The Encyclopedia of Crime and Punishment*, ed. Wesley G. Jennings (Chichester: Wiley-Blackwell, 2014), 983–89.

85. United Nations, "Ad Hoc Committee Established by General Assembly Resolution 51/210 of 17 December 1996." Last modified 16 February 2017. Available at: http://legal.un.org/committees/terrorism/.

86. Patryk Pawlak, "Understanding Definitions of Terrorism," European Parliamentary Research Service, PE 571.320 (November 2015). Available at: http://www.europarl.europa.eu/RegData/etudes/ATAG/2015/571320/EPRS_ATA%282015%29571320_EN.pdf.

87. Legal Information Institute, "22 U.S. Code § 2656f—Annual Country Reports on Terrorism," Cornell Law School. Available at: https://www.law.cornell.edu/uscode/text/22/2656f.

88. Legal Information Institute, "18 U.S. Code § 2331—Definitions," Cornell Law School. Available at: https://www.law.cornell.edu/uscode/text/18/2331.

89. United Kingdom, "Terrorism Act 2000." Available at: http://www.legislation.gov.uk/ukpga/2000/11/schedule/7.

90. For a clear and concise overview of this phenomenon, see: Corinne Squire, Molly Andrews, and Maria Tamboukou, "Introduction: What Is Narrative Research?" in *Doing Narrative Research*, 2nd ed. (London: SAGE, 2013), 1–26. For examples of paradigmatic work, see: Elliot G. Mischler, *Research Interviewing: Context and*

Narrative (Cambridge, MA: Harvard University Press, 1986); Theodore R. Sarbin, *Narrative Psychology: The Storied Nature of Human Conduct* (New York: Praeger, 1986); Donald E. Polkinghorne, *Narrative Knowing and the Human Sciences* (Albany, NY: State University of New York Press, 1988); D. Jean Clandinin and F. Michael Connelly, *Narrative Inquiry: Experience and Story in Qualitative Research* (New York: Jossey-Bass, 2004); Catherine Kohler Riessman, *Narrative Methods in the Human Sciences* (New York: SAGE, 2008); Christine Bold, *Using Narrative in Research* (London: SAGE, 2012).

91. Matti Hyvärinen, "Revisiting the Narrative Turns," *Life Writing* 7 (2010): 72–77.

92. Catherine Kohler Riessman, "Analysis of Personal Narratives," in *Handbook of Interview Research: Context and Method*, ed. J. F. Gubrium and J. A. Holstein (Thousand Oaks, CA: SAGE, 2002), 696–97.

93. Mark Freeman, "Foreword," in S. Cobb, *Speaking of Violence: The Politics and Poetics of Narrative in Conflict Resolution* (New York: Oxford University Press, 2013), vii.

94. D. Lawrence Wieder, *Language and Social Reality: The Case of Telling the Convict Code* (Berlin: De Gruyter Mounton, 1974).

95. Lois Presser, "The Narratives of Offenders," *Theoretical Criminology* 13 (2009): 178.

96. Lois Presser and Sveinung Sandberg, "Introduction: What Is the Story?" in *Narrative Criminology: Understanding Stories of Crime* (New York: New York University Press, 2015), 11.

97. Presser and Sandberg, "Introduction," 1.

Chapter Two

Contemporary Aesthetic Education

The purpose of this chapter is to set out the two most compelling alternatives to my thesis of narrative justice: Gayatri Chakravorty Spivak's theory of global aesthetic education and Sarah E. Worth's theory of narrative education. In section 6, I provide a summary of Spivak's claim that the training of the imagination for epistemological performance detranscendentalises gender, socioeconomic class, religion, and nationality, showing the parallels with Friedrich Schiller's claim that an aesthetic education removes the barriers to individual freedom and personal autonomy. In section 7, I first analyse Spivak's conception of the relationship between the literary imagination and ethical experience and then explore its consequences for global aesthetic education. Section 8 presents Worth's argument for narrative education, explaining why she maintains that the engagement with literary narratives improves both the empathy and the social knowledge of readers. Section 9 examines the empirical evidence Worth provides for her theoretical claim, focusing on five sets of psychological experiments: Raymond Mar, Keith Oatley, Jacob Hirsh, Jennifer dela Paz, and Jordan Peterson (2006); Matthijs Bal and Martijn Veltkamp (2013); David Comer Kidd and Emanuele Castano (2013); Dan Johnson, Daniel Jasper, Sallie Griffin, and Brandie Huffman (2013); and Katrina Fong, Justin Mullin, and Raymond Mar (2013 and 2015).

6. READING, DETRANSCENDENTALISATION, AND EPISTEMOLOGICAL PERFORMANCE

As the title of Gayatri Chakravorty Spivak's *An Aesthetic Education in the Era of Globalization* implies, she is concerned with contemporary aesthetic education, with the relevance of Schiller's theory in the world as it is now, in the early twenty-first century. The current era is the era of globalisation, which Spivak delineates against the preceding era: two worlds (North and South) have replaced three (First, Second, and Third), global has replaced neocolonial, digitally assisted postmodernism has replaced modernism, and neoliberal policy has replaced ideological politics.[1] Globalisation is itself a legacy of the Enlightenment, and Spivak is clear that her work "is about productively undoing another legacy of the European Enlightenment—the aesthetic."[2] She immediately links the aesthetic to the imagination and draws attention to the importance of the double bind. The double bind is a meta-theoretical framework in which two concepts in binary opposition both contradict and construct one another, a development of Jacques Derrida's *différance*.[3] The double bind is particularly important to global aesthetic education because while the aesthetic encourages maximal use of the imagination, globalisation encourages conformity to neoliberal norms.[4] The distinguishing feature of the double bind is not the obvious point that these demands draw the individual in opposite directions, but that the aesthetic and the global construct as well as contradict one another, and Spivak's project is the articulation of a post-structural theory of aesthetic education that both recognises and exploits the double bind at the centre of global aesthetic education.

She issues the following call to action:

> In our dwindling isolation cells, we must plumb the forgotten and mandatorily ignored bi-polarity of the social productivity and the social destructiveness of capital and capitalism by affecting the world's subalterns, in places where s/he speaks, unheard, by way of deep language learning, qualitative social sciences, philosophizing into unconditional ethics.[5]

The subaltern in Spivak is the subjugated or subordinated other, whose agency is not recognised by government, by institutions, or by members of the privileged group.[6] Agency is understood in terms of "institutionally validated action," what might be described as political rather than personal agency, which ceases to exist without institutional recognition.[7] In an interview on *An Aesthetic Education in the Era of Globalization* in 2012, Spivak was explicit about the relationship between recognition and subalternity, explaining that resistance cannot be identified as such without an "infrastructure for recognition" and defining subalternity as "lack of access to social mobility."[8] The lack of access is not only political, reliant upon the socioeconomic status of subaltern groups, but also epistemological, because subalternity can be internalised, as she notes with respect to gender when she writes of the need to acknowledge that "the woman-in-culture may be the site of internalized phallocracy."[9] This is why the intuition of democracy is as important as the institution. Spivak argues that without this epistemological emancipation, people come to accept their poverty as normal: "And when it comes time to starve, they just tighten their nonexistent belts and have to suffer, fatefully accepting this in silence."[10] She therefore understands aesthetic education as both a theory and a practice—a practice that promotes the democratic intuition that facilitates participation in the democratic institution.

The irreducible, essential element of the theory and practice of aesthetic education is "reading in its most robust sense."[11] This type of reading involves the reconceptualisation of belief in terms of the imagination, of what has been conceived of as necessary reconceived as contingent. This reconception from the necessary to the contingent is called "detranscendentalization" by Spivak.[12] Detranscendentalisation is the overcoming of the narrowness of mind that regards certain beliefs as necessarily true. Aesthetic education is teaching aimed at the detranscendentalisation of gender, socioeconomic class, religion, and nationality by means of reading. Spivak has discussed the role of all four of these concepts in creating hegemonies that maintain subalternity in her previous work, and I have placed them in the order of importance with which they are treated in *An Aesthetic Education in the Era of Globalization*.[13] Gender is "our first instrument of abstraction" and is the most problematic because it is both the oldest and the most widespread validator of agency.[14] Sex is conflated with gender, and females/women are provided agency by the institution of "reproductive heteronormativity (RHN)."[15] RHN thus establishes a hegemony within which everyone who is born a female becomes subaltern, their political agency reduced to their gender roles of child-bearer, mother, and grandmother, and restricted to the domestic realm, where they are subordinate to father, husband, and son.[16] As such, RHN is the most likely hegemony to be internalised. RHN also has strong links to the other three instruments of abstraction and plays a role in the hegemonies of socioeconomic class, religion, and nationality.

Spivak provides three definitions of aesthetic education, all of which develop her conception of detranscendentalisation through reading:

(a) "training the imagination for epistemological performance."[17]
(b) "the training of the imagination in epistemological performance through a rearrangement of desires."[18]
(c) "the imagination is trained for epistemological performance through language learning."[19]

In an interview on W. E. B. Du Bois in 2014, Spivak was explicit that epistemological performance means "to construct objects of knowledge differently."[20] She was also clear that language learning is "deep language learning," which refers to the learning required to access cultural infrastructures rather than linguistic competence with one's own or with a foreign language (most

often English in the era of globalisation).[21] Another way to understand the
relation between language learning and epistemological performance, to
which Spivak refers only briefly, is language as an episteme as conceived by
Michel Foucault (i.e., as a body of ideas that shape the perception of knowledge).[22] Deep language learning facilitates an epistemological performance
in which the dominant conceptions of gender, socioeconomic class, religion,
and nationality are revealed as contingent rather than necessary, as belonging
to a particular perspective on reality rather than providing direct access to
reality. This epistemological performance opposes the internalisation of the
respective hegemonies and facilitates and promotes the rearrangement of
desires. As the above definitions suggest, aesthetic education operates by
means of the imagination. Spivak defines the "the aesthetic in aesthetic education" as the *philosophico-literary*, and the mode of reading she promotes
involves the literary imagination.[23]

Reading in its most robust sense involves the reconceptualisation of belief
in terms of the imagination, and Spivak explains her emphasis on the role
of the *literary* imagination as follows: "When I say the literary imagination
de-transcendentalizes, when you think of something as literature, you don't
believe in it, and yet you're moved."[24] She thus reveals her commitment to
the relationship between the literary and the fictive stances that I established
in *The Value of Literature*: fiction is a descriptive concept and literature an
evaluative one, but to adopt the literary stance to a work or text—to read it
qua literature—is to adopt the fictive stance, to appreciate its inventiveness
and imaginativeness.[25] I identified a literary work by the combination of
the intention of the author to invoke a literary response and the practice of
the reader in adopting the literary stance. Spivak does not employ literary
response or literary stance but writes of the literary register, which is "the
register of the singular and the unverifiable."[26] This is a statement of what
I call literary anti-cognitivism, the view that truth is not a value of literature
qua literature (i.e., that there is no necessary relation between truth and literary value).[27]

In a further similarity, however, Spivak is also committed to a close relationship between work or text and world, to literature referring to reality.
I characterised this pro-reference, anti-cognitivist position as *aboutness*,
which I explained in terms of *literary thickness*, a concept that describes a
particular relation between literary form and literary content.[28] Spivak has a
corresponding take on the relationship between text and world:

> Because he figures in a novel, I read "Wordsworth" here as a figure. But a figure
> cannot be stripped of content. It says something about the very logic that allows
> us to recognize it as a figure—a logic that rests not only on the history of the
> language but upon "empirical" history.[29]

The literary imagination thus frees us from the constraints of truth without severing the text from the world, which is why one is moved by a literary text without believing in it. The relationship with detranscendentalisation is that the literary imagination provides a paradigm for value without a commitment to truth (i.e., it provides epistemological training in reconceiving the restrictions of gender, socioeconomic class, religion, and nationality as contingent rather than necessary without rendering them valueless). Like Schiller on aesthetic education, Spivak maintains that the education afforded by literature is indirect rather than direct:

> The successful reader learns to identify implicitly with the value system figured forth by literature through learning to manipulate the figures, rather than through (or in addition to) working out the argument explicitly and literally, with a view to reasonable consent. Literature buys your assent in an almost clandestine way and therefore it is an excellent instrument for a slow transformation of the mind.[30]

The type of imagining that robust reading promotes thus invites application beyond the literary text to the cultural and political context and produces a reconception of those contexts. In this way, "deep language learning and literary textuality train the ethical reflex."[31]

7. LITERARY IMAGINATION, ETHICS, AND IMPOSSIBILITY

As conceived thus far, the role of the literary imagination in ethical life can be compared to the role of fitness in sport. Acquiring proficiency in most sports requires the combination of cardiovascular fitness with a specific set of motor skills—for example, boxers with their fists. Cardiovascular fitness underpins the motor skills for the simple reason that fitness reduces fatigue, which has a negative impact on motor skills. Improving one's cardiovascular fitness thus improves one's performance in boxing, but proficiency in boxing requires the application of one's improved endurance to the practice of the relevant motor skills. There is no necessary relation between fitness and boxing because one might improve one's cardiovascular fitness for the sake of one's health or for the pleasurable experience produced and never apply the endurance gained to learning to box. Similarly, one could agree with Spivak that the robust reading she advocates does constitute an epistemological performance, but one could argue that this epistemological performance exercises the literary rather than ethical imagination and may never be applied to questions concerning gender, socioeconomic class, religion, or nationality. In other words, deep language learning and literary textuality necessarily train the literary imagination, but this training may merely enrich the literary experience and develop the reader's capacity for appreciation.[32] On this conception, Spivak's theory of global aesthetic education proposes a contingent rather than necessary relation between aesthetic and ethical value: the literary imagination necessarily improves epistemological performance, but contingently improves ethical performance (understood as epistemological performance in ethics). Her theory is in fact more robust than this, however, and the relation between aesthetic value and ethical value is much closer.

In section 3, I mentioned that contemporary aesthetic education was dominated by the ethical turn in criticism and that one of the three constituents of this turn was *Levinasian poststructuralism*, which is exemplified in the work of Derrida. Spivak's aesthetic education belongs to this particular branch of the ethical turn, and her conception of ethics corresponds with Derrida's in two important respects: first, they both employ Emmanuel Levinas's meta-ethical framework, and second, they both accept the normative consequences of this framework as establishing a close relation between the ethical and the impossible. Levinas famously maintained that ethics, not ontology, was "first philosophy," by which he meant that the inquiry into existence presupposed dialogue between self and other.[33] For Levinas, ethics simply *is* the relationship upon which all philosophy is constructed, and responsibility "the essential, primary and fundamental structure of subjectivity."[34] This responsibility is not reliant upon reciprocation by the other, but is prior to and definitive of human agency:

> Responsibility in fact is not a simple attribute of subjectivity, as if the latter already existed in itself, or before the ethical relationship. Subjectivity is not for itself; it is, once again, initially for the other. In the book, the proximity of the Other is presented as the fact that the Other is not simply close to me in space, or close like a parent, but he approaches me essentially insofar as I feel myself—insofar as I am—responsible for him.[35]

The self is thus constituted by the other, and responsibility for and to the other is absolute.

Derrida described Levinas's project as the distillation of "the essence of the ethical relation in general," an *ethics of ethics* as opposed to an ethical theory.[36] Derrida explored the theoretical implications of Levinas's conception of the ethical relation as responsibility and of ethics as prior to ontology in *The Gift of Death*. If responsibility to the other is not reliant upon reciprocation or propinquity, but is infinite and absolute, then the ethical relation appears to paralyse rather than guide ethical behaviour:

By preferring what I am doing here and now, simply by giving priority to my work or my activity as a citizen or professorial and professional philosopher, writing and speaking here in a public language, French in my case, I am perhaps fulfilling my duty. But I am sacrificing and betraying at every moment all my other obligations: my obligations to the other others whom I know or don't know, the billions of my fellows (without mentioning the animals that are even more other than my fellows) who are dying of starvation or sickness.[37]

How, Derrida asks, does one reconcile the finitude of self with the infinity of responsibility to the other? I am responsible to, for example, my family as other, but in devoting time and resources to my family I am failing to devote time and resources to human and non-human animals who have far greater needs than my family. Were I to devote my time and resources to those most in need of them or to those whom they would benefit the most, however, I would be ignoring a responsibility that many, if not most, people hold as more rather than less significant than my responsibility to strangers.

Derrida refers to the "aporia of responsibility," which recognises the paradox between singular responsibility and general responsibility.[38] He illustrates the aporia with the biblical example of the "Binding of Isaac," where Abraham has a dual and conflicting responsibility to both protect his son without hesitation and obey the command of his god without question. In secular language one can understand this conflict in terms of responsibility to the specific others with whom we have personal relationships and responsibility to the general Other with whom we are also in an ethical relation. Derrida's conclusion is that one does not sacrifice oneself for others/Other but sacrifices one other to another other/Other. He states:

I can respond to the one (or to the One), that is to say to the other, only by sacrificing to that one the other. I am responsible to any one (that is to say to the other) only by failing in my responsibility to all the others, to the ethical or political generality. And I can never justify this sacrifice, I must always hold my peace about it. Whether I want to or not, I will never be able to justify the fact that I prefer or sacrifice any one (any other) to the other.[39]

Derrida does not answer the question of how one must choose between (or rather, *among*) these impossible and conflicting demands—or even if one should make a choice—but claims that the choices one does make determine one's singularity and are consequently constitutive of one's character.

Spivak describes the "bottom line of being-human as being-in-the-ethical-relation."[40] The ethical relation places human beings in a frustrating situation because the self is angled toward a quite-other that it cannot reach. The ethical is thus characterised by a gap between the desire to reach the quite-other and the impossibility of fulfilling that desire, and this founding gap is so significant as to extend beyond the ethical into the related discourses of politics and history. "Thus the ethical situation can only be figured in the ethical experience of the impossible."[41] The ethical situation is not just characterised by impossibility but is defined by it because of the impossibility of achieving the desired union with the quite-other. Spivak agrees with Levinas that ethics is fundamentally a relation, and with Derrida that ethics is defined by an aporia. She makes explicit reference to the "double bind of the ethical" in the work of Levinas, Derrida, Melanie Klein, and Luce Irigaray and identifies the kind of situation to which Derrida refers in the "Binding of Isaac" as an experience rather than a dilemma.[42] A dilemma suggests a problem to which a solution can be found, but the ethical relation begins with the gap between self and quite-other and Abraham's situation—caught between responsibility to the other and responsibility to the Other (which is the situation of every human being in every ethical experience)—admits of no ethical resolution. In consequence, "the typecase of the ethical sentiment is regret, not self-congratulation."[43] Ethics is fundamentally a relation, and the ethical situation is an experience of impossibility that produces a sentiment of regret. In a similar manner to that in which Abraham would regret either killing his son or failing to follow his god's command, so I shall regret either failing to donate to Charity B when I donate to Charity A or failing to donate to Charity A when I donate to Charity B. This does not, however, mean that one cannot or should not decide between two options.

Recall that in the double bind the binary oppositions both contradict and construct one another. This is why Spivak states that "the figure of the experience of the impossible *is* the condition of possibility of deciding. In the aporia or double bind, to decide is the burden of responsibility."[44] Ethics is the call of relationship rather than a problem of knowledge, and as such, one should not rely on ideological guidelines to ethical behaviour.[45] Neither utilitarian calculations nor deontological maxims will suffice, because they both grasp the ethical as an epistemological problem. The ethical is, rather, "an interruption of the epistemological, which is the attempt to construct the other as an object of knowledge."[46] This repudiation of epistemological solutions to ethical problems appears to be a return to aporia, to promote either inaction or arbitrary action. Spivak's alternative is robust reading, the "ethical motor that undermines the ideological field."[47] Robust reading trains the imagination for epistemological performance, for reconceiving the necessary as the contingent, but it also exercises and develops the ethical faculty: the "imagination is our inbuilt instrument of othering, of thinking things that are not here and now, of wanting to become others."[48] The literary imagination is the ethical faculty, and robust reading therefore promotes "the habit of mind that can be open to experience ethics as the impossible figure of a founding gap, of the quite-other."[49]

In the analogy with which I began this section, I claimed that the role of the literary imagination in ethical life is similar to the role of cardiovascular fitness in boxing: in both cases the former can—but does not necessarily—contribute to latter. Spivak's claim that the imagination is the ethical faculty changes this relationship, however, because the exercise of the imagination in deep language learning and literary textuality is (also) the exercise of the ethical faculty. So, on this conception, the literary imagination can be compared to shadow-boxing (or, if a more popular contemporary form of exercise is preferred, Boxercise). Shadow-boxing is a means of improving one's cardiovascular fitness, which has all sorts of benefits for one's health and performance in a variety of sports, but it is also the actual practice of and for boxing (i.e., the specific set of motor skills required for proficiency in boxing). Similarly, if the imagination is the ethical faculty in virtue of the definition of ethical experience in terms of impossibility, then deep language learning and literary textuality simultaneously enrich the literary and ethical experiences and develop the reader's capacity for literary appreciation and ethical response. As such, aesthetic education operates at two distinct but complementary levels—or rather, there are two distinct aspects of or elements in aesthetic education:

(a) Robust reading trains the imagination for epistemological performance (i.e., reveals conceptions of necessity as contingent).
(b) Robust reading trains the ethical faculty for the experience of impossibility (i.e., reveals ethics as the call of a relationship rather than a problem of knowledge).

Like the two aspects of shadow-boxing (cardiovascular fitness and motor skills), (a) and (b) operate simultaneously and interactively: (a) encourages an openness to new ideas, including those concerning gender, socioeconomic class, religion, and nationality; and (b) provides practice in identifying with the quite-other, others, and the Other and responding to their calls in a responsible manner, albeit one necessarily characterised by regret.

(a) identifies a contingent relation between literature and ethics and (b) a necessary relation between literature and ethics. Schiller maintained that an aesthetic education was a necessary and sufficient (i.e., the only) means to the end of achieving harmony of character. Spivak does not make such a forceful claim explicitly, but in insisting that the imagination is the ethical faculty, she is maintaining that aesthetic education is a necessary and sufficient means to the end of achieving the detranscendentalisation of gender, socioeconomic class, religion, and nationality. The double bind at the centre of global aesthetic education is revealed as: globalisation facilitates the widespread implementation of robust reading practices to places and people that would not have been reached in the neocolonial era; but at the same time as globalisation facilitates the spread of robust reading, neoliberalism restricts the practice by forcing the humanities into the profit-making model of education and reducing the plurality of values associated with a humanities education to the single economic value of financial profit. In other words, the neoliberal era of globalisation has both disseminated the humanities to more people than ever before and marginalised humanities students as a group of subjects that are not (economically, which is the only measure) useful to local, national, and global economies. While globalisation unquestionably provides new opportunities for aesthetic education, Spivak is not optimistic about its long-term effects:

> If I have learned anything in my forty-five years of full-time teaching, it is the tragedy of the trivialization of the humanities, a kind of cultural death. Unless the polity values the teaching of literature in this way rather than just literary history and content and a fake scientism, the imagination will not be nourished.[50]

This recalls Schiller's pensive reflection at the end of *Letters*, and Spivak's theory is a direct development of his thesis that *political harmony can only be achieved by the cultivation of aesthetic sensibility*:

> *Global aesthetic education*: the detranscendentalisation of gender, socio-economic class, religion, and nationality can only be achieved by the cultivation of the literary imagination (i.e., the literary imagination is a necessary and sufficient condition of the detranscendentalisation of gender, socioeconomic class, religion, and nationality).

8. NARRATIVE UNDERSTANDING

Like Spivak, Sarah E. Worth is troubled by the widespread adoption of the neoliberal imperative in the twenty-first century. The scope of the diversity of values recognised in different cultures is being reduced to a single value, economic advantage or disadvantage, which is readily measurable in financial terms. This ultra-reductive account of value poses a dual threat to the practice of fiction, and Worth's aesthetic education, her theory of narrative education, is intended as a response to neoliberal monism:

> The utility of *reading for pleasure* is under attack in a number of settings because it is perceived as impractical. The value of *reading fiction* is under attack because it presumably does not teach us anything true or useful and, therefore, is not something that school curricula should waste time teaching. The primary purpose of this book is to build a defense against both of these claims.[51]

Like me, Worth is critical of one of the leading defences of fiction: Martha Nussbaum's theory of aesthetic education, which I refer to as *literature as moral philosophy* in *The Value of Literature*.[52] While I endorse the end of all defences of the value of fiction, narrative, and literature, I am rarely compelled by the means employed to mount those defences, and I think that some have the potential to do more harm than good (i.e., to serve as evidence against the practice, values, or institution defended). I have argued that Nussbaum's literary education was one of these, on the basis that it both proposed an unconvincing necessary relation between literary value and moral value and made completely unsubstantiated claims about the behavioural effects of reading.[53] Worth's critique of Nussbaum is also twofold, on an explicit and implicit level. Explicitly, she criticises Nussbaum for making too restricted a claim, for arguing that reading realist novels develops the moral imagination when the salient claim is that reading well-constructed narratives improves reasoning in general.[54] The implicit criticism of Nussbaum is that she shares the common weakness of philosophical accounts of the value of literature, a failure to engage with the scientific evidence of the benefits of literature.[55] In contrast to my take on Nussbaum, Worth employs the literary education established in *Love's Knowledge* and *Poetic Justice* as a springboard for her own theory.[56]

In a further similarity with Spivak, one can identify three levels at which Worth's theory operates. Where Spivak is concerned with language learning, the literary imagination, and the ethical faculty, Worth is concerned with literacy, narrative cognitivism (learning to reason through narrative), and narrative moralism (developing a capacity for empathy). With respect to the first of these, Worth is quick to point out the obvious but nonetheless significant benefits: "Reading literature, in fact, increases literacy, which in turn allows us a broader base of understanding of language and better access to the ways in which meaning is constructed by ourselves and others."[57] She also draws attention to the practical implications of a lack of literacy, pointing out that the most accurate predictor of the size of the prison population in the United States in fifteen years is the current percentage of illiterate ten- to fifteen-year-olds.[58] The most basic and most powerful defence of reading can therefore be calculated in terms of utility and even economic value in that literacy is related to level of education, and level of education is related to earnings.

Worth's primary focus, however, is on the second of the above three levels: narrative cognitivism, or the value of reading a particular type of text rather than the value of reading per se. She begins by identifying literature in terms of narrative and isolating her interest in literature to fictional literature, where fiction is understood as a genre (i.e., "to be read in a particular way") or a text toward which a reader adopts a particular intentional stance.[59] Her

approach to fictional literature is thus consistent with my own conception of
the literary stance and with Spivak's conception of the literary register (as
discussed in section 6).[60] Worth proceeds to discuss narrativity, distinguishes
narratives from annals and chronicles, and delineates narratives in virtue of:

(a) representing two or more states of affairs;
(b) the connection among which is either causally necessary or causally
     relevant;
(c) having a unified subject; and
(d) having a temporal structure.[61]

She defines *plot* as a feature of complex narratives, "the structure through
which events are connected to a narrative."[62] Worth's concern is with narrative
structure or, more precisely, with narrative as the structure of a particular kind
of representation.[63] Her subject matter is thus at the intersection of literary,
fictional, and narrative representations—exemplified by novels, novellas, and
short stories—and specifically with the way in which those representations
are structured. Worth's emphasis on the activity of reading rather than the text
or work (or the intention of the author of the text or work) is reiterated in her
summary of her position on narrative: "narratives are representations of at
least two events with a unified subject and a retrievable temporal order that
generally have an explanatory gap that needs to be filled in by the reader."[64]
   Worth not only shifts the focus of the debate about the value of literature
from its previous emphasis on the work of literature, but also shifts the focus
of the debate about the value of fiction to an analysis of what is distinctive
about nonfiction. The latter shift has two significant effects: the articulation
of a distinction between two different theories of truth in representation, correspondence, and coherence, and the recognition that the distinction between
narrative and non-narrative representation is more salient to the question of
value than the distinction between fictional and nonfictional representation.
Worth then draws both of these effects together in her theory of narrative
knowledge, which she describes as a version of aesthetic cognitivism on the
basis that: "What we gain from engaging with the arts, and with narrative in
particular, is a certain way of making sense of the world."[65] Worth's aesthetic
cognitivism is not a simple version of the literary cognitivism I identified in
section 6, the view that truth is a value of literature qua literature (or narrative
qua narrative in this case), because of her distinction between correspondence
and coherence theories of truth.
   The correspondence model of truth is the default setting in texts or
conversations that take truth as their subject matter (i.e., "a claim is true if
and only if it corresponds to the facts or reality of a situation. It is false if it
does not correspond.").[66] This is the sense in which "fiction" is used as the

antonym of "fact." The denotation does not, however, convey the sense in which "fiction" is used as the antonym of "nonfiction," as narrative nonfiction is more than a set or series of factual descriptions. In the coherence model of truth, "a statement is true if it is logically consistent with other beliefs that are considered true."[67] In narrative representation, coherence can refer to either the external connection between the text and the reader's beliefs about the text or to the internal connection between the parts of the text provided by the plot. "The coherence model of truth nicely accords with the narrative connection and the narrative-type grammars that many fictions follow."[68]

These two models of truth map onto the two models of reasoning identified by Worth: discursive and narrative. "Discursive reasoning relies on logical, direct arguments, while narrative reasoning depends on the narrative aspects of a story to order a certain experience."[69] In narrative reasoning, "we learn through the structure of stories."[70] This is why Worth is primarily concerned with narrative as the structure of a representation, because it is through engaging with this structure that the imagination is extended beyond the thought stimulated by discursive reasoning. The more developed one's narrative reasoning, "the more intelligent one should be able to become—assuming intelligence is related to the ability to retrieve information readily and find coherence where it does not obviously exist."[71] Narrative reasoning is developed by reading and writing stories, and this sensibility facilitates both a more rewarding experience of those stories and an improved ability to retrieve information and identify coherence. Unlike discursive reasoning, which involves the analysis of correspondence with fact, narrative reasoning involves the interpretation of experience for the purpose of the construction of meaning.[72]

Worth's narrative cognitivism has both a theoretical and empirical element, and her theory of narrative reasoning is supported by evidence of narrative comprehension. She cites neuroscientific studies to show that "coherence is the truth condition that trumps correspondence in the case of narrative comprehension."[73] When we read or write narratives we exercise our narrative reasoning, and the actual process of grasping or creating those narratives involves brain activity directed at establishing coherence rather than correspondence. The evidence from narrative comprehension is thus that narrative reasoning is based on the coherence model of truth and that we develop our narrative reasoning by according the distinction between narrative and non-narrative representations greater salience than the distinction between fictional and non-fictional representations.[74] This is why the coherence model of truth trumps the correspondence model of truth: in comprehending narrative representations we primarily employ narrative rather than discursive reasoning, and a focus on the narrativity of the representation provides a more rewarding experience than a focus on the fictionality of the representation. In order to become better readers and writers we therefore need to develop our understanding of narrativity rather than fictionality.[75] Worth summarises narrative comprehension as follows:

> Narrative comprehension is a dynamic interactive system built from the swarm of information bits that materialize and subsequently evaporate within the mind in the midst of both reading and hearing stories. It engages key brain areas in the attempt to build a working, conceptual narrative structure and can hopefully thereby produce narrative comprehension and narrative understanding. This comprehensive structure depends largely on a coherence-based model of understanding.[76]

Narrative cognitivism is the claim that narrative representations can provide knowledge in virtue of their narrativity. Worth has demonstrated how this knowledge is provided—by means of the narrative reasoning employed in reading narratives—and indicated the type of knowledge gained by the reader, knowledge that coheres with the reader's justified beliefs about the representation and about the world. This knowledge differs from knowing that (such and such corresponds with reality) and knowing how (to perform an action) and is described as knowing what-it-is-like. "It is a form of knowledge that helps us to understand *what it is like*: what it is like to be a different gender, in a different age, in a different historical period, or just what it is like to be anyone but me."[77] The knowledge of what-it-is-like provided by narrative reasoning benefits readers in at least three ways—cognitively, morally, and socially—and the movement from the moral to the social is what makes narrative education a theory of aesthetic education over and above a theory of aesthetic cognitivism.[78] Worth compares her theory to Nussbaum's:

> The underlying assumption that Nussbaum uses here, which is the explicit notion that I want to defend, is that through engaging with well-constructed narratives (what Nussbaum focuses on specifically is "good literature" and my scope of narrative is purposefully much broader than that) our own way of reasoning is changed through the moral imagination; our reason is heightened and thereby influenced through the *structure* of what we read.[79]

Unlike Nussbaum, Worth proposes a contingent relation between engaging with well-constructed narratives and the heightening of reason, but one that is nonetheless causal. Worth draws on an article by A. W. Eaton on the subject of pornography, using her example of the relationship between smoking and cancer: smoking is neither a necessary nor sufficient cause of cancer, but there is a general consensus that the link between smoking and cancer is causal rather than correlational.[80] "Chain smoking for 10 hours straight does not *cause* cancer, but smoking regularly for years on end significantly increases the statistical probability that one will develop cancer."[81] Worth's narrative education is also both broader and narrower than Nussbaum's literary education. It is broader in that it applies to well-constructed narratives rather than to the specific subgenre Nussbaum describes as "realist Anglo-American" and "realist social" novels.[82] Worth maintains that this engagement improves readers in the following ways: "the way we develop a capacity for empathy, the way we construct cognition, the way we improve our social interaction, and the way we make sense of the experiences of others."[83] Her narrative education involves the development of the capacity for empathy and is narrower than Nussbaum's in that she specifies "the ways in which narrative structure can help increase a healthy theory of mind for readers."[84] Worth makes a further distinction between two types of theory of mind (ToM)—cognitive and affective:

(i) CTM: "the inference and representation of others' beliefs and intentions."[85]
(ii) ATM: "the ability to understand the emotions of others."[86]

Worth is primarily concerned with ATM as it is positively linked with empathy.[87]

My interest in Worth's narrative education is specifically as a version of aesthetic education, the claim that *the cultivation of aesthetic sensibility develops political harmony*. Before examining the evidence she provides for aesthetic education, however, I want to draw the various elements of her theory together to be clear on her position. Narrative education involves both narrative cognitivism and narrative moralism:

(A) Narrative cognitivism: often, the engagement with well-constructed narratives develops the way we construct cognition.
(B) Narrative moralism: often, the engagement with well-constructed narratives develops our capacity for empathy.

9. EMPIRICAL EVIDENCE

Unlike Nussbaum, Worth does not simply provide a theoretical argument for aesthetic education, make a general claim about cause and effect, and rely on examples to convince her readers. As one might expect from the rigorous manner in which she provides evidence for her claim that narrative reasoning operates on a coherence model of truth (and thus for narrative cognitivism), she presents a detailed discussion of the evidence for the relationship between narrative and empathy. Worth precedes this discussion with a further distinction, between sympathy and empathy:

(a) Sympathy: "we do not feel the emotions ourselves, we just recognize that others are feeling something."[88]
(b) Empathy: "the capacity to feel what another person is feeling *from their perspective*."[89]

She explains empathy in more detail, drawing attention to the importance of the imagination:

> Empathy is *not* about what I would feel if I were going through what someone else is going through. It requires work of the imagination to understand how to adopt as much information about what the other person believes, thinks, and feels to be able to imagine how *he/she* is feeling as he/she experiences various situations. So empathy is what I would feel if I were in someone else's shoes. . . . Since it involves both feeling and believing, it incorporates both affective and cognitive aspects.[90]

Sympathy involves recognising an emotion (for example, sadness) in another person (for example, my friend) and experiencing an emotion in response to their emotion (for example, I feel sad that my friend is sad). Empathy involves recognising an emotion in another person and reproducing their emotion for oneself (for example, I feel my friend's sadness). This ability to reproduce someone else's emotion (rather than to experience an emotion in response to someone else's emotion) is achieved by means of the imagination at the psychological level and mirror neurons at the neurophysiological level. Having distinguished empathy from sympathy, Worth then states the goal of her empirical investigation, "which is some evidence that reading fiction produces higher empathy levels in its readers."[91]

She begins with two experiments conducted by Katrina Fong, Justin Mullin, and Raymond Mar. In the first, Fong, Mullin, and Mar used an expanded Author Recognition Task–Revised (ART–R) to measure genre reading habits, and a Reading the Mind in the Eyes Test–Revised (MIE) to measure interpersonal sensitivity.[92] They concluded that "individuals who exhibited more exposure to fiction tended to have greater interpersonal sensitivity while individuals who had been exposed to more Nonfiction did not show the same relationship."[93] In the second, the researchers used a modified ART to measure genre reading habits, the Traditional Egalitarian Sex Role Scale and Sex Role Stereotyping subscale to measure attitudes toward gender roles, and the Sexual Conservatism subscale to measure sexual conservatism (both of these subscales are from the Sexual Attitudes Survey).[94] They reached the conclusion that "fiction exposure predicted greater egalitarian gender roles, less endorsement of gender role stereotypes, and lower levels of sexual conservatism. In contrast, exposure to nonfiction did not statistically significantly predict any of our measures of sexual attitudes."[95] Worth notes that Fong, Mullin, and Mar make correlational rather than causal claims in both cases, but that the correlations are sufficient for the purposes of accurate prediction.[96]

Matthijs Bal and Martijn Veltkamp conducted two experiments to investigate the relationship between reading fiction and empathy.[97] In both, emotional transportation—the extent to which readers had been emotionally affected by the text—was measured using Busselle and Bilandzic's scale, and empathy was measured using Davis's empathic concern scale. The first experiment used the first third of the Sherlock Holmes story "The Adventure of the Six Napoleons" as its fictional text, and the second used the first chapter of José Saramago's *Blindness*. Bal and Veltkamp concluded that "increase of emotional transportation enhances empathy for fiction readers while it does not for nonfiction readers, such that it leads to higher empathy at relatively high levels of transportation."[98] In other words, reading fiction leads to emotional transportation, and emotional transportation leads to an increase in empathy. Bal and Veltkamp do not explicitly state that the relationship is causal, but neither do they claim it is correlational, and the use of *leads to* is indicative of the former relationship, such that one can summarise their position as: reading fiction causes emotional transportation, which causes an increase in empathy.

The relevant experiment that has received the most attention from both academics and the media was conducted by David Comer Kidd and Emanuele Castano.[99] Kidd and Castano used a series of five experiments to test their "general hypothesis that literary fiction would prime ToM."[100] The first of these compared the effects of reading literary fiction and non-fiction, and the remainder compared the effects of reading literary fiction and popular fiction. Kidd and Castano distinguished ATM from CTM and used MIE (in experiments 1, 3, 4, and 5) and the Diagnostic Analysis of Nonverbal Accuracy 2–Adult Faces test (DANVA2–AF, in experiment 2) to measure the former. They conclude: "Experiment 1 showed that reading literary fiction, relative to nonfiction, improves performance on an affective ToM task. Experiments 2 to 5 showed that this effect is specific to literary fiction."[101] Again, Kidd and Castano do not explicitly state that there is a causal relation between reading literary fiction and enhanced ATM, but their use of *improves* and *effect* is a clear statement that reading literary fiction enhances ATM. Referring to the work of Bal and Veltkamp, and Kidd and Castano, Worth concludes: "All of these experiments have shown that our intuition that reading fictional literature makes us more empathic is empirically veri-fiable."[102] Or, to return to the terminology employed in section 8, there is a causal relation between well-constructed narratives and empathy such that reading well-constructed narratives develops our capacity for empathy.

Worth also discusses two other experiments, which she regards as offering evidence for the social benefits of reading (i.e., benefits that extend beyond the moral). In view of my discussion of Worth's narrative education as a contemporary version of aesthetic education, one can consider the rela-tion she establishes between well-constructed narratives and empathy as the moral component (an empathetic education by narrative means) and the social benefits as the political component supervenient upon the moral. Raymond Mar, Keith Oatley, Jacob Hirsh, Jennifer dela Paz, and Jordan Peterson conducted an experiment to investigate the relationship between lifetime exposure to fiction on the one hand and empathy and social acumen on the other.[103] They used the Interpersonal Reactivity Index (IRI) to measure transportation and empathy, the MIE test to measure empathy, and the Interpersonal Perception Task–15 (IPT–15) to measure social sensi-tivity and skills. Worth summarises their conclusion: "What Mar found was that exposure to narrative fiction is positively related to social ability, and exposure to nonfiction was negatively related to social ability."[104] Mar and his colleagues make no more than a correlational claim, but the correlation is highly suggestive when considered in the context of the causal claims made by Bal and Veltkamp and Kidd and Castano.

Dan Johnson, Daniel Jasper, Sallie Griffin, and Brandie Huffman conducted two experiments to investigate the relationship between reading a fictional narrative and feelings of identification and compassion.[105] In the first, participants were divided into three groups, which read an extract from Shaila Abdullah's novel *Saffron Dreams*; a condensed version of the extract, which was lacking in formal complexity and substantive richness; and a brief his-tory of the automobile, respectively. Implicit and explicit bias toward Arab Muslims was then measured using the Implicit Attitudes Test (IAT) for the former and a six-item measure on a nine-point bipolar scale for the latter. The second experiment reproduced the first, using different measurement: implicit prejudice was measured by means of a thirty-item word fragment completion test in which fragments were accompanied by visual face stimuli, and explicit prejudice was measured by means of a nine-point semantic-differential scale. The results of the second experiment replicated the first, and the researchers make the causal claim that "narrative fiction can be used to induce empathy and reduce implicit and explicit prejudice."[106] Worth concludes that Johnson's "experimental results also provided empirical evidence that readers can gain social benefits from reading narrative fiction."[107] She summarises Mar and colleagues and Johnson and colleagues as both having demonstrated that reading well-constructed narratives provides "social knowledge."[108]

Unlike Spivak, Worth does not identify a necessary relation between an aesthetic means and a moral end, but she does specify a contingent relation that is both causal and common such that—just like the relationship between smoking and cancer—it should be taken seriously both inside and outside the academy. The evidence Worth offers for her theory of narrative education supports the relationship between aesthetic means and moral ends as well as the relationship between aesthetic means and political ends that is supervenient on the relationship between aesthetic means and moral ends and character-istic of traditional and contemporary theories of aesthetic education. As such, narrative education operates on two distinct but related levels:

(i) Often, reading well-constructed narratives develops our capacity for empathy (moral).
(ii) Often, reading well-constructed narratives provides social knowledge in addition to the development of empathy (political).

The qualification, *often*, is required because the empathic and social gains are potentialities that may or may not be realised by readers and may or may not have subsequent behavioural effects. The crux of Worth's theory of narrative education can be summarised as follows, using her own termin-ology: "If simulation is something we do regularly with real others, fictional literature provides an excellent *model* of the way in which we understand other people—characters, if you will."[109] As such, the relation between well-constructed narratives and social interaction, ability, and knowledge can be defined as:

Narrative education: social harmony can be achieved by the cultivation of narrative sensibility (i.e., the cultivation of narrative sensibility develops social harmony).

I shall return to Spivak's global aesthetic education and Worth's narrative education in chapter 6. In the next chapter, I begin to lay the foundations for my own thesis—narrative justice—examining the relationship between narrative representation, moral value, and ethical value.

NOTES

1. Gayatri Chakravorty Spivak, *An Aesthetic Education in the Era of Globalization* (Cambridge, MA: Harvard University Press, 2013 [2012]), 98–100.

2. Spivak, *Aesthetic Education*, 1.

3. See: Spivak, *Aesthetic Education*, 185, 228. Derrida set out *différance* as a meta-theoretical framework in: Jacques Derrida, *Of Grammatology*, trans. Gayatri Chakravorty Spivak (Baltimore, MD: John Hopkins University Press, 1997 [1967/1976]), 59–73; Jacques Derrida, *Writing and Difference*, trans. Alan Bass (Abingdon: Routledge, 2001 [1967/1978]), 248–58.

4. Spivak, *Aesthetic Education*, 2–3.

5. Spivak, *Aesthetic Education*, 27.

6. See: Spivak, *Aesthetic Education*, 430–34; Gayatri Chakravorty Spivak, "Can the Subaltern Speak?" in *Marxism and the Interpretation of Culture*, ed. C. Nelson and L. Grossberg (Urbana, IL: University of Illinois, 1988), 271–313.

7. Spivak, *Aesthetic Education*, 214.

8. Rahul K. Gairola, "Occupy Education: An Interview with Gayatri Chakravorty Spivak," *Politics and Culture*, 25 September 2012. Available at: https://politicsand culture.org/2012/09/25/occupy-education-an-interview-with-gayatri-chakravorty-spivak/.

9. Spivak, *Aesthetic Education*, 231.

10. Brad Evans, "When Law Is Not Justice," *New York Times*, 13 July 2016. Available at: https://www.nytimes.com/2016/07/13/opinion/when-law-is-not-justice.html.

11. Spivak, *Aesthetic Education*, 10.

12. Spivak, *Aesthetic Education*, 297.

13. See, for example, the following: gender in Gayatri Chakravorty Spivak, *Outside in the Teaching Machine* (New York: Routledge, 1993); religion in Gayatri Chakravorty Spivak, *A Critique of Postcolonial Reason: Toward a History of the Vanishing Present* (Cambridge, MA: Harvard University Press, 1999); socioeconomic class in Gayatri Chakravorty Spivak, *Death of a Discipline* (New York: Colombia University Press, 2003); nation in Gayatri Chakravorty Spivak, *Nationalism and the Imagination* (Chicago: Chicago University Press, 2010).

14. Spivak, *Aesthetic Education*, 30, 465. See also: Evans, "When Law Is Not Justice."

15. Spivak, *Aesthetic Education*, 123, 130, 288, 437.

16. For a discussion of the gendered subaltern, see: Spivak, *Aesthetic Education*, 71, 129; Spivak, *Teaching Machine*, chapters 2, 6, and 9.

17. Spivak, *Aesthetic Education*, 122, 301.

18. Spivak, *Aesthetic Education*, 125.

19. Spivak, *Aesthetic Education*, 127.

20. Ryan Rafaty, "Who Will Educate the Educators? An Interview with Gayatri Spivak," *King's Review*, 24 April 2014. Available at: http://kingsreview.co.uk/articles/who-will-educate-the-educators-an-interview-with-gayatri-spivak/.

21. Spivak, *Aesthetic Education*, 131, 133, 461, 472, 474.

22. Spivak, *Aesthetic Education*, 54. See: Michel Foucault, *The Order of Things: An Archaeology of the Human Sciences*, trans. A. Sheridan (London: Routledge, 2005 [1966]), chapter 9.

23. Spivak, *Aesthetic Education*, 464.

24. Spivak, *Aesthetic Education*, 296.

25. Rafe McGregor, *The Value of Literature* (London: Rowman & Littlefield International, 2016), 11.

26. Spivak, *Aesthetic Education*, 332.

27. McGregor, *Value of Literature*, 19.

28. McGregor, *Value of Literature*, 107–8.

29. Spivak, *Aesthetic Education*, 365.

30. Spivak, *Aesthetic Education*, 38.

31. Spivak, *Aesthetic Education*, 27.

32. My use of "merely" is not intended to imply that the literary experience is insignificant, as my central argument in *The Value of Literature* is that this experience has autonomous value, and that this literary value is both significant and distinct from cognitive value and moral value.

33. Emmanuel Levinas, *Totality and Infinity: An Essay on Exteriority*, trans. Alphonso Lingus (Pittsburgh, PA: Duquesne University Press, 2007 [1961]), 47.

34. Emmanuel Levinas, *Ethics and Infinity: Conversations with Philippe Nemo*, trans. Richard A. Cohen (Pittsburgh, PA: Duquesne University Press, 1985 [1982]), 95.

35. Levinas, *Ethics and Infinity*, 96. The book referred to is *Otherwise Than Being, or Beyond Essence*, which was first published in 1974.

36. Derrida, *Writing and Difference*, 138.

37. Jacques Derrida, *The Gift of Death*, in *The Gift of Death (2nd ed.) and Literature in Secret*, trans. David Wills (Chicago: University of Chicago Press, 2008 [1992]), 69.

38. Derrida, *Gift of Death*, 62.

39. Derrida, *Gift of Death*, 71.

40. Spivak, *Aesthetic Education*, 98, 352.

41. Spivak, *Aesthetic Education*, 98.

42. Spivak, *Aesthetic Education*, 104.

43. Spivak, *Aesthetic Education*, 105.

44. Spivak, *Aesthetic Education*, 109.

45. See: Spivak, *Aesthetic Education*, 104, 233.

46. Spivak, *Aesthetic Education*, 374.

47. Spivak, *Aesthetic Education*, 352.

48. Spivak, *Aesthetic Education*, 111, 406.

49. Spivak, *Aesthetic Education*, 111.

50. Spivak, *Aesthetic Education*, 288.

51. Sarah E. Worth, *In Defense of Reading* (London: Rowman & Littlefield International, 2017), 2.

52. McGregor, *Value of Literature*, 37–44.

53. McGregor, *Value of Literature*, 142–48.

54. Worth, *Defense of Reading*, 147, 150.

55. Worth, *Defense of Reading*, xv, 182–97.

56. See: Martha Nussbaum, *Love's Knowledge: Essays on Philosophy and Literature* (New York: Oxford University Press, 1990); Martha Nussbaum, *Poetic Justice: The Literary Imagination and Public Life* (Boston: Beacon Press, 1995).

57. Worth, *Defense of Reading*, 14.

58. Worth, *Defense of Reading*, 23.

59. Worth, *Defense of Reading*, 6, 41, 133.

60. Worth and I differ in that although we both define the literary in terms of the fictive stance, I take this stance to apply to poetry as well as narrative, while her definition is restricted exclusively to narrative.

61. Worth, *Defense of Reading*, 128–31.

62. Worth, *Defense of Reading*, 133.

63. Worth, *Defense of Reading*, 133–34.

64. Worth, *Defense of Reading*, 138.

65. Worth, *Defense of Reading*, xi.

66. Worth, *Defense of Reading*, 57.

67. Worth, *Defense of Reading*, 57.

68. Worth, *Defense of Reading*, 59.

69. Worth, *Defense of Reading*, 138.

70. Worth, *Defense of Reading*, 147.

71. Worth, *Defense of Reading*, 147.

72. Worth, *Defense of Reading*, 149.

73. Worth, *Defense of Reading*, 157. The neuroscientific evidence is drawn from: E. Mellet, S. Bricogne, F. Crivello, B. Mazoyer, M. Denis, and N. Tzourio-Mazoyer, "Neural Basis of Mental Scanning of a Topographic Representation Built from a Text," *Cerebral Cortex* 12 (2002): 1322–30; Robert Mason and Marcel Adam Just, "Neuroimaging Contributions to the Understanding of Discourse Processes," in *Handbook of Psycholinguistics*, ed. M. J. Traxler and M. A. Gernsbacher (Amsterdam: Elsevier, 2006), 765–79; Raymond Mar, "The Neuropsychology of Narrative: Story Comprehension, Story Production and Their Interrelation," *Neuropsychologia* 42 (2004): 1414–34; Véronique Boulenger, Olaf Hauk, and Friedmann Pulvermüller, "Grasping Ideas with the Motor System: Semantic Somatotopy in Idiom Comprehension," *Cerebral Cortex* 19 (2009): 1905–14; Jiang Xu, Stefan Kemeny, Grace Park, Carol Frattali, and Allen Braun, "Language in Context: Emergent Features of World, Sentence and Narrative Comprehension," *Neuroimage* 25 (2005): 1002–15; Rolf Zwaan, "Effect of Genre Expectations on Text Comprehension," *Journal of Experimental Psychology: Learning, Memory, and Cognition* 20 (1994): 920–33.

74. Worth, *Defense of Reading*, 96.

75. Worth, *Defense of Reading*, 169.

76. Worth, *Defense of Reading*, 161.

77. Worth, *Defense of Reading*, 127–28. I discuss these different types of knowledge in detail in chapter 4.

78. Worth, *Defense of Reading*, xi.

79. Worth, *Defense of Reading*, 143–44.

80. Worth, *Defense of Reading*, 177. See: A. W. Eaton, "A Sensible Antiporn Feminism," *Ethics* 117 (2007): 674–715.

81. Worth, *Defense of Reading*, 178.

82. Nussbaum, *Love's Knowledge*, 10, 87.

83. Worth, *Defense of Reading*, 174.

84. Worth, *Defense of Reading*, 176.

85. Worth, *Defense of Reading*, 191.

86. Worth, *Defense of Reading*, 191.

87. Worth, *Defense of Reading*, 191.

88. Worth, *Defense of Reading*, 183.

89. Worth, *Defense of Reading*, 183.

90. Worth, *Defense of Reading*, 183.

91. Worth, *Defense of Reading*, 187.

92. Katrina Fong, Justin B. Mullin, and Raymond A. Mar, "What You Read Matters: The Role of Fiction Genre in Predicting Interpersonal Sensitivity," *Psychology of Aesthetics, Creativity, and the Arts* 7 (2013): 370–76.

93. Fong, Mullin, and Mar, "What You Read Matters," 372.

94. Katrina Fong, Justin B. Mullin, and Raymond A. Mar, "How Exposure to Literary Genres Relates to Attitudes Toward Gender Roles and Sexual Behavior," *Psychology of Aesthetics, Creativity, and the Arts* 9 (2015): 274–85.

95. Fong, Mullin, and Mar, "Exposure to Literary Genres," 277.

96. Worth, *Defense of Reading*, 189–90.

97. P. Matthijs Bal and Martijn Veltkamp, "How Does Fiction Reading Influence Empathy? An Experimental Investigation on the Role of Emotional Transportation," *PLoS ONE* 8 (2013): 1–12. Doi:10.1371/journal.pone.0055341.

98. Bal and Veltkamp, "Emotional Transportation," 8.

99. David Comer Kidd and Emanuele Castano, "Reading Literary Fiction Improves Theory of Mind," *Science 342* (2013): 377–80.

100. Kidd and Castano, "Reading Literary Fiction," 378.

101. Kidd and Castano, "Reading Literary Fiction," 379.

102. Worth, *Defense of Reading*, 193.

103. Raymond A. Mar, Keith Oatley, Jacob Hirsh, Jennifer dela Paz, and Jordan B. Peterson, "Bookworms versus Nerds: Exposure to Fiction versus Non-Fiction, Divergent Associations with Social Ability, and the Simulation of Fictional Social Worlds," *Journal of Research in Personality* 40 (2006): 694–712.

104. Worth, *Defense of Reading*, 195.

105. Dan R. Johnson, Daniel M. Jasper, Sallie Griffin, and Brandie L. Huffman, "Reading Narrative Fiction Reduces Arab-Muslim Prejudice and Offers a Safe Haven from Intergroup Anxiety," *Social Cognition* 31 (2013): 578–98.

106. Johnson et al., "Reading Narrative Fiction," 587.

107. Worth, *Defense of Reading*, 197.

108. Worth, *Defense of Reading*, 198.

109. Worth, *Defense of Reading*, 181.

Chapter Three

Narrative Ethics

The purpose of this chapter is to defend a deflationary account of the ethical value of narrative representation. In section 10, I demonstrate that there is a necessary relation between narrative representation and ethical value, but not between narrative representation and moral value. *Ethical* is conceived in terms of moral as opposed to amoral, and *moral* in terms of moral as opposed to immoral, and the essential value of narrative representation is restricted to the former. Recently, both analytic philosophers and literary theorists have erred in conflating these two distinct kinds of value. In section 11, I defend my deflationary view against a philosophical argument for the moral value of narrative representation, Berys Gaut's ethicism. I analyse a theoretical argument in section 12, Geoffrey Galt Harpham's closural moral order. While I reject Harpham's elevation of ethical value to moral value, I accept his conception of emplotment as entailing movement from the condition of *is-but-ought-not-to-be* to the condition of *is-and-ought-to-be*, which articulates precisely the relationship between exemplary narratives and ethical value that I propose. My conclusion is that while every story does indeed have a moral, that moral may be virtuous, vicious, or somewhere in between.

10. ETHICAL VALUE AND NARRATIVITY

If my definitions in section 1 are accepted, then all narrative representations are concerned with agency in that they represent a minimum of a single agent and two events. The combination of agency and events places narratives in the ethical sphere, as all action (and inaction) is subject to ethical appraisal, even if that appraisal is that the action is permissible (rather than prohibited or obligatory) and therefore raises no ethical concerns. There is thus a necessary relation between narrative representation and ethical value. There are at least four ways of unpacking this relation:

(a) In virtue of their narrativity, narrative representations can be evaluated ethically.
(b) In virtue of their narrativity, narrative representations can provide knowledge when evaluated ethically.
(c) In virtue of their narrativity, narrative representations should be evaluated ethically.
(d) The value of narrative representations qua narrative representation is ethical value.

If the combination of agency and events entails an ethical dimension to narrative representation, as I have suggested, then (a) is obviously—but also trivially—true. Similarly, (b) is obviously and trivially true of some narrative representations but not others (especially minimal narratives, as I demonstrate below). The claim in (d), that the value of narrative qua narrative (which is often conceived of as aesthetic value) is ethical value is the thesis that ethical value is partly or wholly constitutive of narrative value. I make no such commitment and shall therefore defend (c), the claim that narrative representations not only can, but should, be evaluated ethically in virtue of their narrativity. Specifically, I shall defend the following relation between narrative representation and ethical value:

(EN^{NR})   The engagement with a narrative representation qua narrative representation is incomplete without ethical evaluation.

I noted that narrative representation entails dual agency in section 1: even a minimal narrative is the product of an agent in which (at least) one agent is represented. Currie identifies the internal perspective as examining "the world of the story as if it were actual" and the external perspective as seeing "a vehicle, something that represents a sequence of events in virtue of the activity of an agent we call the author."[1] Consider the following pair of minimal narratives, using my example from section 1:

 (i) Katy kicked the stone and missed her bus.
 (ii) Katy kicked the dog and ran away.

Adopting the internal perspective, one evaluates Katy's actions in both cases. In the absence of further information, (i) is ethically permissible and (ii) ethically prohibited. In adopting the external perspective, it is not the agency of the agent in the narrative, but of the producer of the narrative—the author— that is judged;[2] (ii) could be presented for the following purposes:

(A) as an example of shameful behaviour; and
(B) as an example of admirable behaviour.

From the internal perspective, Katy's action is evaluated as unethical in both contexts; from the external perspective, the author is evaluated as ethical if he is criticising Katy's action (A), is unethical if he is demonstrating how clever she was, for example, in being able to inflict harm on the dog without being bitten (B). The problem with (i) and (ii) is that the narratives are so minimal, communicating so little information, that there is barely any evidence to make an ethical evaluation of the represented agent and none at all for an ethical evaluation of the author. Both examples remain the product of an agent for which EN^{NR} is true, but they show that the ethical evaluation of narratives does not necessarily provide knowledge and is not even always possible from the external perspective.

In section 1, I identified the difference between minimal narratives and exemplary narratives as causal relations, thematic unity, and closure. In exemplary narratives, authors combine these three features to create a perspective on the agents, settings, and events represented. Lamarque refers to this perspectival nature as follows:

> narratives are "opaque" somewhat as paintings are opaque. They have the same kind of intentionality, not just as products of intentions, but also, in different ways and to different degrees, through expressing thoughts or a point of view on what they represent. This seems to be true of all narratives, not just those of literary fiction.[3]

I shall employ *opacity* to distinguish the authorial perspective constitutive of an exemplary narrative from the *framework* produced thereby, which Currie identifies as "a preferred set of cognitive, evaluative, and emotional responses to the story."[4] He notes that there are no explicit instructions, but that the framework is expressed in the representation of the sequence of events. From this framework Currie proceeds to

> the *standard mode of engagement* with narrative. Narratives, because they serve as expressive of the points of view of their narrators, create in our minds the image of a persona with that point of view, thereby prompting us to imitate salient aspects of it—notably evaluative attitudes and emotional responses. In taking on those responses, we thereby come to adopt, wholly or in part, the framework canonical for that work.[5]

The standard mode of engagement is thus the adoption, by audiences, of the framework that the author invites one to adopt.

It is this framework—the preferred set of cognitive, evaluative, and emotional responses—that produces a more complex relation between narrative representation and ethical value in the case of exemplary narratives. In contrast to minimal narratives, the necessary relation between narrative representation and ethical value in exemplary narratives is twofold:

(EN^{EX}) The engagement with an exemplary narrative qua narrative is incomplete without a dual ethical evaluation, from both the internal and external perspectives.

The *History of the Conquest of Peru* and *Citizen Kane* therefore invite the following ethical evaluations:

(I) the agency of the characters represented in the narrative, represented as they are by the author within a particular framework; for example, the agency of Francisco Pizarro or Charles Foster Kane.
(II) the agency of the author in telling the story, which includes the decision to represent the characters within a particular framework; for example, the agency of Prescott or Welles.

Both the actions of the characters in the story and the action of the author in telling the story are subject to ethical appraisal, and different authors can provide different frameworks for the same characters and events. In *Triumph of the Will*, for example, Riefenstahl frames Hitler as a messianic saviour who descends from the heavens to lead the German people to glory. In contrast, Oliver Hirschbiegel frames Hitler as an evil megalomaniac who sacrifices millions of people—including the German nation—for his self-aggrandisement in *Downfall*. If one rejects the standard mode of engagement for *Triumph of the Will*—Hitler as heroic—in adopting the internal perspective, then one will make a negative judgement of Riefenstahl for creating that framework in adopting the external perspective.[6]

When discussing closure as a criterion of exemplary narratives in section 1, I mentioned White, who maintains that narrative closure is a resolution that is presented by the author as either moral or immoral.[7] When history is represented in a narrative rather than non-narrative form,

> the demand for closure . . . is a demand . . . for moral meaning, a demand that sequences of real events be assessed as to their significance as elements of a *moral* drama.[8]

In the terminology I am employing, White is claiming that the standard mode of engagement with (historical exemplary) narrative representations requires the adoption of an internal perspective that *prioritises* ethical evaluation. My claim is that the standard mode of engagement with exemplary narratives requires the adoption of an internal perspective that *involves* ethical evaluation. The greater complexity of the necessary relation between exemplary narratives and ethical evaluation on the one hand and minimal narratives and ethical evaluation on the other hand creates the need for a two-part theory:

(T^{NR}) Narrative representations are essentially ethical in virtue of their combination of agency and events.

(T^{EX}) Exemplary narratives are essentially ethical in virtue of both the combination of agency and events represented and the agency of the author in inviting the adoption of a particular framework.

T^{NR} and T^{EX} are neither controversial nor remarkable claims and would perhaps not even be interesting had they not served as springboards for so many erroneous conclusions about the relationship between narrative representation and ethical value. I mentioned the following distinction in my abstract, which I have been employing heretofore and shall continue to employ (unless quoting directly):

(a) *Ethical* as opposed to a-ethical or amoral (i.e., a positive, negative, or ambiguous evaluation of agency or character); and

(b) *Moral* as opposed to immoral or unethical (i.e., a positive evaluation of agency or character).[9]

Returning to the pair of examples above, both *Triumph of the Will* and *Downfall* have ethical value, but only *Downfall* has moral value. My thesis, as articulated in T^{NR} and T^{EX}, is that narrative representation is essentially ethical in virtue of its narrativity. The erroneous conclusion to draw is that every narrative representation is essentially moral (i.e., subject to a positive ethical evaluation in virtue of its narrativity). Conclusions such as this have, however, been reached in both the philosophical and theoretical approaches to narrative representation. In order to avoid conflation with a distinction that can at times be subtle, I shall revise my two-part thesis as follows:

(TR^{NR}) Narrative representations are essentially ethical, but not essentially moral, in virtue of their combination of agency and events.

(TR^{EX}) Exemplary narratives are essentially ethical, but not essentially moral, in virtue of both the combination of agency and events represented and the agency of the author in inviting the adoption of a particular framework.

The arguments that narrative representations are essentially moral focus exclusively on exemplary narratives, and I shall follow suit. In the remainder of this chapter I defend my deflationary account of the ethical value of exemplary narratives, TR^{EX}, against two inflationary accounts—from Berys Gaut and Geoffrey Galt Harpham, respectively.

11. ETHICISM

In *Art, Emotion and Ethics* Gaut presents a meticulous analysis of a variety of proposed relationships between ethical value and artistic value and offers a complex and wide-ranging set of arguments for the theory he calls *ethicism*. He approaches the relation in question in the terms established by what I refer to as the "value interaction debate."[10] The value interaction debate, which was initiated by Noël Carroll with his article "Moderate Moralism" in 1996, is the most recent instantiation of the philosophical interest in the relationship between ethics and art.[11] Gaut's monograph is a development of his early contribution to the debate, "The Ethical Criticism of Art."[12] The value interaction debate focuses on the relationship between moral defects and merits and aesthetic defects and merits in artistic representations. Within the debate, the majority of contributions have argued either for or against the following pair of propositions:

(a) A moral defect in a work of art is (also) an aesthetic defect.
(b) A moral merit in a work of art is (also) an aesthetic merit.

The first half of *Art, Emotion and Ethics* (chapters 1 to 5) provides a conceptual mapping of the numerous positions in the debate, while the second half advances three distinct arguments for ethicism: the moral beauty argument (chapter 6), the cognitive argument (chapters 7 and 8), and the merited response argument (chapters 9 and 10). Gaut presents these arguments in order of both chronology and valence, from moral beauty as articulated during the Enlightenment and the least likely to convince, to merited response as Gaut's original contribution to the debate and the most compelling. As he states of the latter in his introduction, "the upshot of the argument is to show that the aesthetic domain is deeply intertwined with the ethical realm."[13]

Gaut's most concise definition of ethicism is in "The Ethical Criticism of Art," where the theory is defined in terms of the merited response argument, but a succinct definition can nonetheless be constructed by combining the article with the monograph as follows:

> *Ethicism*: Ethical merit is neither a necessary nor sufficient condition of aesthetic value, but an intrinsic ethical merit of an artwork is a *pro tanto* aesthetic merit, and an intrinsic ethical defect of an artwork is a *pro tanto* aesthetic defect.[14]

Ethicism is a theory about the ethical criticism of art, and Gaut employs examples from across a wide variety of art forms, including non-narrative painting. In his defence of the cognitive argument, however, he focuses on the cognitive value of narrative art, and his primary example in his defence of the merited response argument is a novel. As such, ethicism applies to both narrative art and non-narrative art, and there is a clear overlap of my own concerns with Gaut's in the area of artistic narrative representation. Similarly, when Gaut refers to a moral or ethical *merit*, he is concerned with what I refer to in section 10 as the moral value of a narrative representation (i.e., a *positive* evaluation of agency or character). Ethicism can therefore be restated as a theory about the ethical criticism of narrative representation as follows:

(MN^{ET})   Artistic narrative representations are essentially moral in virtue of the relationship between their moral and aesthetic values (i.e., an intrinsic moral merit is a *pro tanto* aesthetic merit).

Although Gaut and I differ in our respective uses of *intrinsic*, his use of *intrinsic* in MN^{ET} is consistent with my conception of the attribution of ethical value to representations as set out in section 2.[15] Gaut defines intrinsic ethical value in terms of attitudes manifested in an artwork, such that "in assessing the ethical value of art we are assessing the ethical quality of the point of view, cognitive and affective, that it takes toward certain situations."[16] In other words, the intrinsic ethical value of an artistic narrative representation is the ethical value of its framework, the evaluative attitudes and emotional responses that the author invites the audience to adopt. Gaut does not distinguish between what I refer to in section 10 as the internal and external perspectives, but he is obviously referring to the latter. He employs an uncontroversial conception of ethical or moral value (terms he employs interchangeably):

> the category of the moral is applied only to actions, feelings and motives directed towards others: that is, to other-regarding actions, feelings, and motives. Where such motives involve active hostility or improper neglect towards the other person, we talk of moral defects; where they involve concern for the other, we talk of moral merits.[17]

He qualifies this definition with the claim that the other-regarding sentiments and motives must be what I refer to in section 2 as non-instrumental (i.e., a concern for the other for his or her own sake rather than instrumentally, for the way in which the other can benefit the self). With the above definition in place, MN^{ET} becomes a thesis of the moral value of artistic narrative representation, a claim that there is a relation between the positive evaluation of the standard mode of engagement and the positive evaluation of the narrative qua narrative. Gaut's use of *aesthetic* in MN^{ET} differs from my use of the term in section 2, which I delineated broadly as the value of either a representation qua representation or a work of art qua art (i.e., its characteristic value, whether that character is understood in terms of being a narrative representation or a work of cinematic art). In his initial paper, Gaut identifies aesthetic value with artistic value, "the value of an object *qua* work of art," which includes "beauty," "cognitive insight," and an "articulated expression of joy," and excludes instrumental values such as "investment value" and "value as status symbols."[18] In his monograph, he addresses five objections to this view before stating:

> We have identified the (wide) aesthetic properties of artworks with their artistic properties, the properties that make something valuable qua art, and so have given an explanation for the otherwise mysterious diversity of aesthetic properties.[19]

Gaut's definition of aesthetic value thus includes several of the values of a work of art—artistic narrative representation in MN^{ET}—that I identified as non-instrumentally valuable in section 2, and I shall return to this definition below.

The moral beauty argument builds on the foundation laid by Wayne Booth in *The Company We Keep: An Ethics of Fiction* and Colin McGinn in *Ethics, Evil, and Fiction*.[20] Gaut's summary of the argument in his introduction reveals his emphasis on Enlightenment value theory, however, on the kind of close relationships among beauty, virtue, truth, and divinity I noted in my discussion of Shaftesbury in section 3. He is subsequently explicit that Schiller's aesthetic education was the apotheosis of the concept of moral beauty, and the implication is that the moral beauty argument for ethicism is in turn a development of aesthetic education.[21] With respect to the explicit claim, Schiller's thesis presents a version of moral beauty, broadly construed, but is also a specific and sophisticated refinement of the broad concept with which Gaut is working. With respect to the implicit claim, there is nothing wrong with relying on Enlightenment value theory—I have, after all, been clear that narrative justice traces its antecedents to Schiller—but the close relation among the various non-instrumental values of art upon which Gaut appears to rely has been the subject of dispute since at least the rise of the Aesthetic Movement in the second half of the nineteenth century. Gaut's argument is presented in the following passage:

> If a manifested author has a morally good character, it follows from the moral beauty view that he or she has, in this respect, a beautiful character. Since the manifested author is the author as he or she manifests herself in the work, it follows that the work has a beautiful aspect, in so far as the author has a beautiful character. The beautiful is undeniably an aesthetic value. So, in so far as the manifested author has a morally good character, the work has aesthetic merit in this respect; and *mutatis mutandis* for a morally bad manifested author, whose presence contributes an aesthetic flaw in this respect.[22]

MN[ET] holds because the manifestation of the moral (immoral) character of the author in the representation is an aesthetic merit (defect) (i.e., a merit [defect] qua narrative).

Gaut's cognitive argument is introduced in an apparently uncontroversial manner, as the notion that audiences can "ethically learn from imaginings guided by artworks."[23] I initiated my discussion of the cognitive value of representations in section 2 by drawing on John Gibson, whose focus is on whether literary representations are in some significant respect informative of extra-textual reality. As discussed in section 8, Worth refers to artistic representations more generally, to the question of what we gain from the arts being a certain way of making sense of the world. I shall discuss the various cognitivist claims in more detail in chapter 4, but aesthetic (or artistic) cognitivism can be defined as the claim that aesthetic (or artistic) representations can provide knowledge in virtue of their aesthetic (or artistic) value. Gaut distinguishes between two versions of this thesis: minimal and strong. In the former, a work manifests understanding in an aesthetically relevant way; in the latter, a work teaches in an aesthetically relevant way. In both cases, however, the cognitive merit (manifesting understanding or teaching) is an aesthetic merit (aesthetically relevant).[24] Gaut argues for the stronger version, presenting three distinct kinds of ethical learning, and states:

> What they possess in common is that they show that we can learn ethically through the exercise of the imagination through the full range of imaginative resources discussed in the previous section, together with the use of universalisation.[25]

He demonstrates a variety of ways in which narrative art in particular can be aesthetically relevant in the strong sense and concludes his argument with a detailed discussion of an apparent counterexample to the cognitivist argument, Vladimir Nabokov's *Lolita*. Gaut is explicit about his aesthetic cognitivism, but less so about his moral cognitivism (i.e., the position that moral statements have truth value [or that truth is a criterion of moral evaluation]). As such, Gaut's argument is actually that a cognitive merit (defect) is an aesthetic merit (defect) and that a moral merit (defect) is one kind of cognitive merit (defect) and therefore an aesthetic merit (defect). The aesthetic cognitivist argument for ethicism is readily adaptable to narrative cognitivism: MN^{ET} holds because the moral-cognitive merit (defect) in the representation is a narrative merit (defect) (i.e., a merit [defect] qua narrative).

As the name suggests, Gaut's most convincing argument for ethicism relies on the notion of merited response. He claims that artistic representations present a point of view on imagined events such that the representations prescribe both imaginings and responses to those imaginings in and by the audience. Gaut employs Donatien Alphonse François, Marquis de Sade, as an example:

> The responses are not simply imagined: we are prescribed by *The 120 Days of Sodom* actually to find erotically attractive the fictional events, to be amused by them, to enjoy them, to admire this kind of activity. So the novel does not just present imagined events, it also presents a point of view on them, a perspective constituted in part by actual feelings, emotions and desires that the reader is prescribed to have towards the merely imagined events.[26]

The 120 Days of Sodom represents its subject (sexual torture), manifests attitudes to the represented subject matter (amusement and arousal), and prescribes a corresponding response to that subject matter in its audience (amusement and arousal to sexual torture). Gaut claims that a "work's attitude is standardly manifested in prescribing certain responses towards the events it describes."[27] *Prescribed response* is thus identical to the *evaluative attitudes and emotional responses* that constitute the framework one is invited to adopt by the author of a narrative representation described in section 10. Prescribed responses or narrative frameworks can be merited or unmerited. Gaut provides two examples of the latter:

(i)   "If I am afraid of a harmless victim in a horror movie, because of her passing resemblance to an old tormentor of mine, my fear is inappropriate."[28]

(ii) "If we actually enjoy or are amused by some exhibition of sadistic cruelty in a novel, that shows us in a bad light, reflects ill on our ethical character, and we can properly be criticised for responding in this fashion."[29]

He identifies an unmerited response as an aesthetic failure, and the circumstance described in (ii) is therefore one in which a moral defect (enjoyment or amusement as a response) is an aesthetic defect (in virtue of being prescribed by the novel). The merited response argument for ethicism as applied to narrative representation can be set out as follows:

(A) An artistic narrative representation manifests an attitude toward characters and events by prescribing a response.
(B) If the response is unethical, it is unmerited.
(C) If the response is unmerited, the audience has no reason to respond in the prescribed way.
(D) The failure to respond as prescribed is an aesthetic defect.
(E) Therefore, an artistic narrative's manifestation of an unethical attitude is an aesthetic defect in the representation.

MN^{ET} holds because the unmerited response (ethical defect) in the representation is a failed prescribed response (narrative defect).

There is much to admire in *Art, Emotion and Ethics*. Gaut's arguments are always valid, and the chapters are interlinked so as to construct an impeccable intellectual architecture. In addition, he employs informed interpretations of a variety of artworks to support ethicism, beginning with Rembrandt van Rijn's *Bathsheba with King David's Letter* and ending with Joel and Ethan Cohen's *Fargo*. Gaut's theory is nonetheless doubly flawed, relying on a pair of false premises that are reproduced in different instantiations in each of the three arguments. These premises become apparent when one considers his arguments in reverse order, starting with the merited response argument as set out in (A) to (E). I have already agreed with (A), that an exemplary narrative prescribes a response by means of its framework, inviting the standard mode of engagement particular to that representation. A representational flaw that interposes between the framework and the standard mode of engagement does indeed seem to be an artistic, aesthetic, or narrative defect, as suggested by (D). The *aesthetic* failure that Gaut attributes to *The 120 Days of Sodom* is, however, actually the *successful* transition from the manifested attitude or framework (sexual torture represented as erotic) to the prescribed response or standard mode of engagement (actual arousal in the audience). Unlike the example of the idiosyncratic response to a victim in a horror film, this is precisely a *merited* response—merited by the acceptance of Sade's invitation to adopt his own perspective on sexual torture. In his original article, Gaut provides other examples of unmerited responses, which include amusement in response to tiresome comedies and excitement in response to dull thrillers.[30] These are clearly aesthetic failures, but they are also clearly in contrast with Sade's success in creating arousal in his audience. Returning to (i) and (ii) above, (i) is a failure on the part of the member of the audience rather than the author, and (ii) is an aesthetic success rather than an aesthetic failure. Gaut is correct in claiming that audience and author alike can be criticised for responding to the framework with the standard mode of engagement, but he does not explain why this immoral action is (also) unmerited beyond identifying immoral responses with unmerited responses.

One must revert to the cognitive argument for ethicism for elucidation, where Gaut controversially—and somewhat surreptitiously—accepts moral cognitivism. He refers to this position as the "cognitive-affective view of art" in his initial article, and its consequence is that an immoral prescribed response is unmerited in virtue of being inaccurate or false.[31] In other words, by promoting an ethically reprehensible attitude, the work advances an immoral perspective as a moral one and therefore commits an epistemic error by representing falsity as truth. Setting aside the question of the contentious identification (or reduction) of virtue with (or to) truth, it is also difficult to understand how Sade—as a writer of fiction—can be regarded as aiming for truth. Both the merited response and cognitive arguments appear to rely on the claim that a moral merit (defect) is (also) a cognitive merit (defect). Recall that Gaut not only identifies aesthetic value with artistic value, but defines aesthetic/artistic value in broad terms, including beauty, cognitive insight, and articulated expression of joy. If one does not accept his definition of aesthetic value in terms of cognitive value or his cognitive-affective view of narrative art, then one must revert to the moral beauty argument for ethicism. The moral beauty argument replicates the strategy of the cognitive argument but identifies aesthetic value with moral value instead of cognitive value. If a manifested author has a good character (moral value), then he or she has a beautiful character (aesthetic value). The combination of the three arguments reveals Gaut's commitment to the popular Enlightenment view that beauty, virtue, and truth are all closely related.

In contemporary terms, Gaut's definition of aesthetic value is so broad that it merely provides a catalogue of some (but not all) of the most important values that have been associated with narrative representation. A candid definition would include *moral attitude* with beauty, cognitive insight, and articulated expression of joy, and would reveal all three arguments for ethicism as tautologous, relying upon the following two premises: (I) ethical value is supervenient on (or reducible to) cognitive value, and (II) ethical-cognitive value is part and parcel of aesthetic value. Gaut comes close to admitting as much in his conclusion, claiming that there is "a sense in which the ethicist position is inevitable."[32] He justifies this statement by appealing to the significance of beauty to early modern aesthetics, the significance of cognitive value to modern aesthetics, and the significance of the affective dimension of art to contemporary aesthetics. Gaut's tracing of the development of historical conceptions of aesthetic value does not offer support for his arguments, but it does reveal their shared and camouflaged (if not concealed) premises. MN[ET] is therefore tautalogous: artistic narrative representations are only essentially moral in virtue of the relationship between their moral and aesthetic values if one accepts that both cognitive and ethical value are part and parcel of aesthetic value.

12. CLOSURAL MORAL ORDER

In his defence of the cognitive value of literature, Fessenbecker states that narrative representation entails commitment to propositions about agency, intention, and other features of subjectivity—which he summarises as "the moral-philosophical commitments inherent in narrative form."[33] In his terminology, therefore, my claim is that narrative form has inherent ethical commitments. Harpham takes this conception a step further, not merely exploring the ethical commitments of narrative form, but reconceptualising narrative representation in ethical terms. His starting point articulates his disillusion with contemporary research:

> One of the most obdurate problems in literary theory is narrative form, the study of which seems to have stalled since Aristotle's statement that the plot of tragedy proceeds towards a moment of reversal, followed by recognition, and ending in a dénouement. . . . But the attempt to define further the basic form of narrative has been virtually abandoned, defeated by the apparent shapelessness and singularity of extended narratives.[34]

Harpham seeks to identify the connection—temporal, causal, or thematic—between agency and event and recommends that narrative form be understood in terms of David Hume's distinction between *is* and *ought*, or fact and value. Both the distinction and Hume's purpose in describing it have been the subject of extensive debate, which has focused largely on what R. M. Hare refers to as Hume's Law, the proposal that no "ought" can be derived from an "is."[35] Harpham's ultimate aim is to employ the relationship between narrative and ethics to establish a reciprocal relationship between literature and philosophy. He maintains that ethics provides an explanation of narrative representation and that narrative in turn contributes to ethics by crossing the chasm between fact and value.[36] My interest is neither in the proposed contribution of narrative to ethics nor the more fundamental relation between literature and philosophy, but in Harpham's explanation of narrative form in exclusively ethical terms.[37] This explanation is made by means of plot.

I deliberately avoided characterising either minimal or exemplary narratives in terms of "plot" in section 1, due to the variety of ways in which the word is employed across the philosophical and theoretical traditions. White claims that narrative form is imposed upon a sequence of events in narrative history, and this imposition is described as follows by Peter Goldie:

> This process, which . . . I will call *emplotment*, is one by which a bare description of events, such as one might find in an annal or chronicle, can be transformed into a narrative, giving coherence, meaningfulness, and evaluative and emotional import to what is narrated.[38]

Emplotment is thus the procedure by which a sequence of real or fictional events is represented in narrative form, and plot distinguishes representations with narrative form from those without. Both White's discussion and Goldie's description imply that plot is restricted to exemplary narratives, and Harpham's definition follows suit:

> The most general and adequate conception of a narrative plot is that it moves from an unstable inaugural condition, a condition that *is* but *ought not*—a severance of the two [fact and value]—through a process of sifting and exploration in search of an unknown but retrospectively inevitable condition that *is* and truly *ought-to-be*.[39]

A narrative representation is formed by the process of emplotment. Emplotment entails movement from the condition of *is-but-ought-not-to-be* to the condition of *is-and-ought-to-be*, and narrative form is therefore essentially ethical.

Two necessarily oversimplified examples will serve to illustrate Harpham's reconceptualisation:

(a) The plot of *Downfall* moves from Traudl Junge's pride at being selected as one of Hitler's personal secretaries in 1942 (*is-but-ought-not-to-be*) to her decision to remain loyal in the *Führerbunker* to the shame she experiences after the war (*is-and-ought-to-be*).
(b) The plot of *Hard Times* moves from Thomas Gradgrind's attempts to inculcate relentlessly pragmatic values in the children of Coketown (*is-but-ought-not-to-be*) to his recognition of the limitations of pure rationalism and thence to his rejection of utilitarian philosophy (*is-and-ought-to-be*).

The *is-and-ought-to-be* captures the significance of closure that I emphasised in section 1, which drew on Carroll's statement that a narrative that concludes gives the feeling that it has ceased at precisely the right point (i.e., is *retrospectively inevitable* in Harpham's terms). Closure contributes to the narrative framework, which forms the basis of the audience's ethical evaluation of the author. The standard mode of engagement with (a) and (b) invites one to view both Junge and Gradgrind as misguided individuals who—to some extent, at least—come to realise the error of their respective ways. As such, both Hirschbiegel and Dickens are subject to positive ethical evaluation from the external perspective.

Although Harpham is critical of others for elevating the ethical value of novels to the moral, he makes a similar error.[40] Here, he identifies a problem in White to which he believes his explanation of narrative form in ethical terms has provided the solution:

> The difficulty, as one of White's critics has pointed out, lies in the apparent suggestion that there are as many moral orders as there are narratives. But if we define closure in the way I have suggested, we can see that closure achieves a moral order that is "other" to that which preceded it, an other to whatever it is in the narrative that *is* but *ought not to be*. There are an infinite number of narratives, but only one closural moral order, which is other not to other narratives but to the incessant questing of all narrative for formal closure. Insofar as our aesthetic education acclimates us to narrative, then, it instructs us in ethics.[41]

Recall from section 10 that White maintains that narrative histories are distinguished from non-narrative historical representations (annals and chronicles) by providing an ethical resolution (i.e., the author passes judgement on the sequence of events represented as either moral, immoral, or morally ambiguous). The criticism mentioned by Harpham is that there are many moral—*ethical*, in my terms—orders because White's theory accommodates both Riefenstahl and Hirschbiegel's representations of Hitler as narrative histories. In contrast, Harpham is pursuing a closural *moral* order and attempting to relate narrativity to moral rather than ethical value.

Harpham has previously made the uncontroversial statement that concern by the self for the other is essential to ethics: "I see this intimate and dynamic engagement with otherness as the key to the kingdom of ethics: where such an engagement is, there is ethics."[42] This conception of moral philosophy, popular in the theoretical tradition, is derived from Emmanuel Levinas.[43] With regard to the ethical turn in criticism, Derek Attridge describes the relevance of Levinas's focus on the other in terms of literature's "apprehension of *otherness*" (i.e., the capacity of literary works to confront and challenge readers' expectations and values).[44] With regard to narrative representation, Harpham's idea is that the *is-and-ought-to-be* of closure is *other* to the *is-but-ought-not-to-be* with which the plot is inaugurated. In (i) and (ii) above, therefore, the respective plots move from an unstable condition, Junge's pride and Gradgrind's pragmatism, to an inevitable closure, Junge's shame and Gradgrind's rejection of utilitarianism. The conditions of closure are different from—*other to*—the conditions of inauguration, and the process of exploration thus involves a *dynamic engagement with otherness* and consequently has moral rather than ethical value. As plot (i.e., movement from *is-but-ought-not-to-be* to *is-and-ought-to-be*) is characteristic of all exemplary narratives, Harpham has established the desired link: all narrative representations that are high in narrativity exhibit a closural moral order, and there is thus a necessary relation between narrativity and moral value.

(MN^{CO})   Narrative representations are moral in virtue of their closural orders (*is-and-ought-to-be*) being other to their inaugural conditions (*is-but-ought-not-to-be*).

Concern for the other is indeed ethical and is also usually, but not necessarily, moral.[45] My objection to Harpham is the case of narrative representations with negative ethical value, which I shall consider in the terminology he employs. In the respective narratives of *Triumph of the Will* and D. W. Griffith's *The Birth of a Nation*, the otherness that the standard mode of engagement requires the audience to apprehend involves the adoption of frameworks that promote the NSDAP and KKK. Levinas is correct in claiming that ethics begins with interest in the well-being of an other instead of—or in addition to—self-interest, but interest in the other is a necessary rather than a sufficient condition of moral agency. The plots of both *Triumph of the Will* and *The Birth of a Nation*, for example, are inaugurated with an *is-but-ought-not-to-be*, explore and apprehend otherness, and close with an *is-and-ought-to-be*. Neither closural order could, however, be considered moral because the otherness that the standard mode of engagement requires one to assimilate is clearly immoral in both cases. Closural orders are not simply made moral by embracing otherness and can be moral, immoral, or morally ambiguous. The necessary relation expressed in the definition of plot as the movement from *is-but-ought-not-to-be* to *is-and-ought-to-be* is thus between narrativity and ethical value and Harpham's attempt to link narrativity with a closural moral order fails.

Despite my criticism of closural moral order, Harpham's reconceptualisation of narrative form in ethical terms is worth preserving for its illumination of the ethical essence of narrative representation. In section 10, I claimed that the combination of agency and events in narratives entails an ethical dimension to narrative representation, the consequence of which is that the engagement with a narrative representation qua narrative representation is incomplete without ethical evaluation. I then argued that the ethical dimension is more complex in exemplary narratives, which are essentially ethical in virtue of both the combination of agency and events represented and the agency of the author in inviting the adoption of the framework particular to the narrative. Harpham's conception of the emplotment characteristic of exemplary narratives as entailing movement from the condition of *is-but-ought-not-to-be* to the condition of *is-and-ought-to-be* articulates the necessity of the relationship between exemplary narratives and ethical value without prioritising ethical value above other narrative values (for example, cognitive value and aesthetic value). The claim that exemplary narratives are essentially ethical is thus restricted to the claim that they are essentially subject to a dual ethical evaluation. From the internal perspective the actions of the characters, whether real or fictional, may be judged as if they were actual; from the external perspective, the author may be judged for the *is-and-ought-to-be* with which he or she concludes the narrative; like the actions of the characters, the author's *is-and-ought-to-be* may be moral, immoral, or morally ambiguous. Harpham's insight can be incorporated into my theory of the ethical value of narrative representation as follows:

(EN^{CO}) Exemplary narratives are essentially ethical in virtue of both the internal perspective (the actions of the characters) and the external perspective (the author's emplotment from *is-but-ought-not-to-be* to *is-and-ought-to-be*).

My conclusion is therefore that there is nothing about narrative representation—whether exemplary or minimal—that entails moral value, only ethical value. In colloquial terms, every story does indeed have a moral, but that moral may be virtuous, vicious, or somewhere in between.

NOTES

1. Currie, *Narratives & Narrators*, 49.
2. For the purposes of this chapter and for the remainder of this book, I shall use *author* to describe the producer of a narrative, regardless of the representational medium employed. Some narrative representations feature a narrator who is distinct from the author, but I shall not discuss the complexities of this distinction (see: Currie, *Narratives & Narrators*, 65–69). I shall also use *audience* to describe the people who engage with a narrative representation regardless of the medium in which that representation is experienced.
3. Lamarque, *Opacity of Narrative*, 9. In this passage, Lamarque uses *all narratives* as similar, if not identical, to *exemplary narratives* (i.e., narrative representations as "complex, involving structure and connectedness and crucially involving a narrator's point of view" [*Opacity of Narrative*, 11]).
4. Currie, *Narratives & Narrators*, 86.
5. Currie, *Narratives & Narrators*, 106.

6. Riefenstahl denied the framework I have described here postwar, which is hardly surprising. For an unsurpassed philosophical discussion of the film, see: Mary Devereaux, "Beauty and Evil: The Case of Leni Riefenstahl's *Triumph of the Will*," in *Aesthetics and Ethics: Essays at the Intersection*, ed. J. Levinson (Cambridge: Cambridge University Press, 1998), 227–56.

7. White, "Value of Narrativity," 23.

8. White, "Value of Narrativity," 24.

9. The difference is usually conceived in terms of "ethics" as a concern with social values and/or the good life and "morality" as a concern with judgement and/or the principles of right conduct. The locus classicus of this distinction is Hegel's critique of Kant's *Moralität* (morality) in terms of *Sittlichkeit* (ethical life) in *Phenomenology of Spirit* and *Elements of Philosophy of Right*. I do not, however, find it useful for the evaluation of narrative representations.

10. Rafe McGregor, "A Critique of the Value Interaction Debate," *British Journal of Aesthetics* 54 (2014): 449.

11. See: Noël Carroll, "Moderate Moralism," *British Journal of Aesthetics* 36 (1996): 223–38. While there has only been one other book engaging directly with the debate, Elisabeth Schellekens's *Aesthetics and Morality* (London: Continuum, 2007), there has been an abundance of individual papers and replies. Since 2000, the debate has expanded beyond aesthetics journals, and contributions have appeared in *Ethics*, *Hypatia*, *Philosophical Forum*, *Philosophy Compass*, *Philosophia*, *South African Journal of Philosophy*, *Journal of Value Inquiry*, *Philosophical Quarterly*, *Ratio*, and *Ethical Perspectives*. The most recent contribution is: Noël Carroll, "Architecture, Art, and Moderate Moralism," *The Nordic Journal of Aesthetics* 25 (February 2017). DOI: http://dx.doi.org/10.7146/nja.v25i52.25618.

12. Berys Gaut, "The Ethical Criticism of Art," in *Aesthetics and Ethics: Essays at the Intersection*, ed. Jerrold Levinson (Cambridge: Cambridge University Press, 1998), 182–203.

13. Berys Gaut, *Art, Emotion and Ethics* (Oxford: Oxford University Press, 2007), 14.

14. See: Gaut, "Ethical Criticism," 183; Gaut, *Art, Emotion and Ethics*, 66.

15. I set out my views on the concepts of *intrinsic* and *extrinsic* as related to literary representations in detail in chapter 1 of *The Value of Literature* (pp. 6–10). My use of both the intrinsic/extrinsic and final/instrumental distinctions, as well as the relationship between them, is identical with respect to narrative representation as it is for that established with respect to literary representation.

16. Gaut, *Art, Emotion and Ethics*, 9.

17. Gaut, *Art, Emotion and Ethics*, 45.

18. Gaut, "Ethical Criticism," 183.

19. Gaut, *Art, Emotion and Ethics*, 40.

20. See: Wayne Booth, *The Company We Keep: An Ethics of Fiction* (Berkeley: University of California, 1988); Colin McGinn, *Ethics, Evil, and Fiction* (Oxford: Oxford University Press, 1997).

21. Gaut, *Art, Emotion and Ethics*, 117.

22. Gaut, *Art, Emotion and Ethics*, 127.

23. Gaut, *Art, Emotion and Ethics*, 13.

24. Gaut, *Art, Emotion and Ethics*, 165–66.

25. Gaut, *Art, Emotion and Ethics*, 164.

26. Gaut, *Art, Emotion and Ethics*, 231.

27. Gaut, *Art, Emotion and Ethics*, 233.

28. Gaut, *Art, Emotion and Ethics*, 231.

29. Gaut, *Art, Emotion and Ethics*, 231.

30. Gaut, "Ethical Criticism," 289.

31. Gaut, "Ethical Criticism," 195.

32. Gaut, *Art, Emotion and Ethics*, 252.

33. Fessenbecker, "In Defense of Paraphrase," 121.

34. Geoffrey Galt Harpham, *Shadows of Ethics: Criticism and the Just Society* (Durham, NC: Duke University Press, 1999), 35.

35. R. M. Hare, *Moral Thinking: Its Levels, Method and Point* (Oxford: Clarendon, 1981), 16. Hume sets out the distinction in Book III, Part 1, Section (i) of the *Treatise*. See: David Hume, *A Treatise of Human Nature*, ed. L. A. Selby-Bigge (Oxford: Clarendon, 1888 [1740]), 469.

36. Harpham, *Shadows of Ethics*, 37, 43.

37. I am sceptical of Harpham's conception of narrative's contribution to ethics, and although the relation he envisages is reciprocal, each of the two aspects can be considered in isolation.

38. Goldie, *The Mess Inside*, 9.

39. Harpham, *Shadows of Ethics*, 36.

40. Harpham, *Shadows of Ethics*, 220–42.

41. Harpham, *Shadows of Ethics*, 43. It is not clear to me that the existence of numerous moral (i.e., *ethical* in my terms) orders in White is problematic, but my interest here is in Harpham's solution, whether or not the problem exists.

42. Harpham, *Shadows of Ethics*, x.

43. See, for example: Levinas, *Totality and Infinity*; Levinas, *Ethics and Infinity*.

44. Derek Attridge, *The Singularity of Literature* (New York: Routledge, 2004), 67.

45. See, for example, Gaut's definition of *moral* quoted in section 11.

Chapter Four

Narrative Knowledge

The purpose of this chapter is to present an argument for narrative cognitivism, the theory that narrative representations can provide knowledge in virtue of their narrativity, regardless of their truth value. I set out the terms of the debate in section 13, distinguishing narrative cognitivism, which is concerned with the ways in which narrative representations provide knowledge, from aesthetic cognitivism, which is concerned with the ways in which art provides knowledge. I discuss three types of knowledge—knowing that, knowing how, and knowing what—and identify *lucid phenomenological knowledge* as a subcategory of "knowing what" that appears to meet both the epistemic and narrativity criteria for narrative cognitivism. In section 14, I test lucid phenomenological knowledge against the epistemic criterion, focusing on lyric poetry as an uncontroversial example of non-narrative representation that presents a disjunctive objection to my argument: either lucid phenomenological knowledge can be reduced to identification and fails to meet the epistemic criterion, or lucid phenomenological knowledge is provided in virtue of aesthetic properties and fails to meet the narrativity criterion. I argue that lucid phenomenological knowledge cannot be reduced to identification. I address the second disjunct, explaining why narrative properties should not be reduced to aesthetic properties, in section 15. My conclusion is that stories provide genuine knowledge just by being stories.

13. KNOWLEDGE AND NARRATIVITY

The question of the cognitive value of art is the most pressing and passionate of the contemporary debates within philosophical aesthetics. Katherine Thomson-Jones provides a neat summary of the issue as currently contested: "Aesthetic cognitivism and aesthetic anti-cognitivism can be defined as opposing responses to two questions: (1) Can art provide knowledge? And, if it can, (2) how is this aesthetically relevant?"[1] The aesthetic cognitivist answers the first question in the affirmative, meeting the epistemic criterion (1). In order to meet the aesthetic criterion (2), a necessary relation between the capacity of a work to provide knowledge and the success (or lack thereof) of that work qua art must be established. The thesis of *aesthetic cognitivism* can thus be defined as follows:

(AC)   Works of art can provide knowledge in a manner that is aesthetically relevant.

This matches my definition of aesthetic cognitivism in chapter 3, which drew my initial characterisation of the cognitive value of representations in chapter 1 together with Spivak's anti-cognitivism and Worth's cognitivism in chapter 2: aesthetic representations can provide knowledge in virtue of their aesthetic value. Anti-cognitivists dispute either the epistemic or the aesthetic criterion. I focused on narrative cognitivism when discussing Worth in section 8 and Gaut in section 11 and took the identification of aesthetic value with the value of a narrative qua narrative as unproblematic. In this chapter, I shall question this assumption and focus exclusively on *narrative cognitivism*, defined as:

(NC)   Narrative representations can provide knowledge in virtue of their narrativity.

The two criteria for NC are: (a) that the narrative representation provides knowledge (epistemic criterion), and (b) that the narrative representation provides knowledge in virtue of its narrativity (narrativity criterion).

Dorothy Walsh employs Gilbert Ryle's *The Concept of Mind* to delineate two distinct types of knowledge:

A philosophical analysis of the meaning of "know" that is at present widely influential is one that finds two fundamental and irreducible meanings in use. There is knowing in the sense of *knowing that* (such and such is so) and there is knowing in the sense of *knowing how* (to perform some act).[2]

She then differentiates between experience as *awareness of* and experience as *living through* and advances the latter as a third type of knowledge:

Recognizing that such and such is so with reference to some kind of human experience is not the same as *realizing* what this might be like as a lived experience. Confession of failure to understand, in the sense of realize, is perfectly compatible with absence of doubt concerning matter-of-fact.[3]

Catherine Wilson refers to this realisation as "knowing what," short for "knowing-what-it-is-like," and John Gibson refers to it as "experiential knowledge."[4] Walsh claims that unlike actual experiences, the virtual experiences of literary works can be experienced by anyone who engages with the work such that they are shareable and can provide knowledge.[5] Alex Burri holds a similar view, maintaining that the practice of art aims at the subjective rather than objective representation of reality, "to conduct some kind of *phenomenological investigation* into how things appear to us."[6] I shall employ the term *phenomenological knowledge*:

(PK)   The realisation of what a particular lived experience is like.

In section 10, I discussed how the combination of causal relations, thematic unity, and closure produced the narrative opacity and narrative framework characteristic of exemplary narratives. Recall that opacity is the authorial perspective constitutive of an exemplary narrative, and framework is the preferred set of cognitive, evaluative, and emotional responses to the exemplary narrative. It is the framework that has the capacity to provide PK. When explaining the ethical value of exemplary narratives, I stated that authors can provide different frameworks for the same characters and events. I compared Leni Riefenstahl's *Triumph of the Will* with Oliver Hirschbiegel's *Downfall* in order to distinguish two types of ethical evaluation, and the same pair serves to illustrate how exemplary narratives provide PK. In *Triumph of the Will*, Riefenstahl frames Hitler as a messianic saviour who descends from the heavens to lead the German people to glory. Hirschbiegel frames Hitler as an evil megalomaniac who sacrifices millions of people—including the German nation—for his self-aggrandisement in *Downfall*. In the former, the audience comes to realise why many Germans supported Hitler; in the latter, the audience comes to realise the full extent of his malevolence in his determination to destroy Germany as well as himself. Gibson shows how art provides PK, using two works that are both exemplary narratives as examples:

> Drawing solely on my own experiences and my preferred books of theory, I will acquire no significant knowledge of what it is like to be a victim of systematic racial oppression or an immigrant struggling to make his way to an unwelcoming country. But I can read Ralph Ellison's *Invisible Man* or watch Elia Kazan's *America, America* and in so doing acquaint myself with a region of human experience that would otherwise remain unknown to me.[7]

In order to acquire PK, it is necessary not just to experience the respective representations, but to adopt the standard mode of engagement to each. If, for example, one fails to adopt the standard mode of engagement to *Invisible Man*—the anonymous narrator as sympathetic—then one will not realise what it is like to be a victim of systematic racial oppression. In an extreme case such as *Triumph of the Will*, the many contemporary viewers who refuse to adopt Riefenstahl's framework will not realise what it is like to see Hitler as heroic. The documentary can provide such viewers with other types of knowledge—for example, knowledge that Hitler was regarded as a saviour by many Germans—but not the PK identified. Viewers who do adopt Riefenstahl's framework do not have to become temporary or permanent National Socialists, but they must temporarily set aside their contempt for Hitler if they are to gain PK. The same would be true of a Ku Klux Klan member reading *Invisible Man*.

The knowledge with which I am concerned is a subcategory of PK that is provided by exemplary narratives—*lucid phenomenological knowledge*:

(LPK)   The realisation of what a particular lived experience is like by means of the reproduction of a particular experience of a particular character for the audience who adopt the standard mode of engagement to the narrative representation.

Tzachi Zamir demonstrates that Shakespeare provides LPK in reproducing a particular experience of a particular character for the audience, not by means of empathy but by structuring the representation so that the experience is acted by the actors and re-enacted by the audience. One of the examples Zamir employs is *Romeo and Juliet*, where Romeo's experience of forgetting about Rosaline—with whom he is deeply in love when the play opens—is reproduced in the experience of the audience.[8] Romeo forgets about his lover, and the audience forgets about the lover of the protagonist of the play: the play therefore provides LPK of what it is like to forget someone who is important. Zamir maintains that Shakespearean drama *conveys* rather than describes this knowledge: "Conveying is a mode of telling that involves con-figuring in highly specific ways the state of mind of recipients. It reenacts an experiential structure that overlaps and resembles the experience that it describes (though is not identical to it)."[9]

The state of mind of the audience who adopt the standard mode of engage-ment, is configured by the framework which—in the case of *Romeo and Juliet*—reproduces an experience of Romeo's in the audience: the forget-ting of Rosaline. The experience may be reproduced for the audience that adopts the framework in part or as a whole, but it must be produced by the framework if it is to provide LPK. The experience is reproduced rather than replicated because the audience does not forget about their own loved ones, like Romeo, but about his lover.. The audience's experiences nonetheless overlap and resemble Romeo's because they both involve forgetting someone who is important (one's own lover for the character and the lover of the protagonist for the audience). Zamir's other examples from Shakespeare vary in their degree of conviction, from a conclusive argument for amoralism as an epistemic defect in *Richard III* to a credible argument for the ambivalence of mature love in *Antony and Cleopatra* to an improbable argument for the limitations of language in *Hamlet*.[10] He is, however, seeking to delineate a fourth type of knowledge altogether: "knowing the shapes through which things may come" rather than identifying a particular kind of "knowing what," which may be why he applies conveying more loosely than I do.[11]

Another example of LPK occurs in my article "Cinematic Philosophy: Experiential Affirmation in *Memento*." Here, I argue that the standard mode of engagement with Christopher Nolan's *Memento* provides the audience with the knowledge that *memory is essential to understanding*, and thus, a version of AC.[12] The means by which the knowledge I described is provided is Nolan's employment of narrative structure. The protagonist, Leonard, has a severe case of anterograde amnesia, and the extraordinary complexity of the narrative places the audience in a similar epistemic situation because of the extreme difficulty of following the sequence of events as represented.[13] To take just one instance, the colour scenes in the film are shown in reverse order such that the audience, like Leonard, does not know the sequence of events that has just occurred, but, unlike Leonard, knows part of the sequence of events that will occur. *Memento* thus provides LPK of what it is like to have anterograde amnesia in virtue of its narrativity. The framework of the film creates an experiential structure for the audience that overlaps and resembles Leonard's because neither he nor the audience are aware of his most recent actions.[14] The LPK in *Memento* and *Romeo and Juliet* is a distinct version of the PK provided by *Triumph of the Will, Downfall, Invisible Man,* and *America, America*. In all six cases, the narrative representation provides knowledge of what a lived experience is like (PK), but only in the first two is that knowledge gained by means of the reproduction of an experience of a character in the experience of the audience (LPK). In the remainder of this chapter I shall argue that LPK meets both the epistemic criterion and the narrativity criterion, and thus, for NC.

14. EPISTEMIC CRITERION

In her discussion of Walsh, Wilson examines D. Z. Phillips's interpretation of *Age of Innocence* and maintains that there is "a wide logical gap between the realization of what it would be like to have Newland Archer's experiences and the realization that a certain popular conception of reasonable action is, in a certain sense, fraudulent."[15] Phillips claims that the novel has provided him with knowledge of the artificiality of an abstract concept of reasonableness, but Wilson argues that this knowledge is not entailed by Walsh's knowledge of what it is like to be the protagonist. The logical gap points to a "serious ambiguity in Walsh's formulation" because there are two senses of PK: shallow and deep.[16] Wilson's view is that in order to meet the epistemic criterion for AC, a literary work must revise or modify the concepts of readers.[17] George Orwell's *Down and Out in Paris and London*, for example, has the potential to provide knowledge in at least the following two ways:

(a) What it is like to be poor and lonely in the big city.
(b) Reconceptualisations of poverty, loneliness, or anonymity.

Wilson's claim is that (a) does not meet the epistemic criterion, but (b) does.

I think that (b) is problematic as an epistemic criterion for AC, but my interest is in Wilson's claim that (a) is a shallow sense of PK. Walsh's argument for the knowledge provided by literary works is restricted to the type of knowledge in (a)—i.e., PK—and she maintains that PK is knowledge despite the fact that (a) has no truth value. Gibson offers further support for (a) as a type of knowledge:

> For all sorts of anatomical, temporal and financial reasons, reality will never offer us the occasion to experience the world as Madame Bovary, Achilles or King Midas did. Art can be seen compensating for the extremely limited way we each encounter the world by offering us an occasion to do in the imagination what real life can never make possible. Surely the occasion to witness this great variety of *kinds* of human experience is a potential source of cognitive insight.[18]

Wilson's criticism that (a) does not meet the epistemic criterion is thus open to dispute, but she has a related concern, which is more convincing: Walsh not only states that PK is not truth-conditional, but that it is inappropriate to demand proof of PK.[19] As Walsh admits, the acquisition of *knowledge that* and *knowledge how* are readily proved—by statement and performance, respectively. To make Wilson's point in another way: even if one accepts that PK meets the epistemic criterion, there is no criterion for PK itself—that is, how does one know that one has gained PK? Or, how can I offer evidence for my claims that *Invisible Man* provides knowledge of what it is like to suffer racial prejudice and *Triumph of the Will* provides knowledge of what it is like to admire Hitler? Walsh's claim that proof is inappropriate to PK will fail to convince many philosophers and theorists and will cast doubt on whether PK is a third type of knowledge.

In contrast to PK, LPK is verifiable. If I am asked to prove that *Invisible Man* provides PK of suffering racial prejudice, I may quote critical interpretations of the novel, but my ultimate response is going to be to direct the inquirer to the novel (i.e., to claim that if a reader adopts the standard mode of engagement, the reader will acquire the PK in question). But if the reader disputes this, then we will have reached an impasse. If I am asked to prove that *Memento* provides LPK of anterograde amnesia, I shall once again direct the inquirer to the film, but the difference is that a clear criterion has been established: if the viewer is not confused by the narrative structure, then he or she has not gained the LPK; if the viewer is confused by the narrative structure, then he or she has gained the LPK.[20] The viewer who keeps Rosaline in the forefront of her mind throughout Romeo's exchanges with Juliet does not adopt the standard mode of engagement to *Romeo and Juliet* any more than the viewer who uses the pause function on his DVD to make notes on *Memento*.

Recall that the model for an LPK claim is that the representation reproduces a particular experiential structure that it represents in respect to a particular character in the narrative for the audience. The criterion for LPK will thus vary in each instance, but is nonetheless verifiable in a way in which PK claims are not:

(i) *Romeo and Juliet* provides LPK by reproducing Romeo's forgetting of Rosaline in the audience. The criterion for LPK in *Romeo and Juliet* is that the audience forgets about Rosaline.

(ii) *Memento* provides LPK by reproducing Leonard's experience of anterograde amnesia in the audience. The criterion for LPK in *Memento* is that the audience is unable to understand the sequence of events represented.

The criteria in both (i) and (ii) can be verified by empirical studies of audiences as well as theoretical studies of the standard mode of engagement for each work. In paradigmatic cases of LPK, both the standard mode of engagement and the knowledge provided by the standard mode of engagement are readily apparent. As such, LPK is not subject to the no-evidence objection to PK.

My argument for NC is reliant upon narrative representations providing LPK in virtue of their narrativity. In order to meet the narrativity criterion for NC, LPK must be provided in virtue of the narrativity of the representation, and I argued that LPK is provided by means of the standard mode of engagement, which is itself determined by the narrative framework. An objection to

NC on the basis of the narrativity criterion would have to show that LPK is not provided in virtue of the narrativity in the representation, but in virtue of something else. It is important to note that I am not arguing for the following, stronger, claim about narrative representations:

(NC*)   Exemplary narratives can provide unique knowledge in virtue of their narrativity.

In order for NC* to hold, LPK would not only have to be provided by representations in virtue of their narrativity, but it would also have to be exclusive to narrative representations. NC is, however, compatible with non-narrative representations—such as lyric poems—providing LPK in virtue of a feature other than narrativity. The case of lyric poetry is worth considering, because although it does not constitute a direct objection to NC, it exposes a disjunction that is problematic.

Anna Christina Ribeiro provides a useful taxonomy of poetry in "Toward a Philosophy of Poetry," dividing poems into three subcategories: lyric, dramatic, and epic.[21] Epic poems are distinguished by having a narrator, dramatic poems by characters having their own voices; both are typically narrative representations. Lyric poems, which are "the prevalent mode of poetic expression," are characteristically—but neither necessarily nor exclusively—non-narrative representations written in verse and in the first person.[22] Gibson agrees that "much lyric poetry is not fictional or even narrative-based: much lyric poetry tells no story, properly so-called."[23] I shall take it as uncontroversial that lyric poetry, which paradigmatically consists of versified, first-person accounts of personal experiences, is a non-narrative mode of representation. As such, if lyric poems provide LPK, it cannot be in virtue of their narrativity.

In section 13, I defined LPK in terms of the standard mode of engagement, which is the audience's adoption of the author's framework. The framework was described as a product of the perspective of an exemplary narrative, and the perspective as composed of causal relations, thematic unity, and closure. If one replaces *narrator* with *poet* in Gregory Currie's definition of the standard mode of engagement, however, the standard mode of engagement might equally apply to poems, and Peter Lamarque claims that the content of poetry—lyric poems written in the first person, in particular—is "filtered through a particular point of view" (i.e., essentially framed by the poet).[24] Both narratives and poems are, in Lamarque's terms, opaque, and employ a framework that invites a standard mode of engagement. One might resist collapsing the standard mode of engagement for narrative and poetic representations by emphasising the difference between the ways in which the respective frameworks are created. If one accepts that most poems are lyric poems and most prose (at least minimal) narratives, then Nigel Fabb's characterisation of poetry as being rich in both formal features and figurative language is promising.[25] Ribeiro reiterates these two characteristics as typically distinctive of poetry, but they are neither necessary nor exclusive, so the question of whether poetic frameworks differ from narrative frameworks in any significant way appears to resist an unequivocal answer.[26]

This ambiguity produces the following disjunction: either

(A) narrative and poetic frameworks are too similar to admit of significant distinction, or

(B) although narrative and poetic frameworks appear similar, the distinction between their different modes of representation is significant.

Both (A) and (B) provide grounds for objections to NC. If (A) is true, then the means by which lyric poems typically invite the standard mode of engagement—identification with the poet—suggests that the LPK provided by narrative representations can be reduced to identification with a particular character. If LPK was provided in virtue of identification, then it would (as I explain below) fail to meet the epistemic criterion for NC. If (B) is true, then the combination of works of poetry and prose in the category of literature suggests that when LPK is provided by narrative representations, it is in virtue of their aesthetic rather than narrative properties. Indeed, the philosophers I have been examining here—Gibson, Walsh, Wilson, Zamir—have all been concerned with the relationship between knowledge and art, literature, or drama (i.e., with AC). If LPK was provided in virtue of aesthetic properties, then it could (as I show in section 15) fail to meet the narrativity criterion for NC.

If narrative frameworks and poetic frameworks are too similar to admit of significant distinction, then my argument for LPK in narrative representations may have erred in its focus on the importance of the narrative features of the framework through which LPK is provided. If lyric poems are typically personal experiences written or voiced in the first person, then one could replace "a particular character" with "the poet" in my definition of LPK and argue that LPK was provided by lyric poems in virtue of non-narrative features. Ribeiro's discussion of the typical audience engagement with poetic representations reveals precisely this possibility and is worth quoting in full:

> When listening to or reading a poem, we begin by hearing someone else's voice, by attending to what the poetic persona might have to share with us. Without presuming to account for *all* poetry reading experiences, I submit that, typically, by the end of the poem we have come to identify with that voice. I do not mean by this that we suddenly come to think that we *are* the poet, or that we

are the *writers* of the poem. I mean an identification in the sense that we feel that we *could* have written those words (if only we had the talent to express ourselves as well), because they express something that we, too, feel or have felt, think or have thought, and sometimes even thoughts and feelings we never realized we had but that now, seeing them expressed, we find resonating with something within ourselves. Our experience of lyric poems is therefore peculiarly *personal*: we either assume the role of the speaker in the poem, or of the one who is spoken to. This makes the reading of poems very immediate and subjective; we are not being told a story, objectively, of what happened to whom and how *they* felt, but instead a very personal account of how *one* felt, in a way that invites us to recognize similar feelings or experiences or thoughts in ourselves.[27]

Ribeiro's description matches LPK closely and suggests that many—if not most—poems provide LPK in virtue of the process of identification she describes. In the standard mode of engagement with a particular poem, one comes to recognise the poet's thoughts, feelings, or experiences as one's own. In reading, for example, T. S. Eliot's "Gerontion," therefore, I identify with the sadness, regret, resignation, and disgust Eliot expresses, appropriating these feelings as my own.[28] The standard mode of engagement with *Romeo and Juliet* causes me to forget about Rosaline and reproduces Romeo's experience in me, but the standard mode of engagement with "Gerontion" seems to be paradigmatic LPK because it is not just one experience of one character (Romeo's forgetting), but a multitude of the poet's thoughts and feelings that are reproduced. There is thus a sense in which the whole poetic experience is an experience of the acquisition of LPK, where the whole narrative experience of *Romeo and Juliet* is not. The problem for my argument for NC is that poems are widely considered to be more resistant to interpretation and paraphrase than narrative representations. In section 13, I distinguished LPK from PK by stating that the former kind of knowledge was specifiable and could therefore meet the demand for evidence. But many poems demonstrate a kind of ineffability that seems to preclude the paraphrasability with which I characterised LPK. On this objection, my conception of LPK is flawed because its paradigmatic occurrence is in lyric poems, which will typically fail to meet the epistemic criterion for NC (as discussed above).

For the purposes of my response, I shall accept that there is no significant distinction between poetic and narrative frameworks and that the standard mode of engagement with poetic representations typically involves the audience's identification with the poet, as described by Ribeiro. The reason that NC is not subject to the no-evidence objection is that the process by which LPK is provided in narrative representations is distinct from identification. The representation (by means of the narrative framework) reproduces (without of course replicating) the structure of experience in a manner that involves a feature which is similar to anagnorisis, the moment of recognition Aristotle identified as an element of narrativity.[29] Recognition is, for Aristotle, "a change from ignorance to knowledge" in the protagonist of a tragedy—for example, Oedipus's realisation that he has both killed his father and married his mother in *Oedipus Rex*.[30] The recognition I have in mind is when the *audience* comes to realise that they have experienced a particular experience of a particular character for themselves in virtue of the narrative framework. This recognition may occur during or after the experience of the representation and occurs when, for example, I realise that *both Romeo and I* have forgotten about Rosaline or that *both Leonard and I* cannot make sense of what is happening to him. In a similar manner to that in which anagnorisis provides the protagonist with knowledge, so the recognition with which I am concerned provides the audience with LPK. The provision of LPK thus requires not only the reproduction of the experiential structure, but the recognition of this reproduction by the audience. In consequence, the acquisition of LPK will be limited to those members of the audience who both adopt the standard mode of engagement and recognise the reproduction.

LPK provided in this manner is related to identification because the acquisition of LPK may encourage identification with, for example, Romeo or Leonard, but identification is an effect of LPK rather than—as in Ribeiro's explanation—its cause. Although Ribeiro mentions recognition as well, her variant is a gradual realisation of the cumulative process of identification that occurs during the course of the poetic experience. Following Aristotle, the recognition by means of which LPK is provided is sudden and instantaneous. Furthermore, and crucially, it is a recognition that a particular experience which can readily be specified and admits of paraphrase has been reproduced. I shall call this recognition, which is characteristically both sudden and specifiable, audience-anagnorisis in order to distinguish it from both Aristotle's anagnorisis and Ribeiro's recognition. In the standard mode of engagement, the audience accepts the author's invitation to adopt a particular narrative framework; in cases where a narrative representation provides LPK, the adoption of that framework will involve the realisation that a particular experience of a particular character has been reproduced in the audience. This realisation—and thus the specific LPK—is acquired in a moment of audience-anagnorisis in which the audience recognises the reproduction of the experiential structure in question. Audience-anagnorisis is the process by which LPK is provided by exemplary narratives and is clearly distinct from the experience of identification that Ribeiro describes. Even if there is no significant distinction between poetic and narrative frameworks, therefore, LPK cannot be reduced to identification.

15. NARRATIVITY CRITERION

If there is a significant distinction between poetic and narrative frameworks, then it is curious that two different types of frameworks invite a similar standard mode of engagement (as noted in section 14). This suggests that the narrative framework with which I am concerned might not be a function of the narrative properties of a representation, but of other properties, and—given that poems and exemplary narratives are often works of art—the obvious choice is aesthetic properties. The objection is thus that when LPK is provided by narrative representations, it is provided in virtue of their aesthetic rather than narrative properties. I do not wish to either commit to a definition of aesthetic properties or to argue for a theory of art, so I shall adopt the following strategy: if there is a narrative representation that is not a work of art but which provides LPK, then the objection that NC does not meet the narrativity criterion (because LPK is provided by aesthetic properties) fails. There is difficulty in selecting such an example because many exemplary narratives that are not canonical works of art—for example, a work of propaganda like *Triumph of the Will*—are often cited as having aesthetic properties. I shall nonetheless employ Morgan Spurlock's *Super Size Me*, on the basis that the work's artistic status has not played a significant role in either its production or reception. The documentary was intended to demonstrate the physical and mental dangers of eating too much fast food and the immorality of companies like McDonald's in not only selling their products, but in maximising their revenue by encouraging people to eat more—*super size*—on each occasion. The film was nominated for the Academy Award for Best Documentary in 2004, and responses have been primarily concerned with the validity of the experiment represented in the narrative, the profundity—or lack thereof—of the narrative's message, and the effect of the narrative on the McDonald's Corporation.

Spurlock's film records the experiment he conducted on himself by eating all of his meals from McDonald's for a period of thirty days. The health dangers were heightened by several factors; for example, he decided to super size his order whenever McDonald's staff made the offer and to finish all of each meal, regardless of his appetite. The narrative is filmed largely from Spurlock's point of view, is narrated by him, and involves him both conducting interviews and addressing the audience directly. The documentary represents Spurlock's experience of his own experiment, and the standard mode of engagement invites one to adopt his framework on the phenomenon of fast food, which changes from curiosity to antipathy as the narrative progresses. In this respect it can be said to provide both *knowledge that* (in the numerous statistics narrated and depicted) and PK (knowledge of what it is like to live on fast food). In addition to the PK provided, the narrative framework provides LPK by reproducing Spurlock's experience of being disgusted by fast food. This is achieved by stylistic choices that employ the narrative perspective to make both indirect and direct links between repulsive images and McDonald's products. There are, for example, several close-ups of a gastric bypass operation on a man whose obesity has become life-threatening. On the second day of Spurlock's experiment (approximately twenty minutes into the ninety-eight-minute documentary) there are close-ups of his physical distress as he struggles to finish a super-size meal and his subsequent vomiting of that meal onto the pavement. Disgust is also stimulated in more subtle ways: Spurlock joins a children's party for his final meal, and images of him eating a sickly-sweet birthday cake are juxtaposed with images of French fries being deep-fried in a sea of fat. The knowledge provided is not merely PK, but LPK, because Spurlock's experience of being disgusted by fast food is reproduced in the audience, who recognise the shared disgust in a moment of audience-anagnorisis. The experience is reproduced rather than replicated because of the difference in stimulus and object: where Spurlock is disgusted by the taste (and probably smell) of fast food, his audience is disgusted by the sight of fast food (and associated imagery). As an exemplary narrative that is both (a) lacking in aesthetic properties and (b) provides LPK, *Super Size Me* thus offers evidence that LPK does meet the narrativity criterion for NC.

My argument for NC is therefore that a subset of narrative representations (exemplary narratives) can provide a particular type of knowledge (LPK) in virtue of their narrativity. I have demonstrated that LPK meets both the epistemic and narrative criteria for NC (i.e., evidence for the acquisition of LPK can be produced, and LPK is provided by the narrative framework through the process of audience-anagnorisis). Finally, I have shown that LPK is acquired in virtue of the narrative properties rather than the aesthetic properties of a representation. Many philosophers and theorists will not be convinced by this last claim. First, *Super Size Me* is not as paradigmatic an example of LPK as *Romeo and Juliet* and *Memento*. If the criterion for LPK in *Super Size Me* is that viewers are disgusted by fast food, there may well be critical debate about the role played by disgust in the standard mode of engagement. Second, if *Super Size Me* does provide LPK, as I maintain, then the techniques I described in creating the audience-anagnorisis seem to be precisely aesthetic techniques, in which case the properties I have discussed throughout this chapter are a subcategory of aesthetic properties, a possibility I mentioned in section 14. If narrative properties are a subcategory of aesthetic properties, then my argument for NC is also an argument for AC: a subset of works of art (those that are also exemplary narratives) can provide knowledge (LPK) in a manner that is aesthetically relevant (in virtue of their narrativity).

There is at least one reason to be cautious about this argument for AC, however, which is that the distinction between narrative and non-narrative representations is more fundamental than the distinction between artistic and non-artistic representations when one is considering the cognitive value of representations. The difference in significance between two distinct but overlapping oppositions can be problematic, as Derek Matravers has shown in *Fiction and Narrative*. Matravers contends that the distinction between confrontations (where action is possible) and representations (where action is not possible) is more fundamental than the distinction between nonfiction and fiction.[31] The failure to recognise the significance of the former distinction has resulted in philosophers restricting certain claims to fictions when they are in fact true of all representations.[32] Employing Ryle's thick-thin distinction, Matravers argues that the engagements with both Tolstoy's *War and Peace* and Faber de Faur's *With Napoleon in Russia* result in a thick experience.[33] What is important about the novel and the memoir is that they are both thick representations (i.e., vivid, rich, and gripping), an insight that is lost when the property of thickness is restricted to fictional representations.

In a mirror image of Matravers's concern, mine is that the failure to recognise the significance of the distinction between narrative and non-narrative representations will encourage the conflation of narrative properties and aesthetic properties such that claims which should be restricted to narrative works of art are extended to (potentially) all works of art. If this seems unlikely, recall the subtlety of the distinction between the identification produced by poetic frameworks and the provision of LPK by means of narrative frameworks discussed in section 14. I am not convinced that non-narrative representations, whether linguistic or visual, can provide LPK. If narrative properties are a subcategory of aesthetic properties—as seems likely—then different subcategories of aesthetic properties appear to have distinct relations to cognitive value. A detailed discussion of aesthetic properties is beyond the scope of this monograph, and my preference is therefore to err on the side of caution and restrict my argument to NC, the provision of LPK by exemplary narratives in virtue of their narrativity. My claim is, in other words, that stories can provide genuine knowledge just by being stories and irrespective of their truth value.

NOTES

1. Katherine Thomson-Jones, "Inseparable Insight: Reconciling Cognitivism and Formalism in Aesthetics," *The Journal of Aesthetics and Art Criticism* 63 (2005): 376.

2. Dorothy Walsh, *Literature and Knowledge* (Middletown, CT: Wesleyan University Press, 1969), 96.

3. Walsh, *Literature and Knowledge*, 103.

4. Wilson, "Literature and Knowledge," 492; John Gibson, "Cognitivism and the Arts," *Philosophy Compass* 3 (2008): 582.

5. Walsh, *Literature and Knowledge*, 105.

6. Alex Burri, "Art and the View from Nowhere," in *A Sense of the World: Essays on Fiction, Narrative, and Knowledge*, ed. J. Gibson, W. Huerner, and L. Pocci (London: Routledge, 2009 [2007]), 310.

7. Gibson, "Cognitivism and the Arts," 582–83.

8. Tzachi Zamir, *Double Vision: Moral Philosophy and Shakespearean Drama* (Princeton, NJ: Princeton University Press, 2007), 113–25.

9. Zamir, *Double Vision*, 147.

10. I discuss Zamir's double vision thesis and the architecture of his argumentation in "Blindness and Double Vision in *Richard III*." See: Rafe McGregor, "Blindness and Double Vision in *Richard III*: Zamir on Shakespeare on Moral Philosophy," in *The Routledge Companion to Shakespeare and Philosophy*, ed. C. Bourne and E. Caddick Bourne (London: Routledge, 2018).

11. Zamir, *Double Vision*, 149.

12. Rafe McGregor, "Cinematic Philosophy: Experiential Affirmation in *Memento*," *The Journal of Aesthetics and Art Criticism* 72 (2014): 58–60.

13. For a comprehensive examination of this structure, see: Andrew Kania, "Scene Tables," in *Memento (Philosophers on Film)*, ed. A. Kania (Abingdon: Routledge, 2009), 13–22.

14. Both of the paradigmatic instances of LPK I have described exploit limitations in the memories of the audience. I am tempted to explore the potential connection between the similar temporal dimensions of theatre and cinema with LPK, but I expect that most people who read *Romeo and Juliet* also forget about Rosaline.

15. Wilson, "Literature and Knowledge," 493–94.

16. Wilson, "Literature and Knowledge," 494.

17. Wilson, "Literature and Knowledge," 494–95.

18. Gibson, "Cognitivism and the Arts," 582.

19. Wilson, "Literature and Knowledge," 492.

20. For readers of this chapter who have not experienced *Memento*, I should note that the narrative complexity is such that Christopher Nolan himself claimed he was unable to predict the sequence in which the scenes appeared, after over a thousand viewings. See: Berys Gaut, "Telling Stories: Narration, Emotion, and Insight in *Memento*," in *Narrative, Emotion, and Insight*, ed. N. Carroll and J. Gibson (University Park, PA: Pennsylvania State University Press, 2011), 23–44.

21. Anna Christina Ribeiro, "Toward a Philosophy of Poetry," *Midwest Studies in Philosophy XXXIII* (2009): 68.

22. Ribeiro, "Philosophy of Poetry," 68.

23. John Gibson, "The Question of Poetic Meaning," *Nonsite* 4, 1 December 2011. Available at: http://nonsite.org/article/the-question-of-poetic-meaning.

24. Peter Lamarque, "Poetry and Abstract Thought," *Midwest Studies in Philosophy XXXIII* (2009): 50.

25. Nigel Fabb, "Why Is Verse Poetry?" *PN Review* 189 (2009): 52–57.

26. Ribeiro, "Philosophy of Poetry," 66.

27. Ribeiro, "Philosophy of Poetry," 69–70.

28. I discussed "Gerontion" as part of my explanation of reference in poetic representation in *The Value of Literature*. See: McGregor, *Value of Literature*, 55–56.

29. Aristotle, *Poetics*, X: 1452a13–23.

30. Aristotle, *Poetics*, XI: 1452a32–33.

31. Derek Matravers, *Fiction and Narrative* (Oxford: Oxford University Press, 2014), 47.

32. Matravers, *Fiction and Narrative*, 87.

33. Matravers, *Fiction and Narrative*, 46–47. See also: Gilbert Ryle, "The Thinking of Thoughts: What Is 'Le Penseur' Doing?" in *Volume II: Collected Essays 1929–1969* (London: Hutchinson & Co., 1971), 480–96.

Chapter Five

Narrative Justice

The purpose of this chapter is threefold: to complete the argument from narrative representation to ethical value, to present the argument from narrative representation to political value, and to set the latter argument in the context of criminal inhumanity (i.e., establish narrative justice as a thesis of aesthetic education). In section 16, I combine the conceptions of narrative value from the previous two chapters to make the claim that some stories can provide ethical knowledge in virtue of their narrativity, regardless of their truth value. I identify both a weak and a strong theory of narrative ethical knowledge. Section 17 employs two similar examples to distinguish the theories, explaining how Amazon Studios' *The Man in the High Castle* television series is illustrative of weak narrative ethical knowledge and how Richard Loncraine's cinematic adaptation of *Richard III* is illustrative of strong narrative ethical knowledge. I address the objection to narrative justice from poetic justice in section 18, understood not in terms of Martha Nussbaum's *Poetic Justice*, but my own *The Value of Literature*, where I was explicit that literary value was independent from both the cognitive and ethical values of literary representations. I set out the argument for narrative justice in section 19, demonstrating that narrative justice applies narrative sensibility to the reduction of criminal inhumanity on the basis of their shared ethical motivation.

16. ETHICAL KNOWLEDGE AND NARRATIVITY

The purpose of chapter 3 was to argue for a deflationary account of the ethical value of narrative representation (i.e., that exemplary narratives are essentially ethical rather than essentially moral or, in colloquial terms, that every story has a moral but that moral may be virtuous, vicious, or somewhere in between). The purpose of chapter 4 was to argue for a version of narrative cognitivism (i.e., that exemplary narratives can provide both phenomenological knowledge and lucid phenomenological knowledge or, in colloquial terms, that stories provide genuine knowledge regardless of whether they are real or imagined). In chapter 3, I proposed a two-part theory, one that explained the ethical value of all narrative representations and one that explained the ethical value of exemplary narratives. In this chapter and in the remainder of this book, I shall be concerned exclusively with exemplary narratives. I employed Harpham's conception of emplotment to explain the essential ethical value of exemplary narratives. I characterised plot in ethical terms, as movement from the condition of *is-but-ought-not-to-be* to the condition of *is-and-ought-to-be*. Exemplary narratives are subject to a dual ethical evaluation: from the internal perspective, the actions of the characters may be judged; from the external perspective, the author may be judged for the *is-and-ought-to-be* with which he or she concludes the narrative. Plot characterised in these terms is the ethical element of the narrative *framework*, the author's preferred set of cognitive, evaluative, and emotional responses that the audience either decides to adopt in the standard mode of engagement or decides to reject. The ethical value of an exemplary narrative is thus embedded in its framework by the author and realised in the standard mode of engagement by the audience.

The framework and standard mode of engagement are also crucial to the provision of both phenomenological knowledge and lucid phenomenological knowledge, which I distinguished in chapter 4. In order to acquire the phenomenological knowledge provided by an exemplary narrative, one must both experience the representation and adopt the standard mode of engagement to that representation. In the examples I used from Gibson, adopting the standard mode of engagement to Ralph Ellison's *Invisible Man* and Elia Kazan's *America, America* provides knowledge of what it is like to be a victim of systematic racial oppression and what it is like to be an immigrant struggling to make his way to an unwelcoming country, respectively. The acquisition of lucid phenomenological knowledge requires an additional step: one must first experience the representation, then adopt the standard mode of engagement to that representation, and then experience audience-anagnorisis (i.e., recognise that the adoption of the standard mode of engagement involved the reproduction of a particular experience of a particular character for oneself). In my examples, the combination of adopting the standard mode of engagement to Shakespeare's *Romeo and Juliet* and Christopher Nolan's *Memento* with audience-anagnorisis provides knowledge of what it is like to forget someone who is important and what it is like to have anterograde amnesia, respectively. Therefore, in a similar manner to ethical value, the cognitive value of an exemplary narrative—whether phenomenological knowledge or lucid phenomenological knowledge—is embedded in its framework by the author and realised in the standard mode of engagement by the audience.

The relation between the two types of value on the one hand and the framework and standard mode of engagement on the other facilitates the combination of the arguments from chapters 3 and 4. In virtue of their preferred set of cognitive, evaluative, and emotional responses, all exemplary narratives convey both ethical knowledge and the realisation of what a particular lived experience is like (i.e., all exemplary narratives convey phenomenological ethical knowledge). There are two points to note: first, the knowledge may be moral, immoral, or in between; and second, different exemplary narratives may provide contrary and even contradictory knowledge of the same lived experience. In chapters 3 and 4, I contrasted Leni Riefenstahl's *Triumph of the Will* with Oliver Hirschbiegel's *Downfall*. In the former, Riefenstahl frames Hitler as a messianic saviour who descends from the heavens to lead the German people to glory; in the latter, Hirschbiegel frames Hitler as an evil megalomaniac who sacrifices the German people for his self-aggrandisement. In the standard mode of engagement with *Triumph of the Will*, the audience comes to realise why many Germans supported Hitler; in the standard mode of engagement with *Downfall*, the audience comes to realise the full extent of his malevolence in his determination to destroy Germany as well as himself.

In section 14, I noted a problem with phenomenological knowledge: even if one accepts that phenomenological knowledge meets the epistemic criterion in the narrative cognitivism debate (i.e., phenomenological knowledge is genuine knowledge), there is no criterion for phenomenological knowledge itself (i.e., for its acquisition). This places phenomenological knowledge in the same category as art criticism with respect to empirical evidence. Most art critics agree that there are no true or false interpretations of a work of art, only more or less convincing ones. If the phenomenological knowledge provided by a particular exemplary narrative is challenged, there appears to be an impasse. *Triumph of the Will* serves as a particularly good example due to the controversy over its ethical value. I stated that the phenomenological ethical knowledge provided by the representation is the realisation of why many Germans supported Hitler, but what if another commentator were to claim that the phenomenological ethical knowledge it provides is the realisation that Hitler actually was a messianic saviour? In section 10, I noted Riefenstahl's disingenuous claim that the representation was a work of documentary rather than a work of propaganda. In her informed essay on the cinematic representation, Mary Devereaux suggests that one cannot both appreciate *Triumph of the Will*'s aesthetic value and distance oneself from its ethical value, because its artistic vision, "its utterly horrifying vision of Hitler and National Socialism," is the essence of the narrative.[1] There is, in other words, a dispute over the extent to which one is required to accept Riefenstahl's *is-and-ought-to-be* in order to gain the knowledge provided by the representation, and this dispute is readily extended to the nature of that knowledge itself. One might argue that the phenomenological ethical knowledge I described above is consistent with an interpretation of the representation as a work of documentary, but not as a work of propaganda. In order for me to convince an opponent that *Triumph of the Will* is both a work of propaganda and that the knowledge provided is the realisation of why many Germans supported Hitler, I would have to construct a critical argument, citing evidence from the film and from critical interpretations of the film. The similarity between art criticism and phenomenological knowledge is not, of course, coincidental, because the phenomenological knowledge with which I am concerned is conveyed precisely by means of representation, and the mode of representation is standardly the subject of art criticism.

In response to this objection to phenomenological knowledge, I argued that lucid phenomenological knowledge was verifiable and used the following criteria for my two examples: the criterion for lucid phenomenological knowledge in *Romeo and Juliet* is that the audience forgets about Rosaline, and the criterion for lucid phenomenological knowledge in *Memento* is that the audience is unable to understand the sequence of events represented. Neither of these examples have particular ethical relevance, however, so I shall return to *Blade Runner: The Final Cut*, discussed in the preface. The lucid phenomenological ethical knowledge provided by the exemplary narrative is that humanity and human beings do not necessarily coincide. The criterion for lucid phenomenological ethical knowledge in *The Final Cut* is that the audience recognises that Deckard is a replicant rather than a human being. In order to acquire this lucid phenomenological ethical knowledge, the audience must not only recognise the significance of the paper unicorn, but they must also undergo audience-anagnorisis and recognise that Deckard's experience of discovering his own biological inhumanity has been replicated in the audience's discovery of the protagonist's biological inhumanity. The advantage that lucid phenomenological ethical knowledge has over phenomenological ethical knowledge—verifiability—comes at great cost, however, and I noted in chapter 4 that the provision of such knowledge by exemplary narratives is rare, perhaps even extremely rare. Phenomenological ethical knowledge and lucid phenomenological ethical knowledge can be defined as follows:

(PEK)   The realisation of what a particular lived ethical experience is like.
(LPEK)   The realisation of what a particular lived ethical experience is like by means of the reproduction of a particular ethical experience of a

particular character for the audience who adopt the standard mode of engagement to the narrative representation.

The combination of advantage and disadvantage is why I shall retain the two categories of narrative ethical knowledge. The argument for LPEK is stronger in virtue of each example being verifiable by empirical means, but the rarity of such cases limits the application of the theory to practice. On the other hand, the argument for PEK is weaker in virtue of its being restricted to the critical level of being more or less convincing, but it has a greater potential for being employed in practice, as every exemplary narrative provides such knowledge to a greater or lesser extent. I shall employ the weaker and stronger conceptions to describe the following two theories of *narrative ethical knowledge*, respectively:

(NEK)   Exemplary narratives convey phenomenological ethical knowledge in virtue of their narrativity.
(NEK*)   Some exemplary narratives convey lucid phenomenological ethical knowledge in virtue of their narrativity.

My claim is no more than that there is a causal relation between the adoption of the standard mode of engagement with an exemplary narrative and ethical development in terms of the acquisition of either PEK or LPEK. That is the theory for which I have argued in chapters 1, 3, and 4. Note also that it is ethical rather than moral knowledge, such that the viewer whose morality was corrupted by Riefenstahl's framework would still have acquired the PEK. Moral corruption constitutes ethical development as much as moral improvement, so the acquisition of immoral knowledge is not problematic for NEK. In section 19 I shall show how the connection between narrative sensibility and ethical value established in NEK and NEK* forms the basis of the connection between narrative sensibility and political value, which I shall then apply to the concept of criminal inhumanity.

17. FASCIST FICTIONS

In this section I shall use two similar examples to differentiate NEK and NEK*. NEK is illustrated by Amazon Studios' *The Man in the High Castle*, a television series consisting of two seasons of ten episodes each (released in 2015 and 2016, respectively).[2] The series is based on Philip K. Dick's disappointing (albeit nonetheless award-winning) 1962 novel of the same name and is an alternative history set in an America of the early 1960s in which the Axis powers won the Second World War. There are two protagonists, Juliana Crain and John Smith. Crain (played by Alexa Davalos) is a young woman living in the San Francisco of the Japanese Pacific States who has managed to remain remarkably free from prejudice given that she has become a second-class citizen in her native country. Smith (played by Rufus Sewell) is an Obergruppenführer (SS general) based in New York within the Greater German Empire, where he is head of what appears to be the American branch of the Geheime Staatspolizei (gestapo, or secret state police). NEK* is illustrated by Richard Loncraine's cinematic adaptation of Shakespeare's *Richard III* (released in 1995). The film is an alternative history set in England in the 1930s, where the fifteenth-century Wars of the Roses are reproduced in the image of the Spanish Civil War (1936–1939), with the fascist House of York battling the democratic House of Lancaster. Ian McKellen plays Richard of Gloucester, and although he completely dominates the exemplary narrative, he is supported by a more than able coterie of co-stars, including Annette Bening (playing Queen Elizabeth), Robert Downey Jr. (playing Rivers), Dominic West (playing the Earl of Richmond), Jim Broadbent (playing the Duke of Buckingham), Kristin Scott Thomas (playing Lady Anne Neville), and Maggie Smith (playing the Duchess of York).

Season 1 of *The Man in the High Castle* successfully captures many of the finer points of the novel and Dick's writing more generally, such as his use of multiple and often apparently unrelated subplots. The audience is introduced to a host of characters without knowing who will drive the narrative or even who will live or die, all of which creates a tense and absorbing atmosphere. The two characters used to advertise the series (who subsequently emerge as its protagonists), Crain and Smith, are linked by a third, Joe Blake (played by Luke Kleintank). Blake is a young American man employed as an undercover agent by Smith, and he meets Crain while on a mission in the Neutral Zone between the two empires, which are separated by the Rocky Mountains. The main plot coalesces around the mystery of documentary film reels that reveal an alternative reality in which the Allied powers won the war (i.e., historical reality). At the end of the season, Crain watches one of the films and sees a representation of Blake, in German uniform executing American prisoners of war. The puzzle of the (alternative) reality in/of the films is set against an arms race between the Greater Japanese Empire and the Greater German Empire and Hitler's failing health.

The documentaries are explained at the beginning of season 2: they are images of possible events that have not happened yet—but might—rather than past events, and they can be used to manipulate the future. The plot then focuses on the geopolitical situation as the Japanese rush to build a nuclear bomb before Hitler dies in order to be able to maintain the Cold War against his successor. The events in the two empires are exacerbated by the presence of jingoistic elements on both sides: Germans who are attempting to preempt a war with Japan before she is capable of nuclear retaliation, and Japanese who want to build a bomb as a precursor to declaring war on Germany. These momentous world events provide the context for the emergence of five interlinked subplots, each of which follows a particular character—the three from season 1; Frank Frink (played by Luke Evans), Juliana's boyfriend and newcomer to the Resistance; and Nobusuke Tagomi (played by Cary-Hiroyuki Tagawa), the trade minister of the Pacific States. This narrowing of narrative focus sets all five characters in pursuit of clear goals as Crain and Frink commit fully to the Resistance, Joe commits to the Germans, Smith remains loyal to Hitler, and Tagomi finds himself capable of moving between the story world and the real world. The season ends with the Third World War averted, Smith's rise to the position of Himmler's deputy, and Crain living under Smith's protection in New York.

In watching the series, the audience that adopts the standard mode of engagement gains PEK of how an America run by right-wing extremists might have looked in the 1960s and might look in the future. The exemplary narrative engages the audience on emotional and evaluative levels and provides this knowledge in virtue of its narrativity rather than the factual accuracy of the alternative history represented. Part of the series' achievement is that it demonstrates how such a society might not only develop but be sustained, and season 1 provides a particularly compelling contrast between Smith's service in the Greater German Empire and those resisting the Greater Japanese Empire. Smith is by far the most captivating (if not appealing) character of the season, despite his National Socialism and participation in genocide during the war. In addition to his credentials as an unequivocal villain, he is fiercely loyal (to his family and the Führer), very shrewd (in outwitting the various German leaders jockeying for power as Hitler's health declines), and pretty much unkillable (whether the assassins are fellow National Socialists or enemies of the Empire). In contrast, the heroes, including Crain, are continually wavering between joining the Resistance and accepting their status as a colonised people, and when the Resistance in the (Japanese) West or (German) East does take action, it is either pointless, useless, or both. What is perhaps most disappointing is the heroes' general selfishness and lack of interest in sacrificing their personal safety for a greater cause—unlike Smith, who has devoted his life to service, albeit to a completely irredeemable cause. In season 2, Crain and other members of the Resistance make a more determined commitment, but Smith's rise to power is nonetheless set within a framework where audience approval is invited (as, aside from the qualities mentioned above, he is opposed to a Third World War). The PEK conveyed thus includes knowledge of how a charismatic leader can win support in spite of being morally repugnant and how difficult resistance to a powerful regime can be, even when the moral basis of that resistance is unquestionable. I shall return to *The Man in the High Castle* shortly.

Richard III opens with a short, intense, and gripping scene in which a tank bursts through the wall of the Lancastrian military headquarters, followed by troops with gas masks that conceal their identity. Richard of Gloucester, distinctive with his severe kyphosis, the hand of his withered left arm tucked into his pocket, and his jerking gait, executes first Prince Edward and then King Henry VI. The scene ends with him removing the gas mask to reveal his face, providing a segue to the second scene, which begins with Richard smoking a cigarette in the back of a car en route to the Palace of Westminster for a celebration of King Edward IV's victory. The soliloquy that opens Shakespeare's play begins with Richard addressing the guests at the ball, then moves seamlessly to a toilet in the palace, where Richard's difficulty in performing basic bodily functions is made all too apparent. These first few minutes of the film are crucial to the framework that Loncraine establishes, in which he departs from the ambiguity about whether Richard is vicious or tragic in the original. The exemplary narrative begins by establishing Richard's courage and martial prowess, the latter an admirable quality in his case as it involves overcoming severe physical disability. The audience is then shown his struggle to perform what for most people is a simple and effortless task—urinating and washing his hands—and the invitation to regard Richard with admiration is now matched by an invitation to pity the everyday struggles and humiliations he faces. From the opening of the film, Loncraine's framework therefore invites a degree of empathy with Richard's desires, emotions, and motivation—or, at the very least, a degree of sympathy for his suffering.

In section 13 I discussed Zamir's insight that Shakespeare provides lucid phenomenological knowledge by reproducing a particular experience of a particular character for the audience in structuring the representation so that the experience is acted by the actors and re-enacted by the audience. I focused on his example in *Romeo and Juliet*, mentioned that his other examples varied in their conviction, and praised his argument for *Richard III*. I also noted that Zamir is attempting to delineate a fourth type of knowledge, which I have elsewhere called *knowledge through*, to distinguish it from *knowledge that*, *knowledge how*, and *knowledge what*.[3] While I am making use of Zamir's examples, I am doing so in order to identify a specific variant of *knowledge what* rather than his *knowledge through*. Zamir argues that *Richard III* conveys knowledge through *amoralism is a deficiency in knowing* (i.e., that amoralism can be an epistemic defect). If his interpretation is correct, then *Richard III* also conveys LPEK, which in turn requires the reproduction of a relevant aspect of Richard's amoralism in the audience. Zamir provides an implicit indication of this reproduction in establishing the premises of his interpretation. After describing *Richard III* as "a literary staging of amoral conduct chosen for its own sake," he states: "I will allow myself to be taken in by a splendid staging of evil."[4] He uses *splendid* to describe the way in which Shakespeare invites an empathic understanding of Richard by the audience. Zamir's statement of intent both reproduces Richard's conscious choice and recommends a mode of audience engagement. In the opening soliloquy of the play, Richard declares:

> And therefore, since I cannot prove a lover
> To entertain these fair well-spoken days,
> I am determined to prove a villain
> And hate the idle pleasures of these days.[5]

Although the third line is ambiguous, Richard appears to be asserting his agency, freely selecting villainy over heroism, hate over love, war over peace. It is on the basis of this conscious choice that Zamir describes the subject of the play as *amoral conduct chosen for its own sake*.

My claim is that Loncraine's *Richard III* conveys LPEK by structuring the dramatic experience so that it is acted by the actor and re-enacted by the audience in the following manner. At precisely the moment when he utters the words "And therefore, since I cannot prove a lover," McKellen turns to address the camera, which zooms in to a close-up (lasting only for the duration of the above lines). As Richard discloses his freely chosen villainy, the audience becomes aware of his clouded left iris and realises that his disability may be even more substantial than previously thought. Richard's early candour (in the 12th minute of a 101-minute film), represented in the context of the previous shots and sequences, invites the audience to regard him as a deeply flawed protagonist rather than a villainous antagonist for the remainder of the narrative. As such, the audience is required to make its own amoral choice, to accept Loncraine's invitation and select the pleasure of the splendid staging of evil rather than anxiety about vicious dictators. The experience is reproduced rather than replicated because the audience does not choose to behave in an amoral manner, like Richard, but to empathise with Richard in spite of his amoral behaviour.[6] The audience's experiences nonetheless overlap and resemble Richard's because they both involve placing pleasure over virtue in their respective choices—the pleasure of villainy for Richard, and the pleasure of Loncraine's adaptation for the audience. In the same way that Richard's choice is made freely, so the audience is free to either accept or reject the standard mode of engagement that Loncraine's framework invites. The audience that declines the invitation is likely to take far less pleasure in the film, which is a vehicle for McKellen, who revels in Richard's villainy from the very beginning to the very end. Unlike Shakespeare, Loncraine denies the audience a moral resolution. In the last minute of the film, while the Battle of Bosworth Field rages in Battersea Power Station, the Earl of Richmond (armed with a pistol) confronts Richard (unarmed), both men high on the exposed metal beams of the ruins. Richard denies Richmond the opportunity to kill him by throwing himself off the building, retaining his agency in his final act. The last few seconds of the film are a slow-motion shot of Richard grinning maniacally as he falls into a raging furnace below, which represents the fires of hell. Richard is smiling because of his success: he chose to be a villain and has succeeded in leading an excessively vicious life, dying in a controversial manner (by his own hand), and going to hell. The audience that accepts Loncraine's invitation prioritises the aesthetic over the ethical, and LPEK is provided by the reproduction of Richard's amoral choice in the audience.

I have employed these two examples because their superficial similarity makes for a particularly effective contrast of the ways in which NEK and NEK* convey knowledge. I stated that *The Man in the High Castle* provides PEK of how an America run by right-wing extremists might have looked in the 1960s and might look in the future. I think the framework of the studio is clear that such a society is highly undesirable. Despite the complexity of Smith's character, for example, his commitment to an immoral cause places him in a situation where he is required to authorise his son's euthanasia when Thomas is diagnosed with a genetic disease. The series is nonetheless open to an alternative interpretation wherein Smith is straightforwardly heroic and there is thus no guarantee that the NEK of the film is moral rather than immoral. I also noted two other aspects of the PEK provided by the exemplary narrative: (1) how a charismatic leader can win support in spite of being morally repugnant, and (2) how difficult resistance to a powerful regime can be, even when the moral basis of that resistance is unquestionable. In consequence of the lack of verifiability associated with PEK, however, it is difficult to establish a criterion for any of the three statements above and even to identify whether the second and third are indeed conveyed by the film. In contrast, the LPEK conveyed by *Richard III* is verifiable. I stated above that the exemplary narrative reproduces Richard's amoral choice (villainy over heroism) in the audience (aesthetic over ethical). The criterion for the LPEK is that the audience makes an aesthetic rather than ethical choice in their engagement with the narrative and chooses the pleasure of Loncraine and McKellen's splendid staging of evil over ethical qualms about taking pleasure in the representation of vicious actions. LPEK is both more specific and more readily identifiable as valid than PEK. It is also more difficult to achieve, however, with examples relatively rare, which is why I advance both NEK and NEK* as a joint foundation for the thesis of narrative justice.

18. POETIC JUSTICE?

In a similar manner to that in which Aristotle distinguished truth in poetry from truth in history, so Thomas Rymer contrasted poetic justice with historical justice. Aristotle maintained that "poetry speaks more of universals, history of particulars" and accorded greater significance to the former with the result that poetry was more significant, serious, and philosophical than history.[7] Rymer coined the term *poetical justice* to denote a type of justice that was more significant, complete, and satisfying than historical justice, which he regarded as legal justice at a particular spatiotemporal location. He states of poetical justice:

> It would require that the satisfaction be compleat and full, e're the *Malefactor* goes off the *Stage*, and nothing left to God Almighty, and another World. Nor will it suffer that the Spectators trust the *Poet* for a *Hell* behind the *Scenes*; the fire must roar in the conscience of the *Criminal*, the *fiends* and *furies* be conjur'd up to their faces, with a world of *machine* and horrid spectacles; and yet the *Criminal* could never move *pitty*.[8]

In other words, as part of the closure, thematic unity, or both of exemplary tragic narratives, the author had to achieve two aims: first, there must be an unequivocal resolution to the injustice, with nothing left to the audience's imagination; and second, justice must be entirely appropriate to the crime committed, a perfect match to the transgression of the antagonist, neither too severe nor too lenient. At a broader level, Rymer conceived of poetical justice as the moral (rather than ethical) value of tragedy, whereby the virtuous protagonist and vicious antagonist receive their just deserts. Jonathan Kertzer describes Rymer as invoking the necessity of "a moral demand that will be satisfied with aesthetic exactitude."[9]

In its contemporary use, *poetic justice* standardly combines the moral with the aesthetic to denote a resolution that is both moral and exactly appropriate. A poetic and historical example will illustrate the point clearly. Shakespeare coined the phrase *hoist with his own petard* in *Hamlet*. A petard was an explosive device used to breach walls during sieges, so the literal meaning is to be raised—blown up—by one's own explosive. Shakespeare's idiomatic use of the phrase is as follows:

> There's letters seal'd, and my two school-fellows,
> Whom I trust as I will adders fang'd,
> They bear the mandate, they must sweep my way
> And marshal me to knavery; let it work,
> For 'tis the sport to have the engineer
> Hoist with his own petar, and 't shall go hard

But I will delve one yard below their mines,
And blow them at the moon: O 'tis most sweet
When in one line two crafts directly meet.[10]

Claudius has sent Hamlet, Rosencrantz, and Guildenstern to England with
a sealed letter to the king that contains a death warrant for Hamlet. Hamlet
believes that Rosencrantz and Guildenstern are complicit in the plot to
murder him and alters the letter so that it contains a death warrant for them
rather than him. Thus, the very means by which they intend to murder him—
the letter—becomes the instrument of their own demise in the same way that
the engineer is blown up by his own device.

Oskar-Paul Dirlewanger was one of the most prolific and feared of National
Socialist Germany's war criminals. After serving with distinction in the First
World War, German Civil War, and Spanish Civil War, his conviction for
having sexual relations with a thirteen-year-old girl was quashed, and he was
given command of a company-sized penal unit in the Waffen SS, the party's
own branch of the armed forces. Over the next five years, Dirlewanger carved
a path of murder, rape, and pillage across Belarus, Poland, and Slovakia.
The combination of personal patronage from Himmler, National Socialist
ideology, and the downturn in German fortunes from 1942 created a situation
in which he roamed across German-occupied territory like a medieval robber
baron, disobeying orders from his superiors, dispensing corporal punishment
to his own troops, and assisting the Einsatzgruppen (mobile death squads) in
their genocidal purges. He reached the rank of Oberführer (senior colonel),
was awarded the Knight's Cross of the Iron Cross (the highest decoration in
the Third Reich) for his part in suppressing the Warsaw Uprising, and was
in command of a brigade by the time he left the front line in February 1945.
Dirlewanger then disappeared and is believed to have been trying to ship his
extensive war booty to Switzerland when he was captured by French troops
in Altshausen in May. The cells in which he was detained were guarded by
Polish soldiers, however, and he was recognised for his part in the razing
of Warsaw. His guards—and others—proceeded to beat and bayonet him to
death over a period of four days.[11] Dirlewanger's end is a particularly good
example of poetic justice, because not only was the means he used to kill
others—torture—used to kill him, but he was killed by soldiers from the
nation where he had wreaked the most havoc.

The question is why poetic justice should present a problem for narrative
justice. As a concept it does not, and I suggested a complementary formulation of the two concepts on Twitter, defining the former as "the suitability
of the ends of justice" and the latter as "the means employed to reach those
ends."[12] A potential problem arises with Martha Nussbaum's conception of
poetic justice, explained in her monograph of the same name, the full title of

which is *Poetic Justice: The Literary Imagination and Public Life* (mentioned in section 8). This is the book in which Nussbaum establishes her theory of aesthetic education in the most concise and explicit manner. She uses Dickens's *Hard Times—For These Times* as her main example to argue for a two-stage theory in which there is first a necessary relation between realist novels and a unique type of moral knowledge, and then a necessary relation between realist novels and the development of liberal democratic ideals. There are nonetheless two reasons that Nussbaum's poetic justice does not present a problem for narrative justice, both noted in section 8: first, I have discussed Nussbaum's literary education in detail in *The Value of Literature*, where I concluded that her thesis was both unconvincing and unsubstantiated; second, I have taken Worth to be advancing a more sophisticated and rigorous version of Nussbaum's theory and address the objection presented by her theory of narrative education in chapter 6. Mention of *The Value of Literature* does, however, raise another potential problem with poetic justice—understood not as the justice represented in poetry, but in all three categories of literary art (poems, plays, and novels)—for narrative justice.

My claim in that monograph was that there is a distinctively literary value common to poetry and narrative (a category I took to include both plays and novels) and that this literary value is *sui generic* (i.e., independent of the values commonly associated with literature, in particular cognitive value and ethical value). I employed the concept of literary thickness to articulate and argue for a particular type of satisfaction as the characteristically literary value and distinguished this value from the truth or virtue of literary representations.[13] Because NEK does not involve a commitment to the moral value of exemplary narratives, literary thickness is not contradictory to narrative justice: both can accommodate the separation of literary (or aesthetic) and ethical value in examples such as Harriet Beecher Stowe's *Uncle Tom's Cabin* (low and high, respectively) and Henry Miller's *Tropic of Cancer* (high and low, respectively). The problem arises in the cognitive value of exemplary narratives because literary thickness involves a commitment against cognitivism such that cognitive value is not part and parcel of literary value.[14] In contrast, NEK is a narrative cognitivist theory because the knowledge provided—PEK and LPEK—is provided in virtue of the narrativity of the representation and meets both the epistemic and narrativity criteria set out in section 13. I shall take Ralph Ellison's *Invisible Man* as an uncontroversial example of a text that is both a work of literature (my concern in *The Value of Literature*) and an exemplary narrative (my concern here). Either the knowledge of what it is like to be a victim of systematic racial oppression is part and parcel of the novel's literary or narrative value, or it is not part and parcel of the novel's literary or narrative value—it cannot be both. Alternatively, literary value and narrative value could be two completely different kinds of value, but both are usually included in the broader category of aesthetic value, so this does not seem like a promising line of defence to pursue. The objection is thus that my position is inconsistent: according to *The Value of Literature*, the PEK provided by *Invisible Man* is not part and parcel of its aesthetic value, but according to *Narrative Justice* it is.

I gestured toward this objection in section 15, when I raised an objection against narrative cognitivism by suggesting that poetic and narrative frameworks might both be produced by the aesthetic rather than narrative properties of a representation. I selected Morgan Spurlock's *Super Size Me* as an example of an exemplary narrative for which artistic considerations appeared to be absent in both production and reception, but which nonetheless conveyed lucid phenomenological knowledge. I concluded that while the narrative properties I identified were very likely also aesthetic properties, I was cautious about extending my argument for narrative cognitivism to an argument for aesthetic cognitivism. I noted that my concern was the close relation between aesthetic and artistic properties and the potential conflation between the narrative/non-narrative distinction and artistic/non-artistic distinction. This close relation applies to *Invisible Man* as follows: if *Invisible Man* is being read qua literature, then the PEK provided is not part and parcel of the literary value realised in the reading; if *Invisible Man* is being read qua narrative, then the PEK provided is part and parcel of the narrativity of the representation. While literary value and narrativity may both be categorised as aesthetic value, this is a step I neither wish to, nor am I required to, take. *Invisible Man* is indeed both a work of literature and an exemplary narrative, and although there is an overlap between the two distinctions, they are different ways of experiencing the novel. As such, my position in *Narrative Justice* is not incompatible with my position in *The Value of Literature*, and the concept of narrative justice (to which I proceed next) can be regarded as distinct from all of the above conceptions of poetic justice.

19. NARRATIVE JUSTICE

With the ethical value of exemplary narratives established in terms of NEK and NEK*, the question is now if and how the political value of exemplary narratives can be established (i.e., whether NEK and NEK* can provide the basis for the elevation of the value of exemplary narratives from the ethical sphere to the political sphere). In common with Sarah E. Worth but not Gayatri Chakravorty Spivak, my thesis of aesthetic education is contemporary rather than traditional and must thus demonstrate that the cultivation of aesthetic sensibility develops political harmony. Once again in common with Worth but not Spivak, my thesis is specifically concerned with narrative sensibility rather than aesthetic sensibility. Recall from section 9 that Worth's narrative education is the theory that the cultivation of narrative sensibility develops social harmony. My concern with the political sphere differs from both Spivak and Worth, however, in that I shall conceive of political value in terms of criminal inhumanity. Recall from section 4 that criminal inhumanity refers to serious crimes committed by a state or non-state actor against a civilian population, government, or public for ideological reasons. Criminal inhumanity thus involves a category—or a combination of categories—of political crime such that the reduction or prevention of criminal inhumanity constitutes a development of political harmony.

Although narrative justice is a contemporary rather than traditional version of aesthetic education, it follows Schiller's thesis in the *Letters* in two important respects: (a) the structure of the argument (i.e., the movement from aesthetic-ethical [narrative-ethical] to aesthetic-political [narrative-inhumanity]); and (b) practical implications, which are intended to drive political (criminal) change. I shall discuss (a) first. The argument for narrative justice begins as follows:

(i) All exemplary narratives are ethically valuable in virtue of their narrativity.
(ii) Narrative sensibility enables the realisation of ethical value in exemplary narratives.
(iii) Therefore, the cultivation of narrative sensibility increases the realisation of ethical value in exemplary narratives (i.e., develops ethical understanding).

The above argument is based on NEK and NEK*, both of which claim that exemplary narratives convey a variant of phenomenological ethical knowledge in virtue of their narrativity. If an exemplary narrative conveys PEK or LPEK in virtue of its narrativity, then greater narrative sensibility will, ceteris paribus, produce an increase in the acquisition of the knowledge conveyed. Both Spivak and Worth make more specific claims than I do at this point: the former establishes a link between the literary imagination and the ethical imagination, and the latter between narrative sensibility and the capacity for empathy. In contrast, the link between the cultivation of narrative sensibility and ethical understanding, set in the context of NEK and NEK*, is uncontroversial.

The second part of the argument concerns criminal inhumanity:

(A) Criminal inhumanity refers to a category of crimes motivated by ideology (i.e., a category of political crime).

(B) Political ideology is supervenient on ethical principles, such that there cannot be a change in the former without a change in the latter.
(C) The supervenience relationship is one of legitimacy (i.e., the political ideology is justified by the ethical principles).
(D) Therefore, criminal inhumanity is a category of crime that is justified by ethical principles.

Recall, again, that the ethical justification of criminal inhumanity—just like the ethical value of exemplary narratives—can be positive, negative, or neutral, so that National Socialism's justification by means of social Darwinism is an ethical justification, albeit an immoral one. Note also that (A) to (D) above is unaltered by criminal inhumanity motivated by religion. For religious devotees, religious value underpins ethical value such that political value is supervenient upon ethical value, which is in turn supervenient upon religious value. During the period of National Party rule in South Africa, for example, the various crimes committed by the state in the name of apartheid were justified by the ideologies of both Afrikaner nationalism and the Dutch Reformed Church. Although the ideologies were complementary, some servants of the state would have been motivated by one rather than the other. (D) holds for those motivated by the religious doctrine as well as those motivated by the political ideology because the theory of racial hierarchy (ethical) that justified apartheid (political) was underpinned by the Dutch Reformed Church's version of Protestantism (religious).

The step from (iii) and (D) to any kind of crime reduction or prevention is a large one, but it draws on a crucial assumption in the discipline of criminology. Criminology is primarily concerned with the reduction of crime. *Prevention* is sometimes used instead of *reduction*, but I prefer the latter as a realistic goal for criminologists at the theoretical level and criminal justice professionals at the practical level. The aim of crime reduction is achieved by employing theoretical and empirical investigation and verification to direct or inform public policy and evidence-based practice. The chain of causation from criminology to crime reduction is thus as follows: criminological inquiry identifies the cause or causes of a particular crime or, more ambitiously, of crime in general; the findings of the research are translated into a policy for one or more government or private agencies with the aim of reducing or removing the causal factor or factors; and the policy is put into practice resulting in the reduction of certain types of crime or the commission of various crimes by certain types of offender. The key factor that links criminological research to crime reduction is the explanation of the cause of crime.

Here is an example from Robert Agnew, the pioneer of general strain theory, taken from an article in between publication of his initial paper in 1992 and publication of the theory in full in 2005. The first quote is from the beginning of the article, summarising general strain theory, and the second is from the end, discussing its crime reduction potential:

(I) General strain theory (GST) argues that strains or stressors increase the likelihood of negative emotions like anger and frustration. These emotions create pressure for corrective action, and crime is one possible response (Agnew 1992). Crime may be a method for reducing strain (e.g., stealing the money you desire), seeking revenge, or alleviating negative emotions (e.g., through illicit drug use).[15]

(II) Agnew (1992) argued that two major policy recommendations flow from GST: reduce the exposure of individuals to strain and reduce the likelihood that individuals will cope with strain through crime (by targeting those individual characteristics conducive to criminal coping). This article suggests a third recommendation: alter the characteristics of strains in ways that reduce the likelihood they will result in crime. Despite our best efforts, many individuals will be exposed to strain. For example, parents, teachers, and criminal justice officials will continue to sanction individuals in ways that are disliked. We can, however, alter the ways in which these sanctions are administered so as to reduce the likelihood that they will (1) be seen as unjust, (2) be seen as high in magnitude, (3) reduce social control, and (4) create some pressure or incentive to engage in crime. In fact, this is one of the central thrusts behind the restorative justice and related movements.[16]

If narrative justice provides a convincing explanation of criminal inhumanity— or a convincing series of explanations—then it has the potential to reduce criminal inhumanity. I shall argue in chapters 7 and 8 that narrative justice has precisely this explanatory potential, with respect to, specifically, explaining responsibility for criminal inhumanity and explaining the psychology of criminal inhumanity. In chapter 9, I take a more direct approach, focusing on how a convincing explanation can be employed to undermine criminal inhumanity.

I can now draw the disparate strands from the above, from the previous sections of this chapter, and from chapters 3 and 4, together into an argument for narrative justice as follows:

(a) The cultivation of narrative sensibility can develop ethical understanding.
(b) Criminal inhumanity is a category of crime that is justified by ethical principles.
(c) Theories have crime reduction potential in virtue of explanation (i.e., developing understanding of the causes of crime).

(d) Therefore, the cultivation of narrative sensibility has the potential to
    reduce criminal inhumanity.

This argument establishes narrative justice as a thesis of aesthetic education
by elevating the link between narrative representation and the ethical sphere
in NEK and NEK* to a link between narrative representation and the political
sphere. Following Schiller, Spivak, and Worth, the link between the aesthetic
and the political is made in virtue of the ethical (i.e., narrative sensibility
impacts political crime because both narrative representation and political
crime are essentially ethical). It is important to note that both my theory of the
ethical value of narrative representation and my thesis of aesthetic education
are deflationary. Exemplary narratives are essentially ethical rather than essentially moral, in consequence of which the plot of an exemplary narrative can
be virtuous, vicious, or somewhere in between. Similarly, narrative sensibility
has the potential to both decrease and increase criminal inhumanity. Narrative
justice establishes a link first between exemplary narratives and ethical value
and then exemplary narratives and criminal inhumanity, but this link is neither essentially moral nor essentially humane. The thesis can be exploited to
either decrease or increase criminal inhumanity, and although my interest is
exclusively in the former, I do not deny the latter. The cultivation of narrative
sensibility for the purpose of increasing criminal inhumanity does not, however, constitute an objection to narrative justice. On the contrary, examples of
this kind offer evidence for narrative justice because they provide evidence of
the link between narrative representation and political crime.

    With this caveat—which I would call *narrative injustice* were it to form a
part of my thesis—in place, I can define narrative justice as follows:

> *Narrative justice*: criminal inhumanity can be reduced by the cultivation of
> narrative sensibility (i.e., the cultivation of narrative sensibility reduces criminal
> inhumanity).

Or, in colloquial terms, stories can reduce ideologically motivated crime.
Narrative justice is a contemporary rather than traditional thesis of aesthetic
education. It is a thesis of aesthetic education because the link between the
cultivation of narrative sensibility and the reduction of criminal inhumanity
links the aesthetic sphere to the political sphere by means of the ethical
sphere. It is contemporary rather than traditional because it proposes aesthetic
sensibility as one of the means—not the only means—by which political
harmony can be achieved. Narrative justice is a philosophical theory with
criminological implications, applications, and effects, which I shall explore in
chapters 7 to 9. Narrative justice is also an example of narrative criminology,
as I shall demonstrate that stories can instigate and sustain the reduction of

and desistance from ideologically motivated harmful action. Before doing so, however, I pick up where I left off in chapter 2, explaining why narrative justice constitutes an improvement on both global aesthetic education and narrative education.

NOTES

1. Mary Devereaux, "Beauty and Evil," 244.

2. At the time of writing there is a third season in production, but the particularly effective way in which the second season ends—so as to both provide closure and offer scope for a continuation of the series—allows me to focus on the first two seasons as a single exemplary narrative.

3. McGregor, "Blindness and Double Vision," forthcoming.

4. Zamir, *Double Vision*, 65, 66.

5. William Shakespeare, *Richard III* (London: Penguin, 2005 [1592–1593]), I.i.28–31.

6. This should be understood in terms of Worth's definition of empathy, discussed in section 9 (i.e., the audience does not just recognise Richard's emotions and respond to them in a positive manner, but actually reproduces his emotions—shame, contempt, frustration, and disgust, for example—and experiences them for themselves).

7. Aristotle, *Poetics*, IX, 1451b7–8.

8. Thomas Rymer, *The Tragedies of the Last Age Consider'd and Examind by the Practice of the Ancients, and by the Common Sense of All Ages* (London: Richard Tonson, 1678), 26. University of Oxford Text Archive. Available at: http://tei.it.ox.ac.uk/tcp/Texts-HTML/free/A58/A58024.html.

9. Jonathan Kertzer, *Poetic Justice and Legal Fictions* (Cambridge: Cambridge University Press, 2010), 11.

10. William Shakespeare, *Hamlet* (London: Penguin, 2001 [1604]), III.iv.224–232.

11. Christian Ingrao, *The SS Dirlewanger Brigade: The History of the Black Hunters*, trans. Phoebe Green (New York: Skyhorse Publishing, 2011), 176–80; French L. Maclean, *The Cruel Hunters: SS-Sonderkommando Dirlewanger Hitler's Most Notorious Anti-Partisan Unit* (Atglen, PA: Schiffer Military History, 1998), 223–26.

12. Rafe McGregor, @rafemcgregor, 12 August 2017.

13. McGregor, *Value of Literature*, 117.

14. McGregor, *Value of Literature*, 24.

15. Robert Agnew, "Building on the Foundation of General Strain Theory: Specifying the Types of Strain Most Likely to Lead to Crime and Delinquency," *Journal of Research in Crime and Delinquency* 38 (2001): 319. See also: Robert Agnew, "Foundation for a General Strain Theory of Crime and Delinquency," *Criminology* 30 (1992): 47–87; Robert Agnew, *Pressured into Crime: An Overview of General Strain Theory* (New York: Oxford University Press, 2005).

16. Agnew, "Specifying the Types of Strain," 352.

Chapter Six

Narrative Value

The purpose of this chapter is to explain why narrative justice provides greater scope for achieving political harmony than either Gayatri Chakravorty Spivak's global aesthetic education or Sarah E. Worth's narrative education. I employ *political harmony* loosely, so as to include all three specific aims of the theories involved: the detranscendentalisation of gender, socio-economic class, religion, and nationality; social harmony; and the reduction of criminal inhumanity. In section 20, I explore the consequences of Spivak's hyperbolic ethics and identify the practical problems they present for political harmony. Section 21 examines the difficulty of establishing conclusive evidence of the effects of reading by discussing the extended debate between David Comer Kidd and Emanuele Castano (2013, 2016) and Maria Panero, Deena Weisberg, Jessica Black, Thalia Goldstein, Jennifer Barnes, Hiram Brownell, and Ellen Winner (2016, 2017). In section 22, I explain why I am not convinced by what I consider to be the most promising empirical evidence presented thus far—two studies by Dan Johnson, Daniel Jasper, Sallie Griffin, and Brandie Huffman (2013, 2014). I extend my inquiry to the debate concerning the relationship between media violence and aggression in section 23. I show that despite four decades of empirical investigation, the evidence for a causal relation is regarded as legally insufficient, and I consider the consequences for Worth's narrative education. In section 24, I conclude by situating my position with respect to not only Spivak and Worth, but Gregory Currie and Martha Nussbaum.

20. HYPERBOLIC ETHICS AND
DECONSTRUCTIVE POLITICS

In selecting the two most compelling alternatives to narrative justice, I used theoretical rigour and practical feasibility as my criteria, which accounts for my choice of Spivak and Worth above more popular (and more fashionable) contemporaries such as Rancière and Nussbaum. Despite emerging from distinct traditions—Levinasian poststructuralism and neo-Aristotelianism, respectively—Spivak and Worth both focus almost exclusively on the practice of reading. In their shared conception, aesthetic education is concerned with reading rather than instruction, and the learning that takes place is achieved by virtue of the reading. They nonetheless have completely opposing views on the relationship between their theories of reading and the empirical evidence of the effects of reading. In contrast to Worth, Spivak is adamant that the effects with which she is concerned are unverifiable. Her reflection on her own work is at its most persuasive in the following personal anecdote:

> When I was a graduate student, on the eve of the Vietnam War, I lived in the same house as Paul Wolfowitz, the ferocious Deputy Secretary of Defense who was the chief talking head for the war on Iraq. He was a Political Science undergraduate, disciple of Allan Bloom, the conservative political philosopher. As I have watched him on television lately, I have often thought that if he had serious training in literary reading and/or the imagining of the enemy as human, his position on Iraq would not be so inflexible. This is not a verifiable conviction. But it is in view of such hopes that humanities teaching acts itself out.[1]

One should not conflate a lack of verifiability with a lack of pragmatism, as the length of Spivak's teaching career suggests. I shall return to her position on verifiability in section 24, but one of its consequences is that any critique of global aesthetic education must focus on the theory itself.

Recall that global aesthetic education claims that the literary imagination is a necessary and sufficient condition of the detranscendentalisation of gender, socioeconomic class, religion, and nationality. I concluded section 7 by identifying Spivak's theory as a direct development of Schiller's, which justified my claim that it is a traditional rather than contemporary version of aesthetic education (i.e., political harmony can only be achieved by aesthetic sensibility). *An Aesthetic Education in the Era of Globalization* consists of a preface, an introduction, and twenty-five essays, and there are occasions where Spivak seems to retreat from the stronger, traditional claim. In "Nationalism and the Imagination," for example, she writes: "I will never be foolish enough to claim that a humanities education alone (especially given the state of humanities education today) can save the world!"[2] Given the context of the statement, Spivak appears to be making a point about the extent to which political harmony is an achievable goal rather than the extent to which global aesthetic education can contribute to political harmony. Although I am confident that my classification of global aesthetic education is accurate, I shall not criticise Spivak on the basis that there may be other means to the end of political harmony. I shall, instead, concentrate on the lynchpin of global aesthetic education, the ethical faculty.

In keeping with the mechanism set out by Schiller, the relationship between the aesthetic and the political is indirect, made by means of the ethical (i.e., the literary imagination is linked to the ethical faculty, which is in turn linked to the detranscendentalisation of gender, socioeconomic class, religion, and nationality). In section 7 I noted Spivak's definition of the ethical situation in terms of impossibility, which draws on both Levinas's argument that ethics is fundamentally a relation and Derrida's argument that ethics is defined by aporia. There is no ethical resolution to Abraham's dilemma in the "Binding of Isaac" because—like every human being experiencing every ethical situation—he must sacrifice either an other or the Other. Derrida recognised, for example, that in apparently sacrificing my time or money to Charity A, I am not sacrificing myself for Charity A, but Charity B (which has an equally strong claim on my time or money) to Charity A. He employed Vladimir Jankélévitch's phrase *hyperbolic ethics* to describe an ethics that recognises the kind of absolute responsibility proposed by Levinas.[3] Kelly Oliver elucidates this concept, explaining it in terms of not only Levinas, but Kant.[4]

In his *Critique of Pure Reason* Kant famously claims:

Pure reason, then, contains, not indeed in its speculative employment, but in that practical employment which is also moral, principles of the *possibility of experience*, namely, of such actions as, in accordance with moral precepts, *might* be met with in the *history* of mankind. For since reason commands that such actions should take place, it must be possible for them to take place. Consequently, a special kind of systematic unity, namely the moral, must likewise be possible. We have indeed found that the systematic unity of nature cannot be proved *in accordance with speculative principles of reason*. For although reason does indeed have causality in respect of freedom in general, it does not have causality in respect of nature as a whole; and although moral principles of reason can indeed give rise to free actions, they cannot give rise to laws of nature. Accordingly, it is in their practical, meaning thereby their moral, employment, that the principles of pure reason have objective reality. I entitle the world a *moral world*, in so far as it may be in accordance with all moral laws; and this is what by means of the freedom of the rational being it *can be*, and what according to the necessary laws of morality it *ought to be*.[5]

Kant's description of the moral world establishes a relation between possibility and morality that is often described as the principle that *ought
implies can*. According to this principle, actions that I ought to perform are
by implication actions that I can (am able to) perform. In other words, one
only has moral responsibility to perform a particular action if one is capable
of carrying out that action. For example, I am only morally responsible for
saving a drowning child if I can swim myself. If I cannot swim then there
is no moral obligation to drown in a futile attempt to reach the child, and
given my awareness of my athletic limitations, my moral obligation seems
to be bringing the child's plight to the attention of a lifeguard rather than
committing to a course of action that is likely to result in two deaths.

Oliver presents the historical movement from Kant's morality to Levinas's
ethics as evidence that Derrida's hyperbolic ethics is actually a reversal of
Kant's principle. Derrida argues that reconciliation between the finitude of
self and the infinity of responsibility is impossible. Recall that he replaces
the concept of ethical dilemma with aporia of responsibility. The certainty
of unethical action is not restricted to rare cases of ethical dilemma, such
as Abraham in the "Binding of Isaac," but is present in all cases. In consequence, Oliver asks, "But what if the reverse were true? What if *ought implies
cannot*? What if our obligations always outstrip our intentions?"[6] It is precisely this reversal of the Kantian principle upon which Spivak's global aesthetic education relies. The imagination is the instrument of thinking things
that are not present, both possible and impossible, and the ethical situation
is the experience of impossibility. Impossibility thus provides the essential
link between the literary and ethical experiences such that the imagination
simply is the ethical faculty, and robust reading develops the reader's capacities for literary appreciation and ethical response simultaneously. The
political value of global aesthetic education—the detranscendentalisation
of gender, socioeconomic class, religion, and nationality—is supervenient
on the ethical value, and the development of the political value by means of
the literary imagination takes place in virtue of the ethical value. Why is this
problematic? There are two reasons, one relatively minor and the other more
damaging.

The first is Oliver's claim that hyperbolic ethics poses a challenge to the
traditional supervenience relationship between ethical and political value
(which I discussed in section 2). According to Oliver, Derrida sets ethics
against politics because a politics based on hyperbolic ethics requires absolute
hospitality, which involves democracy without citizenship and undermines
the conditional essence of politics. "Politics necessitates calculation, perhaps
even cost-benefit or risk analysis, while ethics needs universal principles."[7]
If Oliver is correct, then the transition from the imagination as the ethical faculty to the various aspects of detranscendentalisation may not be as

straightforward as Spivak suggests. I think that Spivak is well aware of this implication, however, and her sophisticated and nuanced explanations of the processes of detranscendentalisation with respect to gender, socioeconomic class, religion, and nationality in the various essays in *Aesthetic Education* acknowledge the complexities of both hyperbolic ethics, deconstructive politics, and the relation between them. Oliver's summary of Derrida on this point is thus entirely applicable to Spivak: "Derrida's notions of justice and democracy to come try to maintain the tense but necessary relation between ethics and politics, for the sake of a more ethical politics."[8]

The second problem is that Kant's principle of *ought implies can* is not merely widely, but extensively, accepted. This applies to both branches of normative ethical theory—consequentialist and non-consequentialist (which includes both deontological and virtue-based theories)—as well as non-traditional approaches such as moral particularism. The implications of this general theoretical acceptance are revealed at the level of practical application. Ethical experience and moral practice usually begin when one becomes self-conscious about morality. Typically this is by means of experiencing an ethical situation as an ethical situation—when one asks, perhaps for the first time, "What should I do?" The other great question asked by the self-conscious ethical agent is "How should I live?" One or both of these questions are standardly employed by teachers to introduce students to the moral world. Neither question appears, however, to admit of an answer that refers to the impossible. There is no point in asking what to do or how to live if the answers present options that are beyond my ability; one might even consider the questions elliptical, such that they both conceal the phrase "given my capabilities." So, regardless of whether the antimony between hyperbolic ethics and deconstructive politics can be negotiated, *ought implies cannot* is a highly controversial principle upon which to base one's conception of ethics. The principle is not merely controversial, but requires a radical reconceptualisation of ethical theory, practice, and value. This principle and the reconceptualisation may be valuable—perhaps very valuable indeed—but they require too substantial a revision of contemporary ethical theory to provide the basis for a widespread programme of political reform.

21. LITERATURE, EMPATHY, AND EXPERIMENTATION

In contrast to Spivak, Worth takes the empirical evidence for the effects of reading very seriously and maintains that the results of the few studies undertaken support narrative education, the theory that the cultivation of narrative sensibility develops social harmony. I am less optimistic about both the reliability and validity of most of these studies. In order to make my point, I shall analyse the work of Kidd and Castano (2013), selected on the dual basis of being the most well-known of the studies cited by Worth and the extensive dialogue that followed the initial study. In section 9, I summarised Kidd and Castano's use of a series of five experiments to test their hypothesis that literary fiction primes theory of mind (ToM). The first experiment compared the effects of reading literary fiction and nonfiction, and the remainder compared the effects of reading literary and popular fiction. They concluded that literary fiction, in contrast to both nonfiction and popular fiction, improves performance on an affective ToM task. Referring to Kidd and Castano and two other sets of experiments, Worth concludes that reading well-constructed narratives develops our capacity for empathy. At the time *In Defense of Reading* was going to press, there was an attempt to replicate Kidd and Castano's findings by Maria Panero, Deena Weisberg, Jessica Black, Thalia Goldstein, Jennifer Barnes, Hiram Brownell, and Ellen Winner (2016). Kidd and Castano (2016) subsequently published a reply to Panero and her colleagues, and Panero and colleagues (2017) then replied to Kidd and Castano. There are thus four papers currently available: two by Kidd and Castano and two by Panero and colleagues, the combination of which provides an unprecedented level of detail about the kinds of experiment in which Worth is interested.

Panero and colleagues begin their replication by acknowledging the correlation between lifetime engagement with fiction (measured by the Author Recognition Test, ART) and ToM (measured by the Reading the Mind in the Eyes Test, RMET) proposed by Kidd and Castano. They then ask the crucial question:

> But do people develop their mindreading capacities by reading fiction, or do people with a strong interest in psychological states seek out fictional texts because of fiction's exploration of psychological states?[9]

With this doubt in mind, Panero and colleagues suggest that the specific conclusion reached by Kidd and Castano on the basis of their evidence—which is that a brief exposure to literary fiction causes an instant improvement in social cognition—is unlikely.[10] Working in three independent research groups, Panero and colleagues replicated Kidd and Castano's experiments using a similar number of participants (a total of 792 as opposed to 697).[11] They employed a different method of analysis to Kidd and Castano and divided their results into three categories: literary fiction versus nonfiction, literary fiction versus popular fiction, and literary fiction versus no reading. In all three cases they found that once ART was taken into account, there was no difference in RMET between the participants who had read literary fiction and those in one of the other conditions.[12] Panero and colleagues conclude: "In short, we found no support for any short-term causal effects of reading literary fiction on theory of mind."[13] They quote several recent studies (including Bal and Veltkamp, cited by Worth) that suggest a variety of reasons for Kidd and Castano's results, such as: personality traits, prior exposure to literature, verbal cognition, and the way in which people read.[14] They complete their study by noting the possibility that whatever the effects of reading literary fiction may be, they may well not be experienced immediately after reading.[15]

In response, Kidd and Castano claim that Panero and colleagues employed different methods and did not therefore replicate their experiments.[16] They also argue that the results are unreliable on the basis of two problems with internal validity. First, Panero and colleagues failed to ensure that the participants had in fact read the required texts (i.e., that they followed instructions). Kidd and Castano accounted for this possibility by establishing thirty seconds as a threshold below which results were discounted, whereas Panero and colleagues used a threshold of only four seconds.[17] Second, Kidd and Castano allege that Panero and colleagues did not randomly assign participants to the four different conditions. They claim that while there was an appearance of equal distribution, the reasons for the actual distribution are opaque.[18] Kidd and Castano then applied their time threshold to Panero and colleagues' study, which eliminated seventy participants, and eliminated a further eight on the basis that they had no ART measurement.[19] With this adjusted sample, they reanalysed the replication. The results confirmed their initial conclusion, that reading literary fiction led to a stronger performance on RMET than reading popular fiction.[20]

Panero and colleagues' reply to Kidd and Castano's response addresses both of the internal validity problems. They suggest that reading time is not as simple as Kidd and Castano claim, that readers who are familiar with genre fiction in particular read it very quickly, and that establishing the precise point at which a threshold should be set becomes "somewhat arbitrary" once these complicating factors are considered.[21] Panero and colleagues accept the criticism of the assignment of participants, describe their efforts to rectify the problem in detail, and disagree that the differences in participant numbers across the four conditions compromise internal validity.[22] They then consider the question of whether participants with no measure on the ART should have been excluded from the results. Panero and colleagues again suggest that the question is more complicated than Kidd and Castano claim and provide evidence to demonstrate that the exclusion of this group would not alter their results.[23] They complete their response with what may be the most telling point against Kidd and Castano, which is that in reanalysing Panero and colleagues' results in order to prove that Panero and colleagues did not replicate their study, Kidd and Castano actually fail to replicate their own results. In the original study, the participants who had read literary fiction scored higher on the RMET than those in all the other conditions, whereas in their reanalysis Kidd and Castano found that the literary fiction and nonfiction participants had similar scores and that both conditions outscored the popular fiction condition.[24] Kidd and Castano acknowledge this new finding in their response to Panero and colleagues, identifying it as a subject for further research, but Panero and colleagues claim that it is highly significant, as the nonfiction reading was also non-social in subject matter.[25] In other words, if Kidd and Castano's original hypothesis that there is a causal relation between literary fiction and empathy is correct, then one would expect the evidence to show a closer relation between non-literary fiction and empathy rather than nonfiction and empathy.

One can summarise the debate thus far as having reached both a methodological and interpretative impasse. Panero and colleagues disagree with all three methodological objections raised by Kidd and Castano: two are rejected as oversimplifications, and the third is accepted in principle but rejected in practice. With respect to interpretation, Kidd and Castano do not regard the new evidence in their reanalysis as contrary to their hypothesis, whereas Panero and colleagues do. Kidd and Castano are correct to indicate that the relation between nonfiction and empathy requires further investigation, but they may be disingenuous in claiming to have produced results "consistent with prior research."[26] This impasse does not surprise me at all, and I think it is indicative of a more general problem with measuring the effects of reading, noted by Panero and colleagues in their first response. The suggestion that the effects of reading literature, narrative, or fiction on cognition, emotion, or behaviour are immediate seems highly implausible to me. Recall Spivak's commentary on literature as an excellent instrument for the slow transformation of the mind, mentioned in section 6. But the longer the interval between the reading and the measurement, the less likely the results are to be valid. So one must either attempt to measure an insignificant effect accurately (which is what I take Kidd and Castano to have been attempting) or attempt to measure a significant effect inaccurately. At the time of writing there has to my knowledge (and according to Worth) been only one of the latter studies, by Gregory Berns, Kristina Blaine, Michael Prietula, and Brandon Pye in 2013. Berns and colleagues conducted an experiment over nineteen days, during which participants read the whole of Robert Harris's *Pompeii: A Novel* in order to determine the effects of reading on resting-state connectivity in the brain. They concluded of the participants that "that there was a detectable and significant common alteration of their RSN [resting-state networks] associated with reading sections of a novel the previous evening."[27] Interestingly, immediately after mentioning Berns and colleagues, Worth herself makes an implicit criticism of Kidd and Castano, stating that "no single literary work, no matter how great a work it is considered, will have the kind of impact that will be immediately measurable, because knowledge from reading is not merely about learning from content."[28]

22. CONCLUSION, COHERENCE, AND CORRESPONDENCE

There is a second set of experiments cited by Worth that has a far greater potential to provide evidence for aesthetic education: Johnson, Jasper, Griffin, and Huffman's (2013) study on narrative fiction and social cognition. The researchers claim that both explicit and implicit prejudice can be reduced, which is relevant not only to Worth's narrative education, but my narrative justice. Worth employs Johnson and colleagues as evidence that reading well-constructed narratives provides social knowledge (i.e., establishes a relationship between narrative sensibility and social harmony). Criminal inhumanity involves ideologically motivated crime, and this motivation is highly likely to involve prejudice against a political or religious other or outgroup. If fiction can reduce prejudice, then there is a strong case for narrative sensibility having the potential to reduce criminal inhumanity. Johnson, Huffman, and Jasper published a second study in 2014, on narrative fiction, race boundary perception, and emotion-related race bias. Racial bias is also relevant to narrative justice, so I shall examine both of these studies.

As discussed in section 9, Johnson and colleagues' study consisted of two identical experiments that were measured using different tests. Participants were divided into three conditions: full narrative, condensed narrative, and non-narrative. The first read seven pages (3,108 words) of Shaila Abdullah's *Saffron Dreams*, the second read a short summary (491 words) of the novel extract, and the third read a brief history of the automobile.[29] Participants in all conditions then completed a series of tests measuring empathy for Muslims and prejudice against Muslims. The results of the second experiment replicated the first, and Johnson and colleagues concluded that narrative fiction can be used to induce empathy and reduce implicit and explicit prejudice. Johnson, Huffman, and Jasper's (2014) study also involved two experiments. In the first, participants were divided into two conditions, using the same full and condensed narratives as above; in the second, participants were divided into three conditions, using the same full and condensed narratives and non-narrative as above.[30] Participants in the first experiment were shown a series of eighteen ambiguous Arab Caucasian faces and asked to determine the race of each.[31] Participants in the second experiment were shown a series of twelve ambiguous Arab Caucasian faces of varying levels of anger and asked to determine the race of each.[32] Johnson, Huffman, and

Jasper concluded that reading the full fictional narrative caused two changes in race boundary perception:

> First, it reduced categorical race perception in favor of perceiving people as being mixed race. Second, it inhibited the tendency to categorize mixed-race individuals with angry expressions as outgroup members.[33]

Taken together, both Johnson and colleagues and Johnson, Huffman, and Jasper thus offer evidence for the capacity of narrative fiction to reduce prejudice against Arab and Muslim populations.

As my argument in chapter 9 will reveal, I believe that narrative justice can be employed as an element of a counterterror strategy and have a particular interest in the phenomenon of Islamophobia. If there is evidence that narrative sensibility can reduce Islamophobia, then there is evidence for the narrative justice thesis. The problem from my point of view is that neither of Johnson's studies provide evidence of narrative sensibility. I am concerned with the effects of engaging with exemplary narratives and recall from section 1 that exemplary narratives are high in narrativity in virtue of representing (i) one or more agents and (ii) two or more events which are (iii) causally connected, (iv) thematically unified, and (v) conclude. (iii) to (v) differentiate exemplary narratives from minimal narratives, which are narrative representations that are low in narrativity. The critical examples I employ throughout this monograph show the significance of the combination of these criteria, in consequence of which no extract from either a novel or a feature film is itself an exemplary narrative. This is not to say that experiments in reading must employ a method analogous to Berns and colleagues (2013), but that participants must read an exemplary narrative in full. The extent to which a presentation is high in narrativity is more important than the length of the narrative. O. Henry's "After Twenty Years," for example, is a short story of only 1,263 words that clearly meets all five criteria for an exemplary narrative.[34] In contrast, the extract from *Saffron Dreams* meets (i) to (iv) at best, but more than likely (i) to (iii) because thematic unity is rarely if ever instantiated in part of an exemplary narrative.

If this seems unnecessarily restrictive or arbitrarily dismissive, consider the three conditions that Johnson and colleagues and Johnson, Huffman, and Jasper employ: the full narrative, the condensed narrative, and a history of the automobile. Both the full and condensed narratives are narrative representations, and the history—in virtue of being a history—is also very likely to be a narrative representation (albeit narrative nonfiction). In other words, participants in all three conditions read narratives, and if there is a significant difference between the first condition and the others rather than the first two conditions and the third, then the investigators must establish a clear distinction between the first condition and the other two. Johnson and colleagues and Johnson, Huffman, and Jasper fail to provide satisfactory criteria to differentiate the first and second conditions: full and condensed will not suffice, as both are not only narrative fictions, but narrative fictions that are part of a more substantial narrative fiction (the novel and the condensed version of the novel, respectively). This is particularly problematic in the absence of either a definition or characterisation of narrative. In order to provide evidence for my thesis, the studies would have to employ an exemplary narrative (for example, "After Twenty Years"), a minimal narrative (for example, a summary of "After Twenty Years"), and a non-narrative representation (for example, an automobile manual). I can agree with Johnson and colleagues and Johnson, Huffman, and Jasper that the full extract is highest in narrativity, but as my interest is in the effects of exemplary narratives, their results are suggestive rather than conclusive.

Worth does not include closure as one of her four criteria for narrative representation and can therefore accept the evidence of both of Johnson's studies. Aside from engaging with me in a long and likely inconclusive argument as to the significance of closure, Worth could defend her position on the basis of her distinction between narrative and discursive reasoning, which is supervenient on the distinction between the coherence and correspondence models of truth (all of which I discussed in section 8). Recall that Worth cited neuroscientific studies to show that coherence trumps correspondence in narrative comprehension (i.e., the empirical evidence reveals that in comprehending narrative representations readers primarily employ narrative rather than discursive reasoning). She describes the complexities of narrative comprehension and claims that this comprehension structure depends largely on a coherence-based model of understanding. She concludes her discussion of narrative reasoning, neuroscientific evidence, the conflation of the correspondence and coherence models of truth, and the apparent paradox of fiction with the following statement:

> Whether a narrative is well-told or not should take precedence over whether it is true, and this seems to be supported by the ways in which we actually process stories. What should take first priority is the narrative coherence that stories have, above and beyond anything else, and as readers we should appreciate the ways in which coherence allows us narrative comprehension.[35]

In setting out a theory of nonfiction and discussing the boundaries of genre and the example of memoir, Worth demonstrates her recognition of how this claim can be problematic when applied to narrative nonfiction and how correspondence and coherence can work against each other in the comprehension of these narrative representations.[36] Like many others, however, she considers the relation between narrative fiction and the coherence model of truth as unproblematic.

In *The Value of Literature*, I discussed a related problem—the question of whether and how works of literature refer—in terms of the substantive axis (reference relation) and formal axis (cross-reference relation).[37] I rejected an emphasis on either one at the expense of the other and concluded that literary representation involved a combination of the two, which I called *aboutness*. My concern with emphasising the formal axis, an interest in the work that is focused on its internal relations, is that it severs the work from the world. In other words, if one's interest in a literary representation is primarily in its internal relations, then it seems difficult to explain how the work is linked to the world at the textual level and why literature is important to human beings at the institutional level. I have a similar concern with Worth's identification of coherence rather than correspondence with narrative knowledge. In addition, the restriction of narrative reasoning to coherence is likely to make Worth's defence of reading fiction and literature more difficult and to be used as evidence against the values she advocates. Regardless of the empirical evidence, it is therefore far from clear that whether a narrative is well told or not should take precedence over whether it is true. This position requires a great deal more argument if Worth is to convince.

23. CORRELATION, CAUSATION, AND THE LAW

In section 21, I used the extended dialogue between Kidd and Castano and Panero and colleagues as evidence that the attempt to demonstrate a link between literature and empathy is thus far inconclusive. In section 22, I argued that neither of Johnson's studies provided satisfactory criteria for narrative representation and that the results are consequently suggestive rather than conclusive. One of the many merits of Worth's work is that she provides a thorough and objective summary of all the experimental evidence available on the relationship between literature, narrative, and fiction on the one hand and cognition, emotion, and behaviour on the other.[38] I think it is uncontroversial to state that there have been very few studies of this relationship to date, and the combination of my arguments in sections 21 and 22 is intended to show that what little evidence there is, is inconclusive. In this section I want to examine an unrelated but nonetheless relevant debate: the relationship between video game violence, media violence, or virtual violence on the one hand and aggressive affect, aggressive cognition, or aggressive behaviour on the other. In contrast to the debate with which Worth and I are concerned, there have been more than four decades of research into the effects of media violence, with the results of one of the first major studies published as early as 1972.[39] The problem with this debate is not that there is too little information available, but that there is too much; so in order to provide an accurate overview, I shall draw on one systematic review and two meta-analyses—published in 1998, 2010, and 2014, respectively.

Karen and Jody Dill (1998) published a narrative review that summarised the results of fourteen experimental and thirteen non-experimental studies of the relationship between violent video games and aggression, all conducted in the fourteen years prior to publication.[40] Dill and Dill stated that the experimental research supported a causal relation between video game violence and both aggression-related outcomes and decrements in prosocial behaviour. While admitting the existence of methodological problems, they argued that these were insufficient to invalidate the proposed relation.[41] They claimed that the descriptive data was less equivocal and more thorough than the experimental data, but that there were both methodological and interpretative problems. When combined with the limited number of studies conducted, Dill and Dill found the non-experimental evidence inconclusive. Their overall summary of the experimental and non-experimental evidence is:

> The preponderance of the evidence from the higher quality experimental studies suggests that short-term exposure to video-game and virtual reality violence engenders increases in aggressive behavior, affect, and cognitions and decreases in prosocial behavior.[42]

The meta-analysis of Craig Anderson, Akiko Shibuya, Nobuko Ihori, Edward Swing, Brad Bushman, Akira Sakamoto, Hannah Rothstein, and Muniba Saleem (2010) supported a stronger relation between video game violence and aggression. Anderson and colleagues used 136 research reports, which included four meta-analyses conducted from 2004 to 2009.[43] They divided the studies into six categories, which involved the relationship between violent video game exposure and aggressive behaviour, aggressive cognition, aggressive affect, prosocial behaviour, empathy, and physiological arousal, respectively. They found that the exposure was "significantly related" to higher aggressive behaviour, cognition, and affect, higher physiological arousal, and lower prosocial behaviour and empathy.[44] With respect to aggressive cognition, aggressive affect, prosocial behaviour, and empathy, these results were "regardless of research design and regardless of whether zero-order correlations or the more conservative partial correlation approach was used."[45] Anderson and colleagues concluded:

> Concerning public policy, we believe that debates can and should finally move beyond the simple question of whether violent video game play is a causal risk factor for aggressive behavior; the scientific literature has effectively and clearly

shown the answer to be "yes." Instead, we believe the public policy debate should move to questions concerning how best to deal with this risk factor.[46]

Malte Elson and Christopher Ferguson's meta-analysis was published at the beginning of 2014, covered a period of twenty-five years, and used a bibliography of 121 entries, including four meta-analyses conducted from 2001 to 2010 (one of which was Anderson and colleagues).[47] They divide the research on the "adversarial effects of digital games" into three categories: experimental studies, cross-sectional and longitudinal studies, and meta-analyses.[48] With respect to the experiments, they claim that the results of the studies on aggressive cognition, aggressive emotions, and aggressive behaviour were "mitigated or even inverted," "inconclusive," and "inconsistent," respectively.[49] The cross-sectional correlation and longitudinal studies suffered from a host of methodological and measurement problems, in addition to which the results were not only inconclusive but contradictory.[50] Elson and Ferguson agreed with the conclusions in two of the four meta-analyses, that "mean effect sizes in meta-analyses are likely inflated due to weak methodology, the use of unstandardized outcome measures (i.e., methodological flexibility), and publication bias."[51] They also noted that the conclusions of Anderson and colleagues differed from all three of the other meta-analyses. Their own conclusion is that "the research has been inconsistent, and often besotted with serious methodological limitations."[52] Elson and Ferguson furthermore accuse the American Psychological Association (APA) of contributing to the urban legend that the relationship between digital games and aggression is similar to the relationship between smoking and lung cancer. They close their article by reiterating the recent legal rulings initially cited:

> In this court case [*Brown v. EMA 2011*], the majority decision of the Supreme Court emphasized that the evidence presented by the state of California in its attempt to ban violent digital game sales to minors was not compelling. The court commented that the state had not presented studies showing a causal link between violent game playing and real-life acts of aggressiveness. Following the same rationale in an extensive literature review that expressed profound criticism of the existing evidence, the Australian attorney-general department (2010) decided to lift the ban on games exceeding the criteria for a 15+ rating. Similarly, a review of the evidence by the Swedish media council . . . declared that the research evidence did not support links between digital games and real-world aggression and many of the existing studies, particularly those conducted in support of the "harm" position were deeply flawed methodologically.[53]

Elson and Ferguson's claim about the APA is interesting for two reasons. First, they refer to the same relationship as Worth (quoting Eaton) between smoking and cancer. The relation was used to argue that while there is insufficient evidence to prove that smoking causes cancer, there is sufficient evidence to show that smoking increases the statistical probability of cancer and that this relation has been recognised in the various legal restrictions placed on the advertising, sale, and consumption of cigarettes in many countries. As discussed in section 8, Worth employed this relation to establish a realistic goal for the empirical evidence for narrative education (i.e., statistical probability rather than scientific proof). With respect to media violence, the legal trend at present—at least in the United States, Australia, and Sweden—is the reverse, as the above three examples show. Second, the APA issued a resolution on violent video games a year and a half after the publication of Elson and Ferguson's meta-analysis, in August 2015. The association claimed that the "link between violent video game exposure and aggressive behavior is one of the most studied and best established," in consequence of which, the

APA strongly encourages the Entertainment Software Rating Board to refine the ESRB rating system specifically to reflect the levels and characteristics of violence in games in addition to the current global ratings.[54]

The controversial nature of this resolution is indicated by the immediate response from researchers such as Ferguson and Mark Coulson, who claimed that the problems to which they had drawn attention in 2013 had not been resolved.[55] Ferguson, Coulson, and 236 other academics from universities across the globe sent an open letter to the APA in September 2013 in which they claimed that the evidence did not support the strength of the APA's 2005 policy statement and identified problems with both the composition of the APA task force and its methodology.[56]

The three meta-analyses and subsequent controversy suggest that the evidence for the relation between video game violence and aggression is either inconclusive or, at best, contested. If this is the situation for an issue that has been debated for so long and for which so many experimental and non-experimental studies have been conducted, then the inconclusive nature of the evidence for the various versions of aesthetic education is to be expected. Set in the context of the much more extensive debate, it is highly unlikely that the few studies cited by Worth show either a causal relation or even a statistical probability between literature, narrative, or fiction and cognition, emotion, or behaviour. The evidence is simply not as strong as Worth suggests, and although it may eventually indicate a relationship parallel with that of smoking and cancer, this would probably require dozens if not hundreds more studies. Worth's exhaustive and astute engagement with the empirical evidence is indicative of a more general problem in defending the humanities, to which I now turn.[57]

24. GREGORY CURRIE AND MARTHA NUSSBAUM

Worth's writing of *In Defense of Reading* is primarily driven by the desire to counterbalance two actively misleading and potentially harmful perceptions of literature.[58] The first is Currie's scepticism, articulated in two newspaper articles in which he expresses his doubts as to whether the effects of reading literature can be measured.[59] The second is the devaluation of literature in particular and the humanities in general, courtesy of the rise of the neoliberal university. Recall Spivak's claim in section 7 that the double bind of global aesthetic education is constituted by the contradiction that the neoliberal era of globalisation has both disseminated the humanities to more people than ever before and marginalised humanities students as a group of subjects that are not useful to local, national, and global economies. The erosion of the value of the humanities and literature is a consequence of the neoliberal demand for quantification, a demand that ultimately aims at the reduction of every aspect of human life to its financial value. In a sense, therefore, Worth is both arguing for and against the measurement of the effects of reading. These are not, however, contradictory motives.

Although he has specialised in narrative, much of Currie's work is concerned with the ontological status of fiction and art. His analyses and arguments are precise and rigorous, but they betray little enthusiasm for stories or storytelling. In his most recent contribution to the debate, which appears to have been published at the time *In Defense of Reading* was in press, Currie claims not only that the evidence for a relation between fiction and an increase in empathy is poor, but that there may be equally poor evidence for a relation between fiction and a decrease in empathy. His conclusion is characteristically deflationary and restrained: while it is plausible that there are pathways from fiction to an increase in empathy, it is also plausible that there are pathways from fiction to a decrease in empathy, and both possibilities should be taken seriously.[60] I can understand Worth's desire to reject Currie's conclusions and to respond to his apparent lack of passion for a subject about which so many of us feel so strongly (and to which Currie himself appears to have devoted his life's work).

Any and every contemporary defence of the humanities, literature, narrative, fiction, or reading finds itself on the horns of a dilemma. Either the defender must resist the neoliberal imperative to quantify and risk complete marginalisation, or he or she must conform to the neoliberal imperative and find new ways of quantification. The decision is a dilemma rather than a choice, as both options are likely to fail: resisting quantification suggests that humanities departments have expertise that is irrelevant to contemporary higher education, while accepting quantification reveals those departments as relevant but inexpert (because the humanities inevitably score low on measures such as knowledge exchange and impact factor). Following the *Browne Review* (2010) and the *Higher Education: Students at the Heart of the System* White Paper (2011), the United Kingdom switched from a public to a profit model of higher education in 2012. Stefan Collini uses the unfortunately apt term "HiEdBiz" to describe the results of this change in his most recent defence of the humanities.[61] With the neoliberal underpinning firmly in place, no department that resists quantification will be tolerated. On the other hand, as pressure increases for departments to fund themselves by partnerships with private enterprise and students are encouraged to weigh the cost of extortionate loans with postgraduate earning potential, departments that are unable to secure either high investment or high student numbers are unlikely to survive. The situation for the humanities in the UK at the moment (and in the United States, in Worth's assessment) is a choice between a quick death by suicide or a slow death by a thousand cuts.

In *The Value of Literature* I was critical of Nussbaum's explicitly instrumental defence of the humanities as a means to the end of liberal democracy. I claimed that in emphasising the humanities in general and literature in particular as a tool for moral and political instruction, she was undermining what was most important about the literary use of language, its freedom from limitation and *sui generic* value.[62] I do not have the same objection against Worth, for she grasps both horns of the dilemma, arguing that much of the value of reading is not quantifiable, but that the results of the limited number of experiments that have been conducted are sufficiently promising. While I share her frustration with influential commentators such as Currie, I think that the end if not the means of his approach is correct and that questioning the possibility of evidence is on balance preferable to citing inconclusive evidence. Worth states of Currie:

> He says that we should just accept the fact that we derive pleasure from fictional literature, but he does not see the need to justify our pleasure by making up reasons that it is good for us either cognitively or morally.[63]

This is an accurate summary of a position I believe to be for the most part correct. Where Currie errs is in failing to have anything to say about this pleasure and whether it has any special characteristics or is valuable above and beyond making our nasty, brutish, and short lives a little more bearable. In the context of defending literature, Currie is thus the opposite of Nussbaum: where she makes hyperbolic claims as to its instrumental value, he claims that its value is at best arbitrary, at worst adventitious.

My approach in *The Value of Literature* was to argue that there was no necessary relation between literary representation and cognitive or ethical value (contra Nussbaum), but that literary satisfaction was valuable in itself (contra Currie). In this respect, I am most closely aligned with Spivak. Like her, I agree that most if not all of the benefits of literature are unverifiable. I also agree that a life devoted to the study and teaching of literature is not a life wasted and that one can furthermore make convincing arguments for the value of this life. If neoliberal number-crunching does crush the discipline to death, then my hope is that the harms produced by its absence from the university will prove more convincing (i.e., quantifiable) than the benefits produced by its presence. In this book I have, however, set aside concern with the literary, poetic, and aesthetic and focused on narrative representation alone, specifically on exemplary narratives. While there is a necessary relation between exemplary narratives and phenomenological ethical knowledge, there is no guarantee that this knowledge will be moral rather than immoral. In consequence, if exemplary narratives are to be put to use—to serve, in my case, the end of reducing criminal inhumanity—these narratives must be carefully selected. In other words, the appropriate narrative must be selected for the appropriate task. This is precisely what I intend to do in the remaining three chapters, where I employ particular narratives to reduce criminal inhumanity by evaluating responsibility for inhumanity, by understanding the psychology of inhumanity, and by undermining inhumanity. My aim is to show that narrative representation can be a means to a criminological end and to argue for a closer engagement between the humanities and social sciences.

NOTES

1. Spivak, *Aesthetic Education*, 324–25.

2. Spivak, *Aesthetic Education*, 291.

3. Jacques Derrida, "On Forgiveness," in *On Cosmopolitanism and Forgiveness*, trans. Mark Dooley and Michael Hughes (London: Routledge, 2001), 35.

4. Kelly Oliver, *Technologies of Life and Death: From Cloning to Capital Punishment* (New York: Fordham University Press, 2013), 190–93, 201–202.

5. Immanuel Kant, *Critique of Pure Reason*, trans. Norman Kemp Smith (Basingstoke: Palgrave Macmillan, 2007 [1781]), A807–A808/B835–B836.

6. Oliver, *Technologies of Life and Death*, 190.

7. Oliver, *Technologies of Life and Death*, 202.

8. Oliver, *Technologies of Life and Death*, 202.

9. Maria Eugenia Panero, Deena Skolnick Weisberg, Jessica Black, Thalia R. Goldstein, Jennifer L. Barnes, Hiram Brownell, and Ellen Winner, "Does Reading a Single Passage of Literary Fiction Really Improve Theory of Mind? An Attempt at Replication," *Journal of Personality and Social Psychology* 111 (2016): e46.

10. Panero et al., "An Attempt at Replication," e47.

11. Panero et al., "An Attempt at Replication," e48; Kidd and Castano, "Reading Literary Fiction," 378–79.

12. Panero et al., "An Attempt at Replication," e50–e52.

13. Panero et al., "An Attempt at Replication," e52.

14. Panero et al., "An Attempt at Replication," e52–e53.

15. Panero et al., "An Attempt at Replication," e53.

16. David Comer Kidd and Emanuele Castano, "Panero et al. (2016): Failure to Replicate Methods Caused the Failure to Replicate Results," *Journal of Personality and Social Psychology* 112 (2016): e1.

17. Kidd and Castano, "Failure to Replicate," e1–e2.

18. Kidd and Castano, "Failure to Replicate," e2.

19. Kidd and Castano, "Failure to Replicate," e2–e3.

20. Kidd and Castano, "Failure to Replicate," e4.

21. Maria Eugenia Panero, Deena Skolnick Weisberg, Jessica Black, Thalia R. Goldstein, Jennifer L. Barnes, Hiram Brownell, and Ellen Winner, "No Support for the Claim That Literary Fiction Uniquely and Immediately Improves Theory of Mind: A Reply to Kidd and Castano's Commentary on Panero et al. (2016)," *Journal of Personality and Social Psychology* 112 (2017): e6.

22. Panero et al., "A Reply to Kidd and Castano," e6–e7.

23. Panero et al., "A Reply to Kidd and Castano," e7.

24. Panero et al., "A Reply to Kidd and Castano," e7–e8.

25. Kidd and Castano, "Failure to Replicate," e4; Panero et al., "A Reply to Kidd and Castano," e7.

26. Kidd and Castano, "Failure to Replicate," e4.

27. Gregory S. Berns, Kristina Blaine, Michael J. Prietula, and Brandon E. Pye, "Short- and Long-Term Effects of a Novel on Connectivity in the Brain," *Brain Connectivity* 3 (2013): 598–99.

28. Worth, *Defense of Reading*, 199.

29. Johnson et al., "Reading Narrative Fiction," 582.

30. Dan R. Johnson, Brandie L. Huffman, and Danny M. Jasper, "Changing Race Boundary Perception by Reading Narrative Fiction," *Basic and Applied Social Psychology* 36 (2014): 84.

31. Johnson, Huffman, and Jasper, "Changing Race Boundary Perception," 84–85.

32. Johnson, Huffman, and Jasper, "Changing Race Boundary Perception," 86.

33. Johnson, Huffman, and Jasper, "Changing Race Boundary Perception," 88.

34. "After Twenty Years" was first published in O. Henry's 1906 collection *The Four Million* and has been widely anthologised since.

35. Worth, *Defense of Reading*, 169.

36. See especially: Worth, *Defense of Reading*, 59–61, 114–17.

37. McGregor, *Value of Literature*, 107–8.

38. I discuss Worth's summary in section 9. See also: Worth, *Defense of Reading*, chapter 7.

39. J. J. McIntyre, J. J. Teevan Jr., and T. Hartnagel, "Television Violence and Deviant Behaviour," in *Television and Social Behavior 3: Television and Adolescent*

Aggressiveness, ed. G. A. Comstock and E. A. Rubinstein (Washington, DC: US Government Printing Office, 1972), 383–435.

40. Karen E. Dill and Jody C. Dill, "Video Game Violence: A Review of the Empirical Literature," *Aggression and Violent Behavior* 3 (1998): 407–28.

41. Dill and Dill, "Review of the Empirical Literature," 420.

42. Dill and Dill, "Review of the Empirical Literature," 424.

43. Craig A. Anderson, Akiko Shibuya, Nobuko Ihori, Edward L. Swing, Brad J. Bushman, Akira Sakamoto, Hannah R. Rothstein, and Muniba Saleem, "Violent Video Game Effects on Aggression, Empathy, and Prosocial Behavior in Eastern and Western Countries: A Meta-Analytic Review," *Psychological Bulletin* 136 (2010): 157.

44. Anderson et al., "Meta-Analytic Review," 162.

45. Anderson et al., "Meta-Analytic Review," 163.

46. Anderson et al., "Meta-Analytic Review," 171.

47. Malte Elson and Christopher J. Ferguson, "Twenty-Five Years of Research on Violence in Digital Games and Aggression: Empirical Evidence, Perspectives, and a Debate Gone Astray," *European Psychologist* 19 (2014): 33–46.

48. Elson and Ferguson, "Twenty-Five Years of Research," 36.

49. Elson and Ferguson, "Twenty-Five Years of Research," 37, 38, 39.

50. Elson and Ferguson, "Twenty-Five Years of Research," 39–40.

51. Elson and Ferguson, "Twenty-Five Years of Research," 41.

52. Elson and Ferguson, "Twenty-Five Years of Research," 41.

53. Elson and Ferguson, "Twenty-Five Years of Research," 34.

54. American Psychological Association, *Resolution on Violent Video Games*, August 2015. Available at: http://www.apa.org/about/policy/violent-video-games.aspx.

55. See: Mike Futter, "More Than 200 Psychology Scholars Speak Out Against APA Video Game Aggression Task Force," *Game Informer*, 14 August 2015. Available at: http://www.gameinformer.com/b/news/archive/2015/08/14/more-than-200-psychology-scholars-speak-out-against-apa-video-game-aggression-task-force.aspx; Zoe Kleinman, "Do Video Games Make People Violent?" BBC News, 17 August 2015. Available at: http://www.bbc.co.uk/news/technology-33960075.

56. Christopher J. Ferguson, "Scholars' Open Statement to the APA Task Force on Violent Media (Delivered to the APA Task Force, 9/26/13)," 5 August 2014. Available at: http://www.christopherjferguson.com/APA%20Task%20Force%20Comment1.pdf.

57. Note that my argument for the inconclusive nature of the empirical evidence for aesthetic education stands even if one either (i) adopts the APA position on the relationship between media violence and aggression, or (ii) regards the debate about media violence and aggression as irrelevant. In the case of (i), substantial further inquiry is required before the aesthetic education evidence reaches a level comparable to the media violence evidence; in the case of (ii), the evidence from media violence neither supports nor undermines my discussions of the aesthetic education evidence in sections 21 and 22.

58. Worth, *Defense of Reading*, xi–xvii.

59. See: Gregory Currie, "Literature and the Psychology Lab," *The Times Literary Supplement*, 21 August 2011. Available at: https://www.the-tls.co.uk/articles/public/literature-and-the-psychology-lab/; Gregory Currie, "Does Great Literature Make Us Better?" *The New York Times Opinionator*, 1 June 2013. Available at: https://opinionator.blogs.nytimes.com/2013/06/01/does-great-literature-make-us-better/.

60. Gregory Currie, "Does Fiction Make Us Less Empathic?" *Teorama XXXV* (2016): 62.

61. Stefan Collini, *Speaking of Universities* (London: Verso, 2017), 166.

62. McGregor, *Value of Literature*, 147–48.

63. Worth, *Defense of Reading*, 174.

Chapter Seven

Responsibility for Inhumanity

The purpose of this chapter is to demonstrate narrative justice (i.e., to show how an exemplary narrative can be employed to reduce criminal inhumanity by providing an evaluation of responsibility for inhumanity). Specifically, the thesis is used to answer the question of what, if anything, the posthumous accusations of collaboration with the Third Reich revealed Belgian literary theorist Paul de Man to have done wrong. In section 25, I summarise the biographies of first Paul de Man and then Howard W. Campbell Jr., an American intelligence agent. The revelation of de Man's wartime journalism in 1987 provoked heated debate about his character, his work, and the ethics of deconstructive criticism, which I discuss in section 26. I compare the various defences of de Man with an appraisal of Campbell in sections 27 and 28, indicating the ways in which the character of the latter illuminates the character of the former. Section 29 explores the relationship between silence and deceit and demonstrates that de Man's silence was deceptive. In section 30, I explain that silence in the context of collaboration offers evidence of an absence of regret or remorse. I conclude that de Man's silence was indicative of both deceit and remorselessness and that he was therefore responsible for collaborating in criminal inhumanity.

25. TWO WARS

Paul de Man was born in Belgium in 1919 and emigrated to America in 1948. He completed his PhD at Harvard in 1960 and moved to Yale in 1970, where he became a successful and celebrated literary theorist. Four years after his death in 1983, it became public knowledge that he had written 180 reviews—at least one of which was explicitly anti-Semitic—for two newspapers run by the National Socialist authorities in occupied Belgium. Howard W. Campbell Jr. was born in America in 1912 and moved to Germany when his father was transferred to the Berlin office of his company in 1923. He became a successful playwright in the late 1930s and worked as a radio broadcaster for Joseph Goebbels during the war. In 1960, it became public knowledge that he had been living in New York since his disappearance in 1945, and he was imprisoned in Israel. Campbell committed suicide the night before his trial for war crimes and was subsequently revealed to have been an American agent from 1938 to 1945.

De Man's war appears to have taken the following course. When the Germans invaded Belgium in May 1940, he, his pregnant girlfriend Anne, and her husband fled to Spain. They were denied entry at the border and returned to Brussels three months later.[1] De Man's uncle, Henri, was a powerful Marxist politician who advocated for collaboration with the Nazi authorities on the basis of shared socialism and may have been a role model for de Man in the wake of a series of family tragedies that began in 1936. Believing that the war had ended with the surrender of France in June, and with a young son to support, de Man accepted the job Henri had secured for him with *Le Soir* (Belgium's biggest newspaper) in December 1940. Anti-Semitic legislation in Belgium was introduced from October 1940, and de Man's most controversial review was published in March 1941.[2] A year later, the first of ten articles was published in *Het Vlaamsche Land*.[3] At the end of 1941, the occupiers began deporting Belgians to work in Germany as slave labour, and Henri exiled himself to France. By the beginning of 1942, de Man was also working for the *Agence Dechenne* and *Toison d'Or*, both of which were key elements of Belgian media collaboration.[4] In May 1942 Belgian Jews were required to wear the Yellow Star, with deportations to concentration camps beginning in August. De Man offered various levels of assistance to Jewish friends and acquaintances during this time, including sheltering a Jewish couple from the authorities for a few days.[5] In the latter half of 1942, he was involved in the distribution of *Messages*, a resistance journal published in Paris, beginning with a volume titled "Exercice de Silence."[6] A combination of overreaching ambition and negligence resulted in the loss of all three of his publishing jobs by April 1943.[7] De Man spent the rest of the war in Kalmthout, near Antwerp, translating *Moby-Dick* and preparing to set up a publishing house named *Hermès*. He married Anne, by whom he would have two more children in the next two years, in May 1944. De Man was questioned by the Auditeur Général in July 1946, but he was released without charges of collaboration.[8]

In Campbell's confession, he stated the following. He achieved early success as a playwright in Germany, and although his works were apolitical medieval romances, they were very popular with the Nazi hierarchy. He married Helga Noth, an actress whose father was the Berlin chief of police, in 1938. Shortly after, he was approached by Frank Wirtanen, an American military officer, who asked him to become an agent. When Campbell's parents left Germany in 1939, he remained, and—unbeknownst to his wife—transmitted coded messages to the Allies by means of the propaganda he broadcast over the radio. His propaganda, like his plays beforehand, was much admired by leading Nazis, and he was given an honorary rank in the German military. Helga died while entertaining German troops on the Eastern Front, and he was captured by the Americans in April 1945, by which time he was a high-profile war criminal. Wirtanen told him that the American government would not acknowledge his war service for political reasons, and he was returned to America in secret, living under his own name in Greenwich Village. In 1958, the KGB became aware of his presence, leaked the information to the American public, and planned to kidnap him. The plot was foiled, but Campbell gave himself up to the Israeli government, revealing his identity to a neighbour who was a survivor of Auschwitz. The night before his trial began, Campbell received a letter from Wirtanen stating that he was prepared to disobey his orders and disclose Campbell's war service to the Israeli authorities. With his acquittal certain, Campbell committed suicide, apparently due to guilt over his collaboration.

26. THREE CHARGES

This chapter is an attempt to answer a single, deceptively simple question: *What, if anything, did the posthumous accusations of collaboration reveal de Man to have done wrong?* As such, most of the details of his life subsequent to 1946 are beyond the scope of my interest. In light of Evelyn Barish's recently published and extensively researched biography, *The Double Life of Paul de Man*, it is nonetheless worth completing the thumbnail sketch from section 25. In 1948 de Man was charged with multiple counts of fraud in connection with *Hermès* and evaded prosecution by fleeing to New York, with Anne and their three children joining her parents in Buenos Aires.[9] De Man began teaching French at Bard College in 1949, where he met Patricia Kelley. Patricia became pregnant by him, and they were married bigamously in June 1950.[10] For reasons that are disputed, de Man was accused of collaboration in 1955. He told the Harvard Society of Fellows that he had stopped working for the newspaper when Nazi policies had curbed freedom of speech.[11] De Man taught at Cornell and Johns Hopkins in the 1960s and rose to fame as the Sterling Professor at Yale, where he remained from 1970 until his death.

Barish characterises de Man as a narcissist and an opportunist, traits that may have been exacerbated by his deeply dysfunctional family, which included a brother who appears to have been a serial rapist and a mother who was clinically depressed (both of whom were dead by 1939). The portrait that emerges from her biography, supplemented by David Lehman's investigations, is of a charismatic sociopath with absolutely no sense of responsibility in either his personal or professional relationships.[12] De Man's frauds and forgeries were as imaginative as they were frequent, and the curriculum vitae that secured his job at Bard contained fictional dissertation, thesis, and publication titles when he had failed to complete any higher education whatsoever.[13] De Man published for and against the Nazis, he contributed to anti-Semitism while maintaining friendships with Jews, and although I shall discuss the complexity of collaboration in section 27, he seems to have had little interest in either cause. Louis Menand may well be correct when he accounts for the duality upon which Barish focuses by describing de Man as a nihilist (i.e., "he believed in nothing").[14] I am not, however, concerned with broader judgements of de Man's character, and I shall therefore omit discussion of the details beyond those sketched in section 25 from my argument.

In a lecture given in 1984, Jacques Derrida recalled his relationship with de Man with great fondness:

> It was in 1967, when he directed the Cornell University Program in Paris, that I first came to know him, to read him, to listen to him and there arose between us an unfailing friendship that was to be utterly cloudless and that will remain, in my life, in me, one of the rarest and most precious rays of light.[15]

Derrida would reiterate this sentiment during and after the furor caused by the discovery of de Man's collaboration. The accusations that were levelled at de Man, his friends, and deconstructive criticism as an intellectual movement unleashed a particularly passionate anger in Derrida, and the tone of his replies to respondents in the *Critical Inquiry* symposium in the summer of 1989 is nothing short of vicious in six of seven cases.[16] This is especially evident in his response to Jean-Marie Apostolidès's brief comment on de Man. While researching Georges Rémi (Hergé, the creator of Tintin), who worked for *Le Soir* throughout the occupation, Apostolidès discovered that several of de Man's colleagues at Harvard were aware of his past.[17] He does not include Derrida in this number, but Derrida nonetheless took the accusation personally, and I shall have more to say about his reaction to de Man's wartime journalism in section 29. Whether deconstructive criticism was especially vulnerable to unethical practitioners or whether its popularity caused resentment by academics is not, however, my concern. Setting aside the personal accusations, the resultant discussion fuelled the broader debate about the relationship between literary theory and ethics and was, in Geoffrey Galt Harpham's opinion, responsible for the ethical turn in criticism at the end of the twentieth century.[18] If he is right, then it is some consolation that the effects of the scandal were not exclusively negative.

The question of what de Man's collaboration reveals him to have done wrong has been asked many times since 1987, but the combination of three decades of hindsight with recent research brings, I believe, an unprecedented clarity to a complex issue, the import of which extends beyond de Man's case considered in isolation.[19] I begin my answer by returning to 1989, to Shoshana Felman's defence of de Man, where she identifies three separate targets of moral judgement:

1. the collaborationist political activities in themselves;
2. de Man's apparent erasure of their memory—his radical "forgetting" of his early past; and
3. the silence that de Man chose to keep about his past: the absence of public confession and public declaration of remorse.[20]

According to Felman, therefore, there are three potential answers to my question: collaboration, forgetting, and keeping silent.

27. DEFENDING DE MAN

I agree with Derrida when he describes the anti-Semitism in "Les Juifs dans la littérature actuelle" published in *Le Soir* on 4 March 1941, as "unbearable."[21] I also accept that de Man may have had reasons for working for *Le Soir* that had nothing to do with Nazi sympathies.[22] At their extremes, collaboration and resistance are easy to identify: abroad, Belgian units served in both the German and British armed forces; at home, Rexist militia assisted the policing of the occupation while resistance groups undertook sabotage operations. In between these extremes lay more passive forms of collaboration and resistance, and a third option—the most prudent given the Nazi predilection for use of force—*cooperation*. The distinction between collaboration and cooperation (and between cooperation and resistance) is much more difficult to make. Should every journalist who worked for *Le Soir* from May 1940 to September 1944 be regarded as having collaborated rather than cooperated? If so, why should it have been incumbent upon a journalist rather than a farmer to sacrifice his livelihood? Cooperation by journalists inevitably involved publishing Nazi propaganda, but farmers had their produce either bought or confiscated by the Nazis and thus made a more substantial contribution to the well-being of the invaders, whether willingly or unwillingly. No one seems to have expected the farmers of occupied nations to stop feeding those nations on the basis that they were also feeding the occupying forces. Is it fair to judge journalists by different standards?

Here is Frank Falla, the deputy editor of the *Guernsey Star*, defending his own work for the Nazi authorities from July 1940 to April 1944:

> I had no option but to agree that the German war communiqué, news items and Lord Haw-Haw's daily outpourings should be given due prominence—the front page, nothing less! This I did with my tongue in my cheek and the front page was duly filled with Nazi-supplied news. We thus schooled our own public into accepting the front page as nothing but Nazi news in which we had no hand, and turned their full attention to pages two, three, and four as exclusively ours in which we featured local news, official notices and civilian affairs. If the Guernsey reader did anything about the front page, he read it cursorily and laughed it to scorn.[23]

It is difficult to portray the publication of William Joyce (Lord Haw-Haw) as anything other than outright collaboration—tongue-in-cheek propaganda is still propaganda—yet one can immediately see the difficulty of the situation in which Falla found himself. Had he resisted relinquishing control of the front page to his Nazi overseer, Kurt Goettmann, he would simply have been dismissed and/or imprisoned and his position filled by another. If no Channel Islander had accepted the position, then the paper would have been run by Goettmann, whose command of English was sufficient to the task. What would Falla have achieved, other than placing his own livelihood and that of his dependents at risk? Falla appears to have exemplified all three stances toward the invaders during the occupation: he published Joyce, continued to work as a journalist under the new authorities, and ran an illegal newsletter for islanders. There is a direct parallel with de Man, for whom the publication of "Les Juifs dans la littérature actuelle" offers evidence of collaboration, the assistance to Jewish associates evidence of resistance, and the majority of his employment evidence of cooperation. One should, furthermore, be wary of judging the actions of an individual from the certainty of hindsight and—more importantly—the safety of a prosperous and stable society where one does not live in day-to-day fear of losing one's life or day-to-day fear of losing one's liberty for voicing dissent. Although he finds evidence of anti-Semitism beyond the above-mentioned review, Frank Kermode refers to de Man's "youthful errors" and concludes his own review with the suggestion that academics direct their critical attention to more worthy projects.[24] That de Man collaborated is difficult to deny, but that collaboration—however reprehensible—was limited in scale and duration.

I am not sure what to make of Felman's second point, the judgement of forgetting or erasure. If "forgetting" is employed in its literal sense, then the charge should be dismissed, because no one except de Man can know how much of the war—if any—was erased from his memory. If Felman is employing "forgetting" metaphorically, perhaps as the erasure of the war in de Man's later writings or in his academic persona, then I think that judgement can be subsumed under her third point, his silence. De Man may have wanted to forget his collaboration—indeed the whole war—but one cannot choose to forget. One can choose to ignore, but the very desire to forget an event maintains its presence in one's mind, ensuring that it is not forgotten. Forgetting about forgetting, therefore, one is left with the collaboration and the silence: unlike the former, the latter cannot be attributed to the circumstances in which de Man was living.

Both Derrida and Kermode disagree with the condemnation of silence. Derrida identifies "several reasons" for de Man's lack of disclosure and states that

> to provoke spontaneously an explanation on this subject was no longer an obligation. It would have been, moreover, an all the more distressing, pointlessly painful theatricalization in that he had not only broken with the political context of 1940–42, but had distanced himself from it with all his might, in his language, his country, his profession, his private life. His international notoriety having spread only during the last years of his life, to exhibit earlier such a distant past so as to call the public as a witness—would that not have been a pretentious, ridiculous, and infinitely complicated gesture?[25]

Derrida suggests that de Man's "modesty" motivated his silence,[26] a claim that Kermode appears to support:

> Generally speaking, few writers, of whatever kind, and even if conceited enough to think anybody else would be interested, would volunteer to bring their juvenilia to judgment, even if they didn't contain opinions later seen to be embarrassing or perverted.[27]

Barish offers an indirect defence of de Man in her contention that silence was a habit that began in his teens and became more entrenched as he matured. By the time he left the Royal Athenaeum in 1937, he already had plenty of reasons to keep his own counsel: his brother's sexual violence, his mother's suicide attempts, his father's many affairs, and his grandfather's slow and painful death from cancer.[28] Contra the defences from modesty and a defence from habit, I shall argue that silence about an ethically tainted past constitutes an ethical failure for at least two reasons. But first I return to Campbell, to

show why he is worthy of admiration even if one disagrees with his decision
to take his own life.

28. COMMENDING CAMPBELL

Howard W. Campbell Jr. is in fact a fictional character, the protagonist and
narrator of Kurt Vonnegut Jr.'s 1961 novel *Mother Night*.[29] Although Major
Campbell of the Free American Corps is entirely fictional, he has historical
counterparts on both sides of the Atlantic. The most notorious are probably
two British broadcasters: William Joyce, mentioned in section 27, an Irish
American who held a British passport; and John Amery, an Englishman who
also raised a unit of British Empire prisoners of war to fight on the Eastern
Front. Joyce and Amery had several lesser-known counterparts in America,
including Jane Anderson, Robert Best, Herbert Burgman, Douglas Chandler,
Donald Day, and Edward Delaney—all of whom broadcasted from Germany
during the war. Amery's Britisches Freikorps never had more than thirty
recruits, but it seems likely that there may have been a larger number of
American citizens scattered throughout the units of the Waffen SS.[30] Accurate
contemporary records are unavailable and, unlike the British government,
American authorities did not pursue these German American soldiers after
the war. Vonnegut was himself of German extraction, served in the American
infantry, and was captured in the final weeks of 1944, during the Battle of
the Bulge. He is well known for surviving the firebombing of Dresden by
taking refuge in an underground meat locker, an experience he recounted in
the novel *Slaughterhouse Five*, and he took part in the subsequent search for
corpses. The Britisches Freikorps was based in Dresden at the time and was
also involved in the aftermath, so Vonnegut may have been inspired by an
encounter with the unit.[31]

The title of *Mother Night* is from Mephistopheles's autobiographical
sketch in Goethe's *Faust* and sets the scene for Campbell's engagement with
Nazi Germany as a demonic alliance and for Campbell as a fallen angel of
a sort.[32] There are two passages that are particularly relevant to disclosing
Campbell's motivation for his subsequent actions, both of which describe
events that occur in 1945.[33] Campbell's second meeting with his handler,
whose real name is Harold J. Sparrow, follows his capture, and he is surprised
by Sparrow's bitterness toward him. Although Campbell has proved to be
America's most successful agent, he has also been a very successful Nazi
broadcaster, and his identity as an agent is known to only three people
aside from Campbell himself. Discussing whether Campbell was a Nazi as
well as an agent, Sparrow asks him what he would have done in the event

of Germany winning the war and establishing the empire of which Hitler boasted. Campbell responds:

> So I projected myself into the situation he described, and what was left of my imagination gave me a corrosively cynical answer. "There is every chance," I said, "that I would have become a sort of Nazi Edgar Guest, writing a daily column of optimistic doggerel for daily papers around the world. And, as senility set in—the sunset of life, as they say—I might even come to believe what my couplets said: that everything was probably all for the best."[34]

Vonnegut does not invite negative judgement on Campbell for his honesty. In his short introduction to the novel, while describing the experience of clearing the ruins of Dresden of 135,000 corpses, he states:

> If I'd been born in Germany, I suppose I would have been a Nazi, bopping Jews and gypsies and Poles around, leaving boots sticking out of snowbanks, warming myself with my secretly virtuous insides. So it goes.[35]

But the question eats away at Campbell. Prior to the war, he had succeeded in avoiding a position on the Nazis by his obsessive love of his wife; after the war, there is a brief opportunity for a similar redemption with his sister-in-law, which ends in tragedy. Once she is dead, the question of his identity becomes all-consuming, and Campbell's decision to hand himself over to the Israeli authorities comes as no surprise.

The decision is both explained and foreshadowed by the second incident, Campbell's last visit to his father-in-law. After the war, Campbell reads a magazine article on his father-in-law's death at the hands of a mob of slave labourers, written by a former British prisoner of war (reminiscent of Vonnegut himself). The journalist notes that Werner Noth was the head of the criminal—as opposed to political—police in Berlin and that his only crime was to have been a city police chief in a country ruled by the Nazis.[36] The reader has, however, already been privy to Noth's evacuation of his home. Campbell describes the scene when one of Noth's labourers nearly drops a valuable vase:

> Werner Noth shook her a little, trying to arouse an atom of intelligence in her. He pointed to another woman who was carrying a hideous Chinese, carved-oak dog, carrying it as carefully as though it were a baby.
>
> "You see?" Noth said to the dunce. He wasn't intentionally tormenting the dunce. He was trying to make her, in spite of her stupidity, a better-rounded, more useful human being.
>
> "You see?" he said again, earnestly, helpfully, pleadingly. "That's the way to handle precious things."[37]

While the journalist may be correct about Noth's dedication to the pursuit of murderers, rapists, and traffic flow rather than Nazi oppression, his "principal offense" was not simply his complicity in Nazi law and order.[38] The offence was adopting the Nazi view that selected races were subhuman, that it was acceptable to employ slave labourers from these races, that the vase had value but the human being holding it did not. Noth is clearly not a malicious or evil man. He speaks to the labourer in a paternal but kindly manner, as if she were an employee or a child in need of instruction. He has completely lost sight of the fact that she is a slave, sent to Germany against her will, with the aim of working her to death in service of the war effort. That is Noth's crime, and all that prevents Campbell from conspiring in the same crime is his secret identity as an American agent.

Campbell is more than an undercover angel sent to hell, however, as his relationship with his wife shows. His feelings for her are not only deep but obsessive, yet he fails to disclose his recruitment to her. Vonnegut never describes Helga firsthand, but she is obviously an enthusiastic German patriot and appears to accept the Nazi rulers without reservation. Helga is thus at least as complicit in crimes against humanity as her father, and if Campbell is an undercover angel, he is also to some extent a fallen angel. As such, Sparrow's disturbing question prompts further introspection for Campbell. What was his real motivation for remaining in Germany? Was it for the purpose of serving a country he left at the age of eleven, for the love of his wife, for the desire to continue his glamorous lifestyle, or a combination of all three? What, on balance, is the nature of his war service? In pure utilitarian terms, it is unclear whether his net contribution falls on the Allied or Axis side of the ledger. These questions, and others, produce a desire in Campbell to confess his sins to the public and to be judged. He is an imperfect angel, for when a chance arises to re-create his *Das Reich der Zwei*—nation of two—with his sister-in-law, he seizes it. Once this opportunity is lost, however, he can no longer suppress his desire for confession and judgement. When Campbell's eleventh-hour reprieve arrives, he states:

> So I am about to be a free man again, to wander where I please.
> I find the prospect nauseating.
> I think that tonight is the night I will hang Howard W. Campbell, Jr., for crimes against himself.
> I *know* that tonight is the night.[39]

Campbell is not merely bent on suicide—he could have committed suicide in New York at the end of his romantic adventure or let himself be killed as the victim of an assassination attempt. The act of suicide is not, therefore, particularly significant in judging his character. It is a last resort, the result of his desperation in the face of a freedom to which he feels he is not entitled, and it matters little whether one condones or condemns his decision. What is unquestionably admirable is Campbell's desire to stand trial, because he believes that he is guilty of crimes against humanity in the same way that his father-in-law and wife were, and can no longer live with that guilt. What one admires about Campbell, I suggest, reveals precisely what should be condemned in de Man.

29. SILENCE AND DECEIT

There is nothing intrinsically wrong with habitual silence or with the decision to keep silent about one's past. Derrida, for example, rarely broke his silence about his Jewish identity and the discrimination he faced under the Vichy regime as a child in French Algeria. In one of the few discussions of his ethnicity, at a colloquium titled "Judéités: Questions pour Jacques Derrida" in 2000, he made a comment that was crucial to understanding the de Man case:

> It is a bit as if a certain way of keeping quiet, of silencing oneself, as if a certain secret had always represented, regarding judaism, regarding jewishness, regarding the condition or situation of being *jew*, regarding this appellation that I hardly dare, precisely, to call mine—it is as if such silence, a determined silence and not just any silence (for I have never, absolutely never, hidden my jewish descent, and I have always been honored to claim it), as if nonetheless such obstinate reserve had represented a kind of guard, a kind of care-taking, of safekeeping: a silence that one protects and that protects, a secret that perhaps keeps *from* judaism, but keeps as well a certain jewishness in oneself—here in me.[40]

Derrida's retreat from speaking about his ethnicity is explained by his desire to avoid being associated with Zionism and as a form of protection against the wound that the early experience left on him, "the wound that will not heal, that anti-Semitism has left in me."[41] I shall return below to the concept of anti-Semitism as a wound, but my immediate concern is the distinction Derrida makes between keeping silent and hiding. He leaves no room for doubt that he *never, absolutely never*, hid his Jewish descent. To hide suggests shame or deception, and in the case of an ethically tainted past, the latter is particularly problematic.

Derrida sets great store by de Man's response to the university authorities in 1955, stating: "He explained himself publicly and in my opinion that is a reason, whatever we might do from now on, not to organize today a trial of Paul de Man."[42] There are two causes for concern in this claim. First, de Man can be accorded no credit for this confession—it was not in fact a confession at all, but an explanation in response to a denunciation (though the reason for the denunciation remains uncertain). De Man was thus, at least to some extent, under duress to provide an explanation. Second, his explanation, like his whole postwar career, was characterised by ellipsis at best and deceit at worst. Felman quotes from de Man's letter to Renato Poggioli, the director of the Harvard Society of Fellows: "de Man explained that he stopped writing for Le Soir 'when nazi thought-control did no longer allow freedom of statement.'"[43] The Nazis took control of *Le Soir* in 1940, and de Man stopped writing for the paper in 1942, so he seems to be suggesting that in the first two years the Nazis did allow freedom of statement. I take this as an outright lie, but if I am wrong, then de Man's explanation implies that "Les Juifs dans la littérature actuelle," published more than eighteen months before he put down his pen, was his freely expressed viewpoint. De Man's statement is thus either deceitful or an unintended confession of anti-Semitism, and the evidence suggests the former.

Barish's research has unearthed de Man's only other explanation, which was also under duress, made to prosecutor Roger Vinçotte at the Palais de Justice in Brussels on 30 July 1946. De Man was not questioned about being employed by *Le Soir*, but about "Les Juifs dans la littérature actuelle" specifically. He replied:

> I can explain this matter because I am known as being the opposite of an anti-Semite. I have always had Jewish friends, I helped them during the war, and they have kept my friendship. Meulepas showed me an article by Eemans violently attacking the influence of Jews in literature. I protested to De Becker, who told me I could write another article. The article that you have before you aims to show that the Jewish influence in literature is benign, and above all it responds to Eemans's article. I know that it appeared on a page devoted to anti-Semitism, but I was never warned about that and was not responsible for it.[44]

As noted in section 27, Barish maintains that de Man made a deliberate contribution to the anti-Semitic page in order to secure his own column. She also claims that the reason Vinçotte failed to prosecute de Man was that he only had time to pursue "the major players" in the collaboration.[45] This is, however, inconsistent with the picture Barish paints of de Man as being at the very heart of the collaborationist media, so the reason for his release without charge remains, like the reason for writing the review, opaque.[46] As such, it seems prudent to withhold judgement on de Man's response to Vinçotte, but not his response to Poggioli, which is unequivocally deceitful.

Derrida only mentions silence once in his initial paper—"one may condemn the silence"—when discussing this review, but it seems to haunt him in "Biodegradables."[47] In various contexts, he writes: "to reduce to silence,"[48] "to accuse the silence,"[49] "to silence proper names,"[50] "the silence of the night,"[51] "I should not have silenced this."[52] One of these occurs in a note on ellipsis, and ellipsis as a means of deceit, whether intended or not, is one of the reasons silence is subject to negative ethical judgement.[53] De Man's explanation is an example of ellipsis: by failing to disclose relevant details of his employment, he provided false testimony about his collaboration. His silence from 1949, when he began teaching in America, to 1983 involves a greater ellipsis: by failing to acknowledge his wartime journalism he presented a false impression of his character as an academic. In both cases, pertinent facts were omitted for the purpose of deception. Even if de Man did not intend to deceive, his ellipsis had that effect, which was foreseeable, and for which he was thus responsible. Consider the contrast with Campbell. Campbell has every opportunity to remain silent about his doubts as to what he would have done in the event of Nazi victory, but he deceives the authorities into believing that he was (only) a collaborator in order to confess. De Man has every opportunity to confess his wartime journalism, but keeps silent—to the authorities, friends, colleagues, and students—in order to deceive them about his collaboration. Even where ellipsis is not intended to deceive, but where omitted material itself invites a negative judgement, the ellipsis will be perceived as deception precisely because—in the silence—no alternative explanation is offered. I shall return to this point in section 30.

While Campbell is betrayed by his only friend, George Kraft (who is actually a Soviet agent), de Man betrayed his friend Derrida, both as a friend and as a *Jewish* friend. Derrida unwittingly condemns de Man's ellipsis when he describes his own reaction to "Les Juifs dans la littérature actuelle." If de Man could find no other reason to confess, he should have considered the consequences of exposure for Derrida. That the exposure was posthumous may have been convenient for de Man but was distressingly inopportune for Derrida, who had to defend his friend in absentia. He describes "the wound I right away felt" upon reading the "unbearable" review[54]—which must have cut all the more deep given the childhood wound of anti-Semitism that had never healed—and gives three reasons for his "painful surprise":

(1) some of these articles or certain phrases in them seemed to manifest, in a certain way, an alliance with what has always been for me the very worst; (2) for almost twenty years, I had never had the least reason to suspect my friend could be the author of such articles (I will come back again to this fact); (3) I had read, a short while earlier, the only text that was accessible to me up until then and that was written and signed by Paul de Man in Belgium during the war.[55]

Contra Derrida and Kermode, de Man's silence is indeed blameworthy: it constitutes a case of deception by means of ellipsis or, at the very least, can be reasonably perceived as such.

30. SILENCE AND REMORSELESSNESS

The second problem with silence is related, but distinct: silence is usually understood as consent or assent. Dissent is voiced, but there is no need to voice one's approval—it is simply assumed in the absence of dissent. To be silent about an action is to condone that action, whether the agent is oneself or another. To be silent about one's past is to condone that past, and where that past is ethically tainted the silence expresses a lack of not only regret, but remorse. The distinction is set out by R. M. Hare, who identifies remorse as being accompanied by a desire for reversibility.[56] Hare's most convincing example concerns the master of a ship travelling in a wartime convoy. When a sailor falls overboard the master decides not to break formation and risk losing his ship to a submarine attack and thus leaves the man to drown. Assuming he is not a moral monster, the master would feel regret at the death of a human being for whom he is responsible and which he could have prevented. He does not, however, feel remorse because he does not believe that he ought to have broken formation to save the sailor and would not do so were the situation to recur. If an action is harmful but necessary, one expects a moral agent to feel regret. For some, collaborating with the Nazis may have fallen into this category.

One could—perhaps *should*, as I suggested in section 27—attribute de Man's work for *Le Soir* to an ulterior motive, the need to support his family in a dangerous time and place, but one would at least expect an expression of regret for his collaboration. It is noteworthy that in neither of his responses—to the Auditeur Général or the Harvard Society of Fellows—did he admit to collaboration. And yet he clearly did collaborate, despite Derrida's defence of "Les Juifs dans la littérature actuelle" as ironic and the significance Derrida and Felman attribute to de Man's use of *vulgar* to describe anti-Semitism.[57] The issue at stake is *why* he collaborated, not *whether* he collaborated, which is why I characterised his silence as deceit by ellipsis in section 29. If, as Derrida seems to suggest, there was duress of some sort—perhaps, contra Barish, he had been instructed to contribute to the anti-Semitic page on which his review appeared at the risk of dismissal—then one would expect a subsequent expression of regret, even if that expression was delayed.[58] If there were no such conditions, then the anti-Semitism was de Man's opinion at the time, and one would expect a subsequent expression of remorse. Neither regret nor remorse were expressed in 1955. In the absence of such expressions, one can only regard his silence as evidence that he neither regretted his collaboration nor experienced remorse for his actions. And, as with silence and ellipsis, even if the motivation for silence was not remorselessness, de Man should have realised that it would be perceived as such and taken action to avoid this (mis)perception.

It might be argued that silence is not, in the circumstances under discussion, evidence of remorselessness and that what is most important is whether de Man experienced regret or remorse, not whether he communicated these feelings privately or publicly. Consider two contrasting possibilities: (a) de Man devotes himself to a worthy cause in secret, assisting holocaust survivors, by way of reparation for "Les Juifs dans la littérature actuelle;" and (b) de Man confesses authorship but disowns responsibility for a juvenile error (as suggested by Kermode) or a review written under duress (as suggested by Derrida). In the former case, de Man's private repentance would invite positive judgement in light of which his failure to confess would be of little significance. In the latter case, a public confession would not allay concerns about his sense of remorse and may even invite a more negative judgement than his silence. When discussing Felman's accusation of forgetting in section 27, I noted that no one except de Man could know how much of the war he forgot in the literal sense. The same is true of his sense of remorse. Given that the controversy was posthumous, none of de Man's accusers or defenders in the 1980s could have known whether his conscience was plagued by his collaboration any more than one can know now. Nor, I maintain, would it have been possible during his lifetime. One can profess regret and remorse just as one can profess forgetfulness, but no one except the individual who has—or does not have—the sense of guilt can ever be certain. Human beings lack direct access to other minds and must therefore rely on the testimony of others and observation of their actions. Neither testimony nor actions are completely reliable guides to motivation, and in lieu of an ever-absent certainty, ethical judgements must be based on inferences from the available evidence.

In my discussion of the complexity of collaboration in section 27, I offered a third option in cooperation, but the distinction between collaboration and cooperation is, as noted, opaque. Ethan Hollander raises doubts as to whether cooperation can be distinguished from collaboration by claiming that negotiation is "institutionally indistinguishable from 'collaboration.'"[59] In her rigorous argument for a particular type of cooperation, rhetorical resistance, Cheryl Jorgensen-Earp identifies the problem as epistemic in nature: "It might fairly be asked when we can know that such deference is a performance and not an expression of wholehearted collaboration."[60] Her response establishes "collaborative intent" as the distinctive criterion, such that the same action may have been committed with or without the intention to collaborate and should be classified on the basis of that intention.[61] The criterion is appropriate to her methodology, which employs diaries written by residents of Guernsey when the outcome of the war was uncertain, as well as the documentation of the German authorities.[62] Assuming that the islanders represented their true motives in their private diaries, it seems reasonable to infer that those—such as Frank Falla—who may have at times appeared to be collaborating, were merely cooperating. In Falla's case, his true sympathies were exposed in April 1944, when he and four colleagues were arrested and charged with the distribution of BBC news. All five spent the last year of the war imprisoned in Germany, during which time one of them died.[63] In de Man's case, however, there is no diary and no documentation from the Germans. The evidence is therefore limited to his actions (i.e., his silence and the answer he gave to the Harvard Society of Fellows, neither of which expressed regret or remorse). His silence offers evidence of assent, because he appears to have believed that he had done nothing wrong and therefore had nothing to be regretful or remorseful about. And, as noted in section 29 with regard to ellipsis as deception, silence furthermore offers no alternative explanation.

It is here that the contrast with Campbell is at its clearest. I juxtaposed Campbell and de Man in section 29: one deceived in order to confess and was betrayed by a friend; the other kept silent in order to deceive and betrayed his friends. The opposition extends far beyond these two points and is almost uncanny in its precision. Campbell was a fictional character who wrote fiction, whose collaboration had a significant impact, and who had a belated desire for confession and judgement. De Man was a historical figure who wrote literary criticism, whose collaboration had a negligible impact, and who either dissembled or kept silent about his war. Where Campbell's desire for judgement was so strong that he resorted to an uncompromising self-judgement when no other form was available, de Man successfully avoided being the subject of judgement for his entire life. Campbell's remorse (or regret, he does not specify whether his guilt includes a desire for reversibility) vindicated his tarnished character in the posthumous publication of his confession by Vonnegut; de Man's character was tarnished by the posthumous republication of his wartime journalism. There are numerous further distinctions that could be drawn, but I have already stated the most important, the different attitudes adopted toward their past indiscretions: Campbell had an urgent need to confess, to avoid what he regarded as a deceitful exoneration of his character, and to express his remorse or regret; de Man had an urgent need to hide his collaboration, to deceitfully exonerate his character in his new life in America. The contrast could not be greater and is useful because—in yet another contrast—it is easy to understand what one admires in Campbell, and that admiration sheds light on what one finds distasteful in de Man, which is not immediately obvious.

The motive behind de Man's wartime journalism will, as I have emphasised throughout this chapter, never be known. As such, I am in agreement with the majority of the commentators who did not employ the controversy as an opportunity to attack Derrida or deconstructive criticism, and the charge of collaboration can be dismissed. In section 27 I suggested that forgetting was either subject to the same epistemic problem as collaboration—no one but de Man can ever be certain as to why he collaborated, how much of the war he remembered, or whether he had a guilty conscience—or could be subsumed under the third charge, silence. It is Campbell's admirable refusal to be silent, even when one might think he had earned the right to do so, that reveals the culpability in de Man's silence. Their respective methods of dealing with ethically tainted pasts show precisely what is blameworthy in de Man's silence: the deceit by ellipsis and the absence of remorse or regret. What de Man did wrong was therefore to keep silent about his war. Whatever negative judgements that silence invites—and I have argued for deceit and remorselessness—it was also blameworthy in a third way, for leaving a mess for others to clean up—a *wound* which friends, colleagues, and followers were left to bear. The comparison of the two biographies, one documentary and one fictional, demonstrates that narrative representation can provide a means to the end of answering complex questions about collaboration (i.e., exemplary narratives can be employed to evaluate responsibility for criminal inhumanity).

NOTES

1. Evelyn Barish, *The Double Life of Paul de Man* (New York: Liveright, 2014), 99–103.

2. Paul de Man, *Wartime Journalism, 1939–43* (Lincoln: University of Nebraska Press, 1988), 45.

3. David Lehman, *Signs of the Times: Deconstruction and the Fall of Paul de Man* (New York: Poseidon, 1992 [1991]), 209.

4. Barish, *Double Life*, 136.

5. Barish, *Double Life*, 158.

6. Barish, *Double Life*, 161.

7. Barish, *Double Life*, 163–69.

8. Barish, *Double Life*, 193–202.

9. Barish, *Double Life*, 210–11.

10. David Lehman, "Paul de Man: The Plot Thickens," *New York Times*, 24 May 1992. Available at: http://www.nytimes.com/1992/05/24/books/paul-de-man-the-plot-thickens.html?pagewanted=all&src=pm.

11. Barish, *Double Life*, 349–52; Shoshana Felman, "Paul de Man's Silence," *Critical Inquiry* 15 (1989): 720–21.

12. In both *Signs of the Times* and "The Plot Thickens."

13. Barish, *Double Life*, 260–62.

14. Louis Menand, "The de Man Case: Does a Critic's Past Explain His Criticism?," *The New Yorker*, 24 March 2014. Available at: http://www.newyorker.com/arts/critics/atlarge/2014/03/24/140324crat_atlarge_menand?currentPage=all.

15. Jacques Derrida, "From *Psyche*," in *Acts of Literature*, ed. Derek Attridge (New York: Routledge, 1992), 313.

16. See: Derrida, "Biodegradables Seven Diary Fragments," *Critical Inquiry* 15 (1989): 812–73.

17. Jean-Marie Apostolidès, "On Paul de Man's War," *Critical Inquiry* 15 (1989): 765–66.

18. Harpham, *Shadows of Ethics*, 20.

19. I lack space to discuss how my conclusion regarding de Man may be extended to other cases of collaboration (with the Nazis and other totalitarian regimes), but my failure to accord the details of his personal circumstances too much prominence should be taken as evidence of my belief in the condemnation of similar cases of silence in the context of an ethically tainted past.

20. Felman, "Paul de Man's Silence," 705.

21. Jacques Derrida, "Like the Sound of the Sea Deep within a Shell: Paul de Man's War," *Critical Inquiry* 14 (1988): 621.

22. Barish maintains that de Man wrote the article in order to secure a column for himself—"Our Literary Chronicle," which began on 18 March 1941—and employs it as further evidence of his extreme opportunism (*Double Life*, 117–27). I suspect she is correct, but an argument could of course be made that his ambition was geared toward providing for his rapidly growing family, not to mention a fiancée with extravagant tastes.

23. Cited in Barry Turner, *Outpost of Occupation: How the Channel Islands Survived Nazi Rule 1940–45* (London: Aurum, 2010), 102. Turner is not convinced by Falla's defence, but he lacks sensitivity with regard to the circumstances of the occupation of the Channel Islands in general and Guernsey in particular. I return to Falla in section 30 and Lord Haw-Haw in section 28.

24. Frank Kermode, "Paul de Man's Abyss," *London Review of Books* 11 (16 March 1989): 3–7. Available at: http://www.lrb.co.uk/v11/n06/frank-kermode/paul-de-mans-abyss#.

25. Derrida, "Paul de Man's War," 638.

26. Derrida, "Paul de Man's War," 638.

27. Kermode, "Paul de Man's Abyss."

28. Barish, *Double Life*, 24–29, 57.

29. Kurt Vonnegut Jr., *Mother Night* (St. Albans: Triad/Panther 1979 [1961]).

30. See, for example: Adrian Weale, *Renegades: Hitler's Englishmen* (London: Weidenfeld & Nicolson, 1994); Phil Froom, "Fred Koenig: A SS Grenadier from Chicago USA," *Axis History*, 22 July 2012. Available at: http://www.axishistory.com/axis-nations/germany-a-austria/waffen-ss/124-germany-waffen-ss/germany-waffen-ss-other/6182-fred-koenig-a-ss-grenadier-from-chicago-usa.

31. Critical interest in Vonnegut's *Vergangenheitsbewältigung* in fiction has focused on *Slaughterhouse Five* at the expense of *Mother Night*. Unlike the former, the latter was not particularly well received (Martin Amis in *The War against Cliché: Essays and Reviews, 1971–2000* [London: Jonathan Cape, 2001] is a notable exception) and is usually categorised as an "early" (i.e., pre–*Slaughterhouse Five*) novel. Even in this category, however, interest in *Mother Night* is eclipsed by *Cat's Cradle*, which enjoyed popular success three years after publication in 1963 and earned Vonnegut his first major publishing contract. Discussions of *Mother Night* tend to be brief and restricted to narrowly defined aspects of the novel; for example: Edward Jamosky and Jerome Klinkowitz, "Kurt Vonnegut's Three *Mother Nights*," *Modern Fiction Studies* 34 (1988): 216–20; Lawrence R. Bruer, *Sanity Plea: Schizophrenia in the Novels of Kurt Vonnegut* (Tuscaloosa: University of Alabama Press, 1989), 45–56; Robert Merrill, "Kurt Vonnegut as a German-American," in *Germany and German Thought in American Literature and Cultural Criticism*, ed. Peter Freese (Essen: Blaue Eule, 1990), 230–43. Donald E. Morse displays a broader, thematic concern in *The Novels of Kurt Vonnegut: Imagining Being an American* (Westport, CT: Praeger, 2003), 53–58, but his treatment is also brief. For a recent overview of Vonnegut criticism, which is representative in mentioning *Mother Night* only once—and in conjunction with *Cat's Cradle*—see: Peter Freese, "The Critical Reception of Kurt Vonnegut," *Literature Compass* 9/1 (2012): 1–14.

32. See: "Editor's Note," Vonnegut, *Mother Night*, ix–xi.

33. The narrative of the novel is a-chronological, switching back and forth between decades as Campbell makes his confession from his prison cell prior to his trial.

34. Vonnegut, *Mother Night*, 122.

35. Vonnegut, *Mother Night*, viii.

36. Vonnegut, *Mother Night*, 70–72.

37. Vonnegut, *Mother Night*, 65–66.

38. Vonnegut, *Mother Night*, 71.

39. Vonnegut, *Mother Night*, 175.

40. Derrida, "Abraham, the Other," trans. Gil Anidjar, in *Judeites: Questions for Jacques Derrida*, ed. Bettina Berg, Joseph Cohen, and Raphael Zagury-Orly (New York: Fordham University Press, 2007 [2003]), 6.

41. Derrida, "Abraham, the Other," 16.

42. Derrida, "Paul de Man's War," 637.

43. Felman, "Paul de Man's Silence," 720.

44. Barish, *Double Life*, 196. Joseph Meulepas was an editor at *Le Soir*, Marc Eemans a surrealist painter who had campaigned against degenerate art and wrote occasional articles for the paper, and Raymond de Becker the editor-in-chief appointed by the Nazis.

45. Barish, *Double Life*, 201.

46. Barish, *Double Life*, 135–50.

47. Derrida, "Paul de Man's War," 624.

48. Derrida, "Biodegradables," 819.

49. Derrida, "Biodegradables," 835.

50. Derrida, "Biodegradables," 854.

51. Derrida, "Biodegradables," 862.

52. Derrida, "Biodegradables," 867 fn.

53. Derrida, "Biodegradables," 854.

54. Derrida, "Paul de Man's War," 621.

55. Derrida, "Paul de Man's War," 600.

56. Hare, *Moral Thinking*, 28–30.

57. See: Derrida, "Paul de Man's War," 623–632; Felman, "Paul de Man's Silence," 712–13.

58. Derrida, "Paul de Man's War," 631.

59. Ethan J. Hollander, "The Banality of Goodness: Collaboration and Compromise in the Rescue of Denmark's Jews," *Journal of Jewish Identities* 6 (2013): 42.

60. Cheryl R. Jorgensen-Earp, *Discourse and Defiance Under Nazi Occupation: Guernsey, Channel Islands, 1940–1945* (East Lansing: Michigan State University Press, 2013), 148.

61. Jorgensen-Earp, *Discourse and Defiance*, 150.

62. Jorgensen-Earp, *Discourse and Defiance*, 98.

63. Frank W. Falla, *The Silent War: The Inside Story of the Channel Islands under the Nazi Jackboot* (London: New English Library, 1968 [1967]), 107. See my previous comment on Falla in section 27 n.23.

Chapter Eight

The Psychology of Inhumanity

The purpose of this chapter is to demonstrate narrative justice (i.e., to show how an exemplary narrative can be employed to reduce criminal inhumanity by affording an understanding of the psychology of inhumanity). Specifically, the thesis is used to solve an evaluative problem: the apparent conflict of aesthetic and ethical value in the narrative representation of torturers in South Africa under apartheid. In section 31 I summarise the biographies of Dirk Coetzee, an apartheid assassin, and J. M. Coetzee, the South African–born novelist and critic. Section 32 presents J. M. Coetzee's dilemma: the novelist must either portray the torturer by means of cliché and fail aesthetically or attribute glamour or grandeur to the world of the torturer and fail ethically. I discuss the way in which J. M. Coetzee makes the former failure in *Waiting for the Barbarians*. In section 33 I analyse journalist Jacques Pauw's representation of Dirk Coetzee in *In the Heart of the Whore*, his exposé of torture and assassination under apartheid. I compare the respective representations of torturers in *Waiting for the Barbarians* and *In the Heart of the Whore* in section 34, concluding that J. M. Coetzee's dilemma is false, as a narrative representation can succeed in exploring the psychology of a torturer while simultaneously condemning his or her actions.

31. IN THE HEART OF THE COUNTRY

Jacques Pauw's work is little known outside of South Africa, so I begin with a sketch of the historical context in which both *In the Heart of the Whore* and *Waiting for the Barbarians* were conceived and published. In 1973 the General Assembly of the United Nations declared apartheid—known by the various euphemisms of *separate development*, *multinationalism*, and *plural*

151

democracy in South Africa—a crime against humanity.[1] At twenty-eight, Dirk Johannes Coetzee's star was rising in the South African Police (SAP), with promotion to warrant officer and qualification as a dog handler after only three years of service. John Maxwell Coetzee was thirty-three. He had recently returned to South Africa from the United States and was teaching at the University of Cape Town while writing his first novel. The following year, Dirk Coetzee was selected for deployment to Rhodesia as part of South Africa's military assistance to Ian Smith's government, J. M. Coetzee's *Dusklands* was published by Ravan Press, and the Bureau for State Security (better known by the erroneous acronym BOSS) began assassinating enemies of the state at home and abroad. The year 1977 was a landmark one for both Coetzees: Dirk was transferred to the security branch of the SAP, and John received his first international acclaim as an author with *In the Heart of the Country*, his second novel. Like *Dusklands*, *In the Heart of the Country* employed "nonrealist or antirealist devices," and Coetzee would subsequently be criticised for failing to engage directly with the politics of contemporary South Africa in his fiction.[2] Meanwhile, in order to deflect international attention away from the internal injustices highlighted by the Soweto Uprising and the death of Steve Biko in police custody, Magnus Malan (the chief of the South African Defence Force) attempted to set the defence of apartheid in the context of the Cold War by coining the phrase *total onslaught from Moscow*. When P. W. Botha, the former minister of defence, was elected prime minister in 1978, the country was placed on a war footing, a *total strategy* that included an increase in repressive measures at home, the destabilisation of neighbouring states, and an expansion of espionage activity abroad. The year 1980 was another important one for both Coetzees: Dirk took command of the police unit at Vlakplaas, a farm near Pretoria, and John published *Waiting for the Barbarians*, the novel he subsequently described as being "about the impact of the torture chamber on the life of a man of conscience."[3] Although there are clear allusions to South Africa, the work is allegorical, set on the border of a nameless empire at an unspecified time when soldiers use muskets and policemen wear sunglasses. Dirk's new command consisted of seventeen *askaris*, black nationalist insurgents who had been "turned" with the aim of establishing them as double agents in the armed struggle against apartheid.

Total strategy suffered a setback in 1981 when BOSS's illegal activities were exposed with Gordon Winter's publication of *Inside BOSS*. Botha, with Malan as his minister of defence, reconstituted the agency as the National Intelligence Service (NIS) and secretly switched death squad duties to the SAP's Security Branch. Coetzee reorganised his command, designated C10, as a counterinsurgency unit along the lines of the Selous Scouts in the former Rhodesia.[4] He ran the death squad for five months before being removed as a result of a diplomatic incident he caused in Swaziland and an internal police pornography scandal for which he was made scapegoat. The long disinte-gration of Dirk's career was mirrored by the success of John's, whose fourth novel—*Life & Times of Michael K*—won the Booker Prize in 1983. Two years later, with internal unrest approaching the level of civil war that Coetzee had depicted in his latest fiction, Botha declared a state of emergency, increasing the security services' powers and immunity in thirty-six magisterial districts. In 1986, the state of emergency was extended to the whole of South Africa. As Dirk Coetzee yielded to pressure to resign from the police, J. M. Coetzee published *Foe*—his reimagining of *Robinson Crusoe*—and the article quoted above, in which he identifies two dilemmas for the representation of torture by novelists. At the beginning of 1988 a former military intelligence unit, the Civil Cooperation Bureau (CCB), was established as a second death squad to augment the efforts of C10. Although the CCB comprised former Special Forces operators, police detectives, and convicted criminals, it was established as an independent agency and allowed to operate with total autonomy and impunity. Opponents of apartheid were targeted in Belgium, France, Mozambique, Zimbabwe, South West Africa, and South Africa.

Twelve months later, the last-ditch defence of apartheid came to a sudden end when Botha suffered a stroke. The irreversible dismantling of apartheid began with the United Nations Transition Assistance Group's overseeing of the transition to an independent Namibia and the appointment of the moderate F. W. de Klerk as state president. While de Klerk met Nelson Mandela in prison with a view to releasing him and lifting the ban on the African National Congress (ANC), Pieter Botes—a senior CCB operative—disclosed the exist-ence of the organisation to Adriaan Vlok, the minister of law and order, as a personal insurance policy.[5] In November, after nearly four years of harass-ment by his former colleagues, Dirk Coetzee decided to seek the protection of the ANC and agreed to let Pauw publish his account of C10. Pauw was a jour-nalist employed by *Vrye Weekblad*, a liberal Afrikaner newspaper that opposed white minority rule and published "Bloedspoor van die SAP" ("Bloody Trail of the South African Police") eight days after the fall of the Berlin Wall. In April 1990, with Mandela released, opposition parties unbanned, and the Harms Commission investigating the death squads, Botes contacted Pauw. Five months later, J. M. Coetzee published *Age of Iron*, which has an explicit historical setting of Cape Town in 1986 and engaged with South African pol-itics in a more straightforward manner than his previous novels. In February 1992, with his network of sources extended well beyond Dirk Coetzee and Botes, Pauw published *In the Heart of the Whore: The Story of Apartheid's Death Squads*, his exposé of both C10 and the CCB. The latter unit had been disbanded ten months previously; the former was still operational.

32. THE PERSON OF THE TORTURER

J. M. Coetzee identifies a dual dilemma for an author writing in the context of a regime that condones torture in his commentary on *Waiting for the Barbarians*.[6] The first is that the author either (a) ignores the existence of torture in a society, or (b) represents the torture, propagating the very fear for which it has been employed. The author is thus consigned to either condoning the torture with his or her silence or unwittingly assisting in the terrorising of the population by the state.[7] The second dilemma concerns "the person of the torturer."[8] Either the author (i) resorts to cliché, or (ii) attributes a grandeur to the torturer's world that (A) misrepresents the character of the torturer and (B) fails ethically. Regarding (A), Coetzee has in mind the "paradox in morality" revealed in the Nuremberg and Eichmann trials, the stark contrast between the triviality of the individuals on trial and the magnitude of their atrocities.[9] Coetzee's claim in (B) is that the author is subject to the same criticisms levelled at the realist novelists of the nineteenth century, that they sought out the malicious and unpleasant for their own literary ends and aestheticized the ethically reprehensible. The first dilemma is an ethical one, a question of the proper response by an author to a regime that condones torture. The second dilemma is both ethical and aesthetic: either the author (i) creates a work that is aesthetically flawed by resorting to cliché, or (ii) creates a work that is ethically flawed by attributing a lyricism, glamour, or grandeur to the world of the torturer.[10] My concern is with the second dilemma, Coetzee's claim that authors who are opposed to torture cannot avoid either an aesthetic or an ethical failure in the representation of the person of the torturer.

In "Torture and the Novel: J. M. Coetzee's *Waiting for the Barbarians*," Susan Van Zanten Gallagher interprets Coetzee's novel in the light of his commentary and claims that he solves both of the dilemmas in the work.[11] Van Zanten Gallagher regards the two solutions as related, so I shall include a brief discussion of the first before proceeding to the second. The dilemma of the representation of torture is solved by Coetzee's refusal to portray torture realistically, his use of a deliberately vague spatiotemporal setting of which very little can be stated with authority except that the empire is located in the Northern Hemisphere and that its civilization is largely pre-industrial. "Coetzee creates an allegorical landscape that loosely suggests the Roman Empire on the verge of collapse but undoubtedly points to South Africa today."[12] The allegorical character of the narrative sets the South African situation in the broader context of colonialism and thus avoids either ignoring the employment of torture in South Africa or contributing to the fear inspired by that torture. Coetzee's use of allegory is doubly effective. First, the novel becomes not only about apartheid South Africa, but all regimes that torture their citizens, including those contemporary to its publication—the Soviet Union, Chile, Argentina—and those before and since. Second, the novel reveals South Africa as a European colony in a postcolonial era, pointing to the violence at the foundation of all empires. Coetzee begins his article on *Waiting for the Barbarians* by quoting Nathaniel Hawthorne on the necessity of cemeteries and prisons to colonies and alludes to Hawthorne's description of prisons in the novel itself.[13]

Van Zanten Gallagher identifies the solution to the second dilemma as more complicated than the first, but it is here that we part company, as I shall argue that Coetzee fails to solve the problem of the representation of the person of the torturer.[14] Van Zanten Gallagher claims that Coetzee portrays both of the torturers described in the novel—Colonel Joll and Warrant Officer Mandel of the Third Bureau of the Civil Guard—as moral vacuums. The absence of morality and humanity is reflected in the impenetrability of their eyes, the continual wearing of sunglasses by Joll and the blank quality of Mandel's gaze: "I look into his clear blue eyes, as clear as if there were crystal lenses slipped over his eyeballs. He looks back at me. I have no idea what he sees."[15] In this way, the torturers are represented as distinct from the magistrate, the *man of conscience* who narrates the novel. The world of the secret police is inaccessible and incomprehensible to the narrator, but there are nonetheless similarities between magistrate and torturer. Van Zanten Gallagher maintains that Coetzee represents the person of the torturer by means of the magistrate's comparison of himself with Joll.

The comparison is made explicit when the magistrate's nightly ritual of washing and massaging the barbarian victim of torture takes a sexual turn. The following morning, he is met with blankness from the girl and asks himself:

> "What do I have to do to move you?" . . . "Does no one move you?"; and with a shift of horror I behold the answer that has been waiting all the time offer itself to me in the image of a face masked by two black glassy insect eyes from which there comes no reciprocal gaze but only my doubled image cast back at me.[16]

Once the magistrate has returned the girl to her people, he admits his affinity with Joll, the way in which they have both treated her as a means rather than an end and desired to make their respective marks on her.[17] He concludes,

> For I was not, as I liked to think, the indulgent pleasure-loving opposite of the cold rigid Colonel. I was the lie that Empire tells itself when times are easy, he the truth that Empire tells when harsh winds blow. Two sides of imperial rule, no more, no less.[18]

According to Van Zanten Gallagher, Coetzee resolves the second dilemma by blurring the distinction between the torturer and the man of conscience, thereby asserting that all citizens of the empire share ethical responsibility for the torturer's atrocities.[19] Her claim recalls a comment Pauw would later make when discussing Dirk Coetzee's successor in C10: "It's very important that every white South African takes responsibility for the actions of convicted [death-squad] leader Eugene de Kock, because he did it in our name."[20] J. M. Coetzee's solution to the second dilemma thus draws on the solution to the first: the setting of the story in a generic colonial context allows torture to be represented without promoting fear and allows the person of the torturer to be represented as a product of that colonial context for which all its citizens are to some extent responsible. The shared responsibility for torture is emphasised by the erosion of the distinction between the magistrate and Joll, culminating in their representation as two sides of the imperial coin.

If this resolution of the dilemma is to succeed, the similarity between the torturer and the guilty man of conscience must be unequivocal, but it is not. There are only two clear comparisons between the magistrate and Joll, both of which are quoted above. In keeping with the vagueness that permeates the whole novel and is partly constitutive of its success as an allegory, there are three—or perhaps four—torturers represented. The narrative begins with Joll's arrival in the edge of empire backwater and he mentions his "assistant," an anonymous individual of whom all one learns is his gender.[21] The magistrate is arrested by an anonymous warrant officer from the Third Bureau when he returns from repatriating the girl. When Mandel is finally named, he is also described as having an "underling" of whom one also only learns his gender.[22] The implication is that the assistant and underling are two different men and that the former (though perhaps not the latter) is from the Third Bureau, but it is impossible to be certain.

While the comparisons that Van Zanten Gallagher employs as evidence for her argument are between the magistrate and Joll, it is Mandel the magistrate comes to know best, in the intimacy of the torture chamber. In contrast with his constant antagonism toward Joll, which begins in the first sentence of the novel with his silent ridicule of the sunglasses, the magistrate empathises with Mandel on several occasions:

> The road to the top must be hard for young men without money, with the barest of schooling, men who might as easily go into lives of crime as into the service of the Empire.[23]

The magistrate's various attempts to understand Mandel nonetheless all fail to penetrate beyond the crystal lenses of his blank exterior. When he is released from custody, he asks Mandel how he balances the demands of his job with everyday life, but receives only abuse in response.[24] Mandel thus remains as inaccessible as Joll, and the magistrate concludes that "the care of souls seems to have left no more mark on him than the care of hearts leaves on the surgeon."[25]

Joll's expeditionary force is defeated by the barbarians—or perhaps the elements, uncertainty is all-pervasive—and his flight to the capital is made via the magistrate's town, setting the scene for a final confrontation between the two sides of empire. This crisis is both the only occasion on which the magistrate extends empathy to Joll and the only appearance of Joll without his sunglasses:

> His face is naked, washed clean, perhaps by the blue moonlight, perhaps by physical exhaustion. I stare at his pale high temples. Memories of his mother's soft breast, of the tug in his hand of the first kite he ever flew, as well of those intimate cruelties for which I abhor him, shelter in that beehive. He looks at me, his eyes searching my face. The dark lenses are gone.[26]

The magistrate launches into the lesson he has prepared for Joll, but the torturer does not respond and quickly resumes his flight. There is no insight into the nature of the relationship between the two men beyond that already gained, the magistrate's recognition of shared responsibility for imperial atrocity. Joll thus departs from the narrative in the same way he entered, blank and incomprehensible, with or without his sunglasses.

In avoiding the ethical pitfalls of representing the person of the torturer, Coetzee impales himself firmly on the aesthetic horn of the dilemma. He describes the aesthetic failing of the author thus:

> If he intends to avoid the clichés of spy fiction—to make the torturer neither a figure of satanic evil, nor an actor in a black comedy, nor a faceless functionary, nor a tragically divided man doing a job he does not believe in—what openings are left?[27]

Mandel and Joll are both faceless functionaries. The fact that Coetzee's lack of characterisation is intentional, that he makes the facelessness conspicuous in the descriptions of Joll's mask and Mandel's blankness, does not eliminate the flaw. Van Zanten Gallagher is therefore in error when she claims that Coetzee resolves the second dilemma. He has not solved the problem of the representation of the person of the torturer, but rather opted—commendably, given the context in which he was writing—to create a work that is aesthetically rather than ethically flawed. Better to represent torturers as faceless functionaries than engender sympathy for them, especially in a society where torture and assassination are sanctioned by the state. If aesthetic and ethical values cannot be reconciled in the case of torture, then the latter must take precedence. Coetzee's deliberate resort to cliché is nonetheless a flaw in an otherwise extraordinary work that leaves one with a sense of learning a great deal about the violence essential to empire, but learning very little about the men and women empires employ to do their dirty work. In the remainder of this chapter, I shall show how Pauw succeeds where Coetzee fails, providing a satisfying alternative to the second dilemma.

33. *IN THE HEART OF THE WHORE*

Pauw offers insight into the character of four assassins in *In the Heart of the Whore*. Six of the sixteen chapters in the book are focused on Dirk Coetzee, one each on the stories of Leslie Johannes Lesia and Ronald Desmond Bezuidenhout, and the remainder on the histories of the two death squads, C10 and the CCB. Both Lesia and Bezuidenhout were themselves imprisoned without trial and tortured for long periods, the former by Robert Mugabe's security services and the latter by the ANC's military wing, Umkhonto we Sizwe. Bezuidenhout's story is particularly pathetic because he was employed by the NIS to infiltrate the ANC, was forced to be become a white *askari* and sent back to South Africa as a double agent, and was then attached to C10 for a year before being remanded to a secure psychiatric hospital. Pauw's book ends with Bezuidenhout on the run from the SAP, his loyalty to his original masters rewarded by becoming one of their targets.[28] I do not have space to discuss the way in which Bezuidenhout and Lesia are portrayed by Pauw in detail; suffice to say that they are represented simultaneously as perpetrators and victims of the apartheid system and that Pauw's pleasure when Lesia is accepted back into his community is palpable.[29] Unlike Bezuidenhout and Lesia, Pauw does not portray Coetzee as a victim or figure of pity. Over the course of his exposé, he presents a mature and nuanced perspective of a complex and immoral—but not irredeemable—individual. Pauw's reaction to Coetzee and the other assassins is nevertheless clear: "I remain aghast and saddened at what I saw and heard."[30] My claim is that he avoids both the ethical horn of the dilemma and the clichés of demon, antihero, faceless functionary, and divided soul in his representation of Dirk Coetzee. Pauw achieves this by means of a simple but effective narrative technique, the creation of a pattern of comparison and contrast between Coetzee and the fourth assassin, Pieter Botes of the CCB.

Pauw first met Coetzee in 1984, spent a great deal of time with him during the course of writing his book, and held an ambivalent attitude toward the assassin:

We did the last of our interviews on the way to the airport. It was an emotional farewell. As I embraced Coetzee I realised that over the weeks, I had grown very close to this man whom I probably would have otherwise despised.[31]

Pauw's overriding concern is admirable, the sense of responsibility he feels for Coetzee. Although Coetzee was a willing participant in the interviews—he had been trying to tell his story for years—the publication of the newspaper article placed his life at risk from both the ANC and the SAP. Pauw attributes Coetzee's death squad activities to his acceptance of National Party ideology, his patriotism, and his immersion in SAP culture, all of which gave him a strong sense of purpose.[32] As such, he was at least dedicated to a creed—albeit an unethical one—rather than committing crimes against humanity for personal gain or pleasure. In this respect, Dirk Coetzee is similar to the fictional John Smith, discussed in section 17. Pauw also depicts Coetzee as pitiless, unrepentant, violent, treacherous, and intolerant, however, and makes no attempt to disguise his many ethical failings.[33] Pauw's sympathy is most evident when Coetzee testifies to the Harms Commission in London, inviting his readers to understand Coetzee's peculiar predicament: in this, his first attempt to take responsibility for his atrocities, he is abandoned by his wife, makes a fool of himself with his poor command of English, and is faced with a hostile judge eager to discredit evidence of death squad activity.[34] Pauw is troubled by Coetzee's lack of remorse, but concedes that "he spoke with great confidence and the sincerity of a man who had to rid himself of a terrible burden."[35] Pauw maintains that Coetzee's decision to confess and seek asylum with the ANC was primarily the result of his desire to give his life the direction he lost when his police career imploded.[36] He was, in other words, neither motivated by purely selfless nor purely selfish considerations. Of Coetzee's character, Pauw concludes:

> The life of Dirk Coetzee, I believe, is one of wasted talents and missed opportunities. He can certainly never be presented as a shining example of a crusader for what is right and proper, but he has always been honest, open and loyal to me.[37]

One should keep in mind that this appraisal is from a man who is a crusader for what is right and proper and has—like Coetzee—placed his own life at risk. The Truth and Reconciliation Commission seems to have concurred with Pauw. Coetzee returned to South Africa in 1993 and was granted amnesty from criminal and civil prosecution in 1997, one of only 12 percent of successful applicants.[38]

Notwithstanding, Coetzee is, like Botes, a death squad commander who demonstrates little if any remorse. Pauw sets up the two men as counterparts—one from C10, the other from the CCB—but uses a variety of narrative means to emphasise the contrasts between them, beginning with his introduction to each:

(a) Sitting cross-legged on the beach under a swaying palm tree, slowly sipping a frosty beer, was Dirk Johannes Coetzee, his handsome face tanned and clean-shaven, a slick of hair over his forehead. . . . Dirk Coetzee is a former security policeman, holder of the police medal for faithful service, the best student of his police college intake nearly twenty years earlier. But Dirk Coetzee was no ordinary policeman.[39]

(b) There are two things that Pieter Botes loves to boast about. The one is how he "stuffed up the enemy" in Mozambique; the other is the "gravy" he made out of Albie Sachs's right arm.[40]

Coetzee is introduced in an apparently casual setting, two men relaxing with drinks on a beach. The initial impression foregrounds positive features—his good looks and success as a police officer—before he is revealed as the killer of Griffiths Mxenge, a human rights lawyer assassinated in 1981. The first mention of Botes is of him boasting, an objectionable trait exacerbated by the fact that he is boasting about men he has killed or maimed. Botes's boasting is not only repugnant, but reveals his lack of intelligence: the bomb he planted was intended to kill Sachs (another human rights lawyer), not disable him, and Sachs was appointed a judge of the Constitutional Court in South Africa in 1994. Pauw keeps Botes's disagreeability firmly in his readers' minds when he notes that after their first meeting, he "constantly referred to the Sachs operation in his smugly macabre way."[41]

   A further comparison between Coetzee and Botes is that both fell afoul of their death squad superiors before agreeing to speak to Pauw. Pauw accords greater priority to their motives than to the actual whistleblowing, however, and thus employs the similarity to establish a wider gap between the two assassins. Where Coetzee is represented as seeking purpose in his life, Botes is represented as seeking only financial reward. Of his former employers, he states: "They haven't paid me or my men. I am going to stuff them up."[42] In 1989, Botes was happy to plan the assassination of Robert Davies despite the lack of proof connecting the academic to Umkhonto we Sizwe.[43] Less than a year later, with the writing on the wall for apartheid, Botes plans to raise a death squad to hunt down CCB operatives on behalf of the ANC in exchange for a quarter of a million rand.[44] Again, the proposal is as idiotic as it is immoral. Perhaps the most damning indictment of Botes's character is revealed in a meeting between Botes, Pauw, and Pauw's editor, Max Du Preez. Pauw and Du Preez have already consumed a considerable amount of alcohol when Botes offers them *mampoer*, an illegal home-brewed spirit that typically has an alcohol content of over 60 percent. After a few drinks each, Pauw and Du Preez politely decline the next.

> "I will show you what I do to people who refuse to drink my mampoer," he said. He left the room and came back with a grain bag, from which he drew a Russian-manufactured RPG rocket launcher. He put the launcher against the wall and said: "Now you will drink my pear mampoer." We finished the bottle. On the way back to Johannesburg, Du Preez was overcome by temporary blindness and stopped the car in the middle of the highway.[45]

The contrast to the relationship of mutual trust Pauw enjoys with Coetzee is stark, but the above passage also works in a subtler manner, setting their respective personalities at odds with each other: sipping beers on the beach with Coetzee versus drinking poison at RPG-point with Botes. As opposed to Pauw's last word on Coetzee as a wasted talent, his final comment on Botes expresses his contempt: "Underneath the bloody bravado of a Pieter Botes and the gleeful torture talk of a James Stevens I have found men of moral straw."[46]

Pauw's play of identity and difference in his portrayal of the two death squad commanders invites a judgement of Coetzee as ethically reprehensible, but not beyond redemption. If one accepts Pauw's perspective on Coetzee, then one also accepts that shock and sadness are more appropriate responses to him than disgust or contempt. As such, Coetzee's story becomes more interesting, and his place as the protagonist of Pauw's narrative makes the work more rather than less compelling. The comparison and contrast of characters or objects is an aesthetic technique common to numerous art forms and modes of representation. With respect to ethical character, the technique is especially effective in narrative representations. Noël Carroll explains this employment in his discussion of the television series *The Sopranos*, of whose protagonist he states, "among an array of ethically challenged characters, he is one of the least deplorable."[47] The result is that, in *The Sopranos*, the audience becomes in some sense allied to Tony Soprano and adopts a pro-attitude toward him. Such a description would be too strong of Coetzee, but Pauw's presentation of him as one of the least deplorable assassins in the tale of apartheid's death squads makes readers more likely to adopt an ambivalent rather than a hostile attitude toward him. To employ Carroll's term, Pauw's construction of the "moral economy" of his exposé identifies Coetzee (as well as Lesia and Bezuidenhout) as being within the sphere of readers' concern.[48]

Returning to J. M. Coetzee, recall that the author wishing to represent the person of the torturer must either fail aesthetically by resorting to cliché or fail ethically by attributing grandeur to the torturer's world. There is no grandeur attributed to either the torturer or his world by Pauw. He does not shy away from Dirk Coetzee's immorality, and there is never any doubt about the extent to which all death squad operatives have committed despicable crimes. There is thus no question of excusing Coetzee from responsibility for his atrocities, and the issue of amnesty and forgiveness is left open. Pauw also avoids transferring the grandeur from the torturer to his world by means of the short chapters devoted to Lesia and Bezuidenhout, respectively. There is no glamour, grandeur, or glory whatsoever in either of these brief biographies. As mentioned above, Bezuidenhout's story—titled "In the Heart of Darkness"—is nothing short of pitiful. The victim of an abusive childhood, his aggression was fine-tuned in the South African Defense Force's (SAD's) Special Forces before he was abandoned by the NIS, tortured by the ANC for three years, and then exploited once again by Eugene de Kock in C10. *In the Heart of the Whore* ends with Bezuidenhout's testimony, and the picture of the world of the death squad with which the reader is left—of a dangerous, mentally unstable, substance-addicted assassin on the run from friend and foe—is disgraceful, appalling, and bleak beyond measure.

My main interest, however, is whether Pauw has avoided the aesthetic horn of J. M. Coetzee's dilemma. Dirk Coetzee is not depicted as a demon, antihero, or faceless functionary. Nor is he depicted as a divided soul, torn between— for example—his duties as an assassin and the demands of family life or his loyalty to the police and his conscience. Coetzee insulated his domestic from his professional life, like most death squad operatives, and failed to recognise the conflict between his duties as a police officer and his lawbreaking. Pauw does not resort to cliché, but one might ask how he represents the man toward whom he invites a combination of condemnation and understanding. The most accurate answer is that Coetzee's character emerges as a paradigm of David Hume's account of personal identity as "nothing but a bundle or collection of different perceptions, which succeed each other with an inconceivable rapidity, and are in a perpetual flux and movement."[49] Coetzee portrayed by Pauw is a complex individual, a discontented mass of contradictions seeking an overriding purpose to unite his various vices and virtues into a stable personality and ultimately failing. The veracity of Pauw's portrayal is to some extent borne out by Coetzee's post-apartheid career. He hoped to be able to return to duty in the reconstituted police service after being granted amnesty, but clashed with his ANC colleagues. He spent the rest of his life as a civilian, a status with which he was never satisfied, and died of kidney failure in 2013 at the age of sixty-seven.[50] Whatever judgement one ultimately makes of Coetzee—a wasted opportunity or beneath contempt—he emerges from Pauw's narrative as a carefully drawn and fully developed character, of much more interest than J. M. Coetzee's Joll. In his depiction of Dirk Coetzee, Pauw therefore solves the problem of the representation of the torturer, succeeding where J. M. Coetzee fails.

34. THE PROBLEM THAT TROUBLES THE NOVELIST

In J. M. Coetzee's defence, he is concerned with the dilemma faced by the novelist rather than the author in general. Coetzee praises anti-apartheid activist Breyten Breytenbach's memoir *The True Confessions of an Albino Terrorist*, with its exploration of

> the spiritual sphere in which the police live. They are human beings who find it possible to leave the breakfast table in the morning, kiss their children goodbye and drive off to the office to commit obscenities.[51]

Because the work is a memoir rather than a novel, a work of nonfiction rather than fiction, Coetzee maintains that Breytenbach is not faced with the dilemma of representing the person of the torturer. He does not have to "justify a concern with morally dubious people involved in a contemptible activity."[52] Coetzee's idea is that the writer of nonfiction avoids the ethical horn of the dilemma as the intention behind his work is not subject to the same criticism as that of the novelist. The nonfiction writer is not accused of perverse fascination with the torturers' world, but is assumed to be motivated by revealing that world to those from whom it is hidden (i.e., exposing the world of apartheid's secret police to white South Africans so that they are aware of the crimes against humanity committed by their government). Pauw offers support for this claim when he states that regardless of one's opinion of Dirk Coetzee's motives, he has performed a service to society:

> Many of the people of Nazi Germany would later say: "Wir haben es nicht gewusst" (We did not know). South Africans will have no such excuse. Dirk Coetzee has warned us all.[53]

The novelist, writing about fictional torturers, cannot claim to be serving such a purpose and therefore—according to J. M. Coetzee—needs to justify his or her literary activity.

One could respond to Coetzee's claim about the difference in the motives attributed to novelists and journalists by pointing to *Waiting for the Barbarians* itself. Despite its status as not only fiction, but allegorical fiction without a clear spatiotemporal location, the novel provides a wealth of information about the nature of empires. As Anthony Burgess writes in his review, the work "is not about anywhere, and hence it is about everywhere."[54] There are two separate questions that bear on the distinction made by Coetzee: first, the various differences between fiction and nonfiction, and second, the relation between fiction and truth. Both have generated a vast amount of philosophical and critical discussion to which I have no wish to contribute beyond my brief comments in chapters 4 and 6. What is significant for my purposes is that both *Waiting for the Barbarians* and *In the Heart of the Whore* are exemplary narratives whose ethical value is realised by narrative sensibility. I shall therefore set aside the question of if and how fictions reveal truth about the world and accept that the novelist faces a dilemma with regard to the representation of torture that the journalist does not: unlike the journalist, the novelist is required to justify his or her concern with the person of the torturer.

I now want to suggest that the structure of *In the Heart of the Whore*—which represents the relevant sequence of events as a narrative in which Dirk Coetzee is the protagonist—places Pauw in a parallel dilemma to that of J. M. Coetzee in *Waiting for the Barbarians*. As noted in section 33, more than a third of Pauw's book is devoted to Dirk Coetzee's story. Pauw is writing an exposé of the death squads rather than a biography of one or more of the members thereof and thus has no need to accord a single assassin such prominence. Coetzee's role in the history of the death squads is furthermore relatively minor. He happened to be in charge of C10 when it was re-designated as a counterinsurgency unit, but he spent only five months on operations. De Kock served as the unit's commander from 1983 until it was disbanded in 1993 and became South Africa's most notorious secret policeman. Coetzee was not even the first assassin whose story appeared in print: four weeks prior to the publication of Pauw's article, Butana Almond Nofemela, one of Coetzee's former *askaris*, disclosed details of his C10 service in an attempt to delay his impending execution for the murder of a white farmer in 1987.[55] Similarly, while the existence of C10 is shocking, the police unit pales in comparison with the CCB, due to the latter's almost complete lack of accountability. The CCB was formed as a private company rather than a branch of the South African government, and its only point of contact with the government was through the chief of the SADF's Special Forces. The absolute autonomy afforded the CCB caused so much confusion that it is still unknown whether the murder of Anton Lubowski in 1989 was part of their attempts to disrupt Namibian independence or an inadvertent blue-on-blue assassination of another apartheid agent.[56] Pauw's exposé is focused on the CCB, formed three years after Coetzee's expulsion from the fold of the South African security services, and his decision to employ Coetzee as the protagonist of his narrative creates a journalist's version of the novelist's dilemma.

In Carroll's introduction to his article on *The Sopranos*, he states his intent as solving the problem of "how a viewer can be sympathetic (care for, or have a pro-attitude) toward a fictional character whose real-world counterpart she would abhor totally."[57] In Pauw's case, the problem is how to maintain the interest of a reader in a real person whom she has every reason to despise. Articulated in this way, Pauw's dilemma is very similar to J. M. Coetzee's. Where J. M. Coetzee is required to justify his literary interest in an ethically reprehensible character, Pauw is required to justify his selection of an ethically reprehensible character as his protagonist. Coetzee cannot excuse himself on the basis of revealing the truth (because he is writing fiction, given my assumptions above), but Pauw cannot excuse himself on the basis of revealing the truth either, because he could simply have devoted a single chapter to Coetzee in the manner of Lesia and Bezuidenhout. Coetzee must justify his selection of the content (the person of the torturer) of his novel, and Pauw must justify his selection of the form of his narrative (Dirk Coetzee as protagonist). J. M. Coetzee's dilemma can be adjusted for Pauw as: either failing ethically by glamourizing Dirk Coetzee's world or failing aesthetically by portraying Dirk Coetzee's character in cliché. Pauw's dilemma is in fact more pressing than J. M. Coetzee's. Many viewers would find no inconsistency in being happy to see Tony Soprano escape the clutches of the law and happy to see his real-world counterpart imprisoned for life.[58] If, however, one takes an interest in Dirk Coetzee's character, motivation, and morality—as Pauw intends—then one faces disturbing questions about justice. These questions have recently been brought into focus with the controversy surrounding the release of de Kock, just twenty years into his sentence of 212 years for a host of death squad activities.[59] Once again, I am approaching the issue of the difference between fiction and nonfiction, so I shall conclude my line of thought by stating that the necessary dilemma faced by the novelist and the dilemma Pauw imposes on himself are sufficiently alike to admit of a similar solution. In other words, J. M. Coetzee could have employed Pauw's solution to the problem of the representation of the person of the torturer, but he did not.

I described Pauw's pattern of comparison and contrast in section 33, and his representation of Dirk Coetzee in *In the Heart of the Whore* exposes J. M. Coetzee's second dilemma as false. J. M. Coetzee's resolution of the first dilemma, the representation of torture in the novel, is—as Van Zanten Gallagher and many others have noted—inspired. He nonetheless fails to resolve the second dilemma, impaling himself on the aesthetic horn and portraying his torturers as (literally) faceless functionaries. In contrast, Pauw's depiction of Dirk Coetzee's character as multifaceted and conflicted, combining serious ethical flaws with virtues like sincerity and loyalty, is neither an ethical nor an aesthetic failing. To this extent, the novelist as well as the journalist can represent the person of the torturer without compromise. For all its much-deserved literary status, *Waiting for the Barbarians* is aesthetically flawed to the extent that it resorts to clichés in the representation of Joll and Mandel. Paraphrasing Pauw and Coetzee, one might call the novel a missed opportunity to fold the flesh of the torturers aside and peer into their souls. The aesthetic flaw in *Waiting for the Barbarians* is revealed by the combination of aesthetic and ethical value in *In the Heart of the*

Whore. The comparison of the two exemplary narratives demonstrates that narrative representation can promote greater responsiveness on the part of readers without promoting an unethical response (i.e., exemplary narratives can provide a means to the end of understanding the psychology of criminal inhumanity).

NOTES

1. For an informed discussion of the various labels employed for apartheid, see: Anne McClintock and Rob Nixon, "No Names Apart: The Separation of Word and History in Derrida's 'Le Dernier Mot du Racisme,'" *Critical Inquiry* 13 (1986): 140–54.

2. Derek Attridge, *J. M. Coetzee and the Ethics of Reading: Literature in the Event* (Chicago: University of Chicago Press, 2004), 2.

3. J. M. Coetzee, "Into the Dark Chamber: The Novelist and South Africa," *New York Times*, 12 January 1986. Available at: http://www.nytimes.com/books/97/11/02/home/coetzee-chamber.html.

4. The unit is most commonly referred to by the name of its base, Vlakplaas, and its counterinsurgency (COIN) role. In keeping with the government's attempts to hide the existence of a police death squad, the official designation was subsequently changed at least once, to C1. I shall use "C10" for the rest of this chapter. See: Pumla Gobodo-Madikizela, *A Human Being Died That Night: Forgiving Apartheid's Chief Killer* (London: Portobello, 2006), 74; Jacques Pauw, *Dances with Devils: A Journalist's Search for Truth* (Cape Town: Struik, 2006), 125–51.

5. Jacques Pauw, *In the Heart of the Whore: The Story of Apartheid's Death Squads* (Johannesburg: Southern Book Publishers, 1992), 180.

6. Coetzee, "Into the Dark Chamber."

7. Coetzee returned to this dilemma in "The Problem of Evil," a short story first published in *Salmagundi* and subsequently included in *Elizabeth Costello* (both in 2003). In "The Problem of Evil" he discusses the *person of the hangman* and focuses on the effects of representing evil on the author rather than on his or her readers. Employing the voice of his fictional alter ego, Elizabeth Costello, he claims: "I do not think one can come away unscathed, as a writer, from conjuring up such scenes. I think writing like that can harm one" (J. M. Coetzee, *Elizabeth Costello: Eight Lessons* [London: Vintage, 2004], 172).

8. Coetzee, "Into the Dark Chamber."

9. Coetzee, "Into the Dark Chamber."

10. The representation of a clichéd agent is a *pro tanto* flaw in an exemplary narrative qua exemplary narrative in virtue of being oversimplified and one-dimensional.

11. Susan Van Zanten Gallagher, "Torture and the Novel: J. M. Coetzee's *Waiting for the Barbarians*," *Contemporary Literature* 29 (1988): 277–85.

12. Van Zanten Gallagher, "Torture and the Novel," 281.

13. J. M. Coetzee, *Waiting for the Barbarians* (London: Penguin, 1980), 79.

14. Van Zanten Gallagher, "Torture and the Novel," 282.

15. Coetzee, *Waiting for the Barbarians*, 118.

16. Coetzee, *Waiting for the Barbarians*, 44.

17. Van Zanten Gallagher, "Torture and the Novel," 284.

18. Coetzee, *Waiting for the Barbarians*, 135.

19. Van Zanten Gallagher, "Torture and the Novel," 284.

20. Jacques Pauw quoted in John Battersby, "Admitting White Guilt," *The World Today* 53 (1997): 24.

21. Coetzee, *Waiting for the Barbarians*, 4.

22. Coetzee, *Waiting for the Barbarians*, 116.

23. Coetzee, *Waiting for the Barbarians*, 84.

24. Coetzee, *Waiting for the Barbarians*, 126.

25. Coetzee, *Waiting for the Barbarians*, 118.

26. Coetzee, *Waiting for the Barbarians*, 146.

27. Coetzee, "Into the Dark Chamber."

28. Pauw, *Heart of the Whore*, 264–69.

29. Pauw, *Heart of the Whore*, 200–202.

30. Pauw, *Heart of the Whore*, iii.

31. Pauw, *Heart of the Whore*, 27.

32. Pauw, *Heart of the Whore*, 64, 71, 112.

33. Pauw, *Heart of the Whore*, 73–75.

34. Pauw, *Heart of the Whore*, 219–26.

35. Pauw, *Heart of the Whore*, 220.

36. Pauw, *Heart of the Whore*, 72.

37. Pauw, *Heart of the Whore*, 71.

38. Tina Rosenberg, "A South African Killer Goes Free," *New York Times*, 11 August 1997. Available at: http://www.nytimes.com/1997/08/11/opinion/a-south-african-killer-goes-free.html.

39. Pauw, *Heart of the Whore*, 12.

40. Pauw, *Heart of the Whore*, 171.

41. Pauw, *Heart of the Whore*, 173.

42. Pauw, *Heart of the Whore*, 174.

43. Pauw, *Heart of the Whore*, 186.

44. Pauw, *Heart of the Whore*, 189.

45. Pauw, *Heart of the Whore*, 176.

46. Pauw, *Heart of the Whore*, 262. James Stevens was a police officer who covered up crimes committed by Eugene de Kock, then worked for the ANC, and finally betrayed them and Coetzee. Like Botes, his motive seems to have been pure self-interest.

47. Carroll, *Minerva's Night Out*, 242.

48. Carroll, *Minerva's Night Out*, 243.

49. Hume, *Human Nature*, I.4.vi: 674.

50. See: Gavin Evans, "Dirk Coetzee: Death Squad Commander Who Helped Expose Apartheid's Killing Machine," *The Independent*, 12 March 2013. Available

at: http://www.independent.co.uk/news/obituaries/dirk-coetzee-death-squad-comm ander-who-helped-expose-apartheids-killing-machine-8530136.html. As a point of interest, J. M. Coetzee also clashed with the ANC government, emigrating to Australia in 2002. See: Lucy Valerie Graham, *State of Peril: Race and Rape in South African Literature* (New York: Oxford University Press, 2012), 3.

51. Coetzee, "Into the Dark Chamber."

52. Coetzee, "Into the Dark Chamber."

53. Pauw, *Heart of the Whore*, 75.

54. Anthony Burgess quoted in Van Zanten Gallagher, "Torture and the Novel," 281.

55. Pauw, *Heart of the Whore*, 22–23.

56. Pauw, *Heart of the Whore*, 165.

57. Carroll, *Minerva's Night Out*, 235.

58. I mentioned this type of dichotomy in my discussion of Ian McKellen's Richard of Gloucester in section 17.

59. David Smith, "South African Death Squad Leader Eugene de Kock to Be Freed from Jail," *The Guardian*, 30 January 2015. Available at: http://www.theguardian. com/world/2015/jan/30/south-africa-eugene-de-kock-released-prime-evil.

Chapter Nine

Undermining Inhumanity

The purpose of this chapter is to demonstrate narrative justice (i.e., to show how a pair of exemplary narratives can be employed to reduce criminal inhumanity by undermining extremist recruitment strategies). Specifically, the thesis is used to identify the white supremacist and Muslim fundamentalist conceptions of victimhood as identical. In section 35, I explain Ajit Maan's narrative counterterror strategy as set out in *Counter-Terrorism: Narrative Strategies*. Section 36 examines "white genocide" as the conceptual core of the white supremacist master narrative and analyses Gustavo Semeria's article "Argentina: A Mirror of Your Future" as an example of a white-genocide-based narrative. In section 37, I examine "crusader" as the conceptual core of the Muslim fundamentalist master narrative, using the pseudonymous Umm Sulaym's autobiographical article "The Hijrah of Umm Sulaym al-Muhajirah" as an example of a crusader-based narrative. I compare the white genocide and crusader concepts in section 38, arguing not only that they are two aspects of the concept of *deliverance* but that their identity can be used as the basis of a soft power counterterror strategy. I conclude, in section 39, with a reflection on the methods employed in chapters 7, 8, and 9, delineating a methodology by means of which narrative justice can be applied in practice.

35. NARRATIVE STRATEGIES

In her slim monograph *Counter-Terrorism: Narrative Strategies*, Ajit Maan argues that narrative representations are essentially strategic and that—despite appearances to the contrary—complex narratives are more robust than simple narratives. She then argues for the employment of alternative narratives rather than counternarratives in the soft power approach to reducing terrorist recruitment. Drawing on the work of Joseph Nye, Alex Schmid distinguishes soft (or non-kinetic) power from hard (or kinetic) power on the basis that the former aims to recruit allies and the latter to kill enemies.[1] Soft power approaches employ rhetoric as a tool of persuasion while hard power approaches employ force as a tool of coercion. Narrative strategies are clearly an element of the former category. The European Commission's Radicalisation Awareness Network (RAN) identifies three types of counternarrative:

(a) Alternative narratives: "Undercut violent extremist narratives by focusing on what we are 'for' rather than 'against;'"[2]
(b) Counternarratives: "Directly deconstruct, discredit and demystify violent extremist messaging;"[3] and
(c) Government strategic communications: "Undercut extremist narratives by explaining government policy and rationale."[4]

Although the purpose of Maan's book is, as the title suggests, to advance a narrative strategy that reduces the impact of terrorist recruitment narratives, she maintains that the work is also itself "a counter-terrorist narrative that confronts terrorist recruitment narratives head-on," on the basis that it both deconstructs those narratives and sketches the framework for successful alternative narratives.[5]

Maan's characterisation of narrative representation is similar to my own in many respects, although she is insistent that there is no generally accepted, universal, and cross-cultural definition of a story or narrative.[6] Narratives nonetheless:

> convey a specific understanding of the events they are about. And this understanding involves a particular way of organizing events. And in this way, narrative, by its very nature, is strategic and its strategic nature is inseparable from its form. Narrative bestows meaning on what were previously just a series of events that are sometimes related and sometimes not related. It ties together events in a certain way for a certain purpose.[7]

The purpose is persuasion, and the means by which the end of persuasion is achieved is identification by the audience. The form of a narrative representation determines its content, and the structure of the fundamentalist or *Master Narrative* manipulates tactically by means of:

1. temporal order (because simply switching the order of events will alter moral responsibility),

2. unity or coherence (because this type of narrative leaves no room for anomalies or exceptions or change), and
3. linearity (because all current events fit into the middle which is the conflict stage. The end is only projected and there will be endless disagreement about where the "beginning" was . . .).[8]

Maan provides two examples of pathologizing master narratives, where *pathologizing narratives* are understood as "narratives that encourage individual audience members to internalize the description of diseased social/political situation."[9] Her first text is "Intro Material for People New to Stormfront," an introduction to Stormfront.org, the internet's first popular hate website, which currently serves as a meeting place for white supremacists worldwide by means of bulletin boards, forums, and chatrooms. The second is the World Islamic Front Statement, "Jihad Against Jews and Crusaders," the *fatwa* issued by Osama bin Laden on 23 February 1998. By performing a comparative analysis of these two texts, Maan reveals a variety of unverified premises, factual inconsistencies, faulty analogies, and logical fallacies. Her analysis not only exposes both texts as flawed, but as two instantiations of the same master narrative:

(i) In the beginning, our people lived in utopia.
(ii) Then others arrived and took over.
(iii) This brings us to the present, where we have two choices.
(iv) We can either do nothing, in which case the situation will remain as it is now, or we can expel these others and restore the utopia in such a way that it is never threatened again.[10]

In the Stormfront version, *our people* are whites and the *others* non-whites; in the World Islamic Front version, *our people* are Muslims and the *others* unbelievers.[11] Both versions "begin with paradise (past), move to paradise lost (present), then foresee paradise regained (future)."[12] Both versions conclude by placing the audience in the postlapsarian present: the fall from grace has already occurred, in consequence of which the in-group has only two options: to live in dystopia or to expel the out-group and regain utopia. The narrative form is nonetheless identical. The purpose of the narrative is to persuade the in-group to take up arms against the out-group, and the means by which this end is achieved is identification—not just with the in-group, but with the in-group represented as victims in virtue of the perspectival, artistic, and rhetorical devices deployed. Maan refers to this master narrative by the title of *Victim*. The power of the victim narrative is "getting the listener first to identify with victim status and then to blame himself for the future victimization of other people ('his' people) unless he takes violent action."[13]

Maan characterises this pathologizing master narrative as a form of psychological warfare, argues that terrorism is simply a variety of colonialism, and that colonising narratives "work to ascribe identity in the interest of getting individuals to regulate themselves."[14] Colonising narratives, including terrorist recruitment narratives, have four essential features: structure, description, identity, and prescription.[15] *Structure* refers to the temporal order of the master narrative, by means of which causation is established. *Description* involves the use of disguised but faulty analogies and the creation of artificial dichotomies—for example, to either expel the out-group or be subject to their rule. *Identity* is performed by the audience, who identifies with the in-group, internalises the victimhood, and takes responsibility for the bifurcated future trajectories. Description becomes *prescription* when the invitation to follow a particular course of action—violence against the out-group—is accepted by the audience.[16] Maan's aim in her comparative analysis is to call the victim narrative into question by exposing the normalising function of master narratives, but the purpose of *Narrative Strategies* is to direct soft counter-terrorist efforts—particularly those in the contemporary United States—toward the use of alternative narratives rather than counternarratives.

Maan claims that the Global War on Terrorism—or War on Terror as it is most commonly called—is primarily an ideological struggle rather than a military conflict. "War on Terror" is derived from the phrase *war on terrorism*, which was employed by President George W. Bush in a press release on 16 September 2001, in which he stated: "This crusade, this war on terrorism is going to take a while."[17] Terrorism is a type of violence, not an enemy in itself, and the religious ideology that inspired the September 11 attacks cannot be defeated by either conventional or unconventional military tactics. Maan is concerned that in consequence of the widespread trauma caused by 9/11, the War on Terror has developed into a master narrative that has become embedded in American national identity.[18] There are two problems with this state of affairs. The first is that master narratives are weak narratives. While they may exert great normative power, they are vulnerable to precisely the kind of deconstructive analysis to which Maan subjects the Stormfront and World Islamic Front narratives. Like all master narratives, the War on Terror involves the imposition of a temporal order, unity, and linearity on a sequence of events in order to prohibit, exclude, or marginalise conflicting interpretations of those events. As such, it is a weak narrative, and a successful counterterror narrative strategy must be complex rather than simple: "Conceptualizing and advertising an American narrative that encompasses difference, even conflict, without being threatened by it is essential. Our narrative should welcome conflict."[19]

The second problem is that even if one is not persuaded by the weakness inherent in the simplicity of master narratives, the War on Terror is a counternarrative rather than an alternative narrative. RAN defines the former in terms of direct opposition to terrorist narratives and the latter in terms of indirect opposition by means of focus on a different narrative. Although RAN employs terms such as a *deconstruct* and *discredit* for counternarratives, Maan is sceptical of the power of the counternarrative as it defines "itself by recourse to the problem as defined and framed by terrorists."[20] In other words, the War on Terror narrative accepts the frame of reference established by the World Islamic Front, fails to engage in the ideological struggle, and results in the reliance of counterterror on hard power—which, at the time of writing, has produced a decade of insurgency in Iraq (followed by an Iraqi Civil War) and seventeen years of insurgency in Afghanistan, not to mention less obvious consequences like the Syrian Civil War. The War on Terror/World Islamic Front narrative is a victim master narrative embraced by both sides in the conflict, each of which identifies with victimhood—as victims of Muslim fundamentalism or as victims of American imperialism. The narrative thus preserves and promotes conflict rather than reducing or terminating it: "The 'war on terror' is the war Al Qaeda thinks of itself as fighting."[21]

Maan argues that narrative counterterrorist strategies must be counter-fundamentalist, but that all master narratives are essentially fundamentalist in virtue of imposing a specific, exclusive linearity and unity on a sequence of events. Complex narratives, which accommodate and even encourage dissent, difference, and coexistent multiplicity, are more robust because of their broader appeal. Although apparently weaker in admitting their own imperfection, inclusive narratives are ultimately stronger:

> long before the events of 9/11 an American narrative has been one of inclusion. An American narrative must carefully avoid mirroring fundamentalist rhetoric by not forcing individuals to make a choice between religious beliefs and nationality.[22]

Accepting the World Islamic Front's terms of reference—identifying as either a Muslim or an American—merely sustains and encourages conflict, and the lengthy and inconclusive nature of hard power attempts to win the War on Terror in spite of the U.S.'s overwhelming military and economic superiority vindicate Maan's view of the conflict as primarily ideological. The War on Terror narrative has not only accepted the frame of reference of its opponents, but has also played into their hands with respect to a particularly powerful conception of victimhood—*crusader*—which I discuss in detail in section 37. I noted Bush's use of *crusade* when coining *war on terrorism* above, of which Maan states: "It is hard to imagine a more counter-productive reference."[23] Maan's message is thus that the military War on Terror is motivated and sustained by a War on Terror counternarrative that motivates and sustains its own opposition. Joe Haldeman's science-fiction masterpiece *The Forever War* was published in 1974, in the context of the Second Indochina War, which is now acknowledged to have lasted twenty years (1955 to 1975). The War on Terror began in 2001 and seems likely to last even longer because, unlike the Second Indochina War, it will not be won (or lost) when territory is secured from (or ceded to) the enemy.

Although Maan makes a convincing case for a revision of counterterror strategy in general and soft power strategy in particular, I want to focus on the initial part of her argument, the comparative analysis of two texts and the critique of the master narrative of which they are both instantiations. She selects her two examples on the basis that each is "a call to global violence" and representative of "the type of strategic communication employed by extremist groups."[24] The World Islamic Front for Holy War against Jews and Crusaders is considered either identical to or part of the International Islamic Front, which was established by Osama bin Laden with the declaration to which Maan refers on 23 February 1998 and followed bin Laden's famous *fatwa* against Americans in the Middle East, published in *Al-Quds Al-Arabi* on 23 August 1996. Where the 1998 declaration is a straightforward call to action and recruitment drive for Al-Qaeda, the link between Stormfront and terrorism is not as explicit or direct. Stormfront is a website rather than an organisation, established in 1995 by Don Black, a former member of the Ku Klux Klan. Stormfront provides services such as chat rooms and a radio network, but it is principally a meeting place for and dissemination point of white supremacist groups and material across the globe, as reflected in the motto "White pride, world wide." The introduction that Maan quotes has been updated to the "Introduction to Stormfront" page and lists thirteen additional "recommended respectable pro-White groups and organizations," including the magazine *American Renaissance*, which I discuss in section 36.[25] In order to explore the implications of Maan's analysis for narrative justice, I shall employ two exemplary narratives from 2017, selected on the basis of being representative of their respective publications and being similar in length (roughly that of a review essay).

36. WHITE GENOCIDE

Following Maan, my first example is from a white supremacist publication rather than a recognised terrorist organisation. I have adopted this approach in consequence of the character of the most significant white supremacist terror attacks, assessed in terms of both loss of life and psychological impact. While first Al-Qaeda and most recently ad-Dawlah al-Islāmiyah (Islamic State, IS) have dominated Islamist terrorism in the twenty-first century, white supremacist terrorism is currently dominated by the phenomenon of the lone wolf, which Ramón Spaaij defines as follows:

> Lone wolf terrorism involves terrorist attacks carried out by persons who (a) operate individually, (b) do not belong to an organized terrorist group or network, and (c) whose modi operandi are conceived and directed by the individual without any direct outside command or hierarchy.[26]

At the time of writing, the two most notorious white supremacist acts of terror have been the 2011 Norway attacks and the Charleston church shooting. In the former, Anders Behring Breivik killed seventy-seven people in two separate attacks in Norway on 22 July 2011; and in the latter, Dylann Roof killed nine people at the Emanuel African Methodist Episcopal Church in Charleston (South Carolina) on 17 June 2015.[27] Breivik and Roof were arrested, tried, convicted, and sentenced as severely as the respective legal systems permitted. Both men made use of the internet to publish manifestos. Breivik emailed a 1,518-word document titled "2083: A European Declaration of Independence" to 1,003 email addresses shortly before he began his attacks. Roof maintained a website called *The Last Rhodesian*, on which he published a five-page manifesto and a photo diary.[28] Both manifestos are explicit about the white race being under threat and about the threat being particularly significant in Europe. Breivik is primarily concerned about the threat from Muslims, and Roof about the threat from blacks. Roof does not use "genocide" at all, but Breivik discusses the Armenian Genocide (1914–1922) as an example of an "anti-Christian jihad" (usually translated as "holy war").[29] The two manifestos nonetheless have their origins in *white genocide*, a concept that motivates and sustains white supremacist organisations worldwide.

The idea that the white race requires protection and defence is not new, but the conception of white victimhood as a call to global violence originates with *The Turner Diaries*, a novel published by William Luther Pierce in 1978.[30] The novel is set in the U.S. in 1999, where a Jewish government attempts to disarm the population by means of black law enforcement officers. The white supremacists revolt and first embark upon a war and then a genocide to restore the country to its racial purity. The work provided inspiration for a terrorist organisation named The Order, which was operational in America from 1983 until 1985, when it was dismantled by the FBI in a series of arrests.[31] One if its members, David Lane, was incarcerated until his death in 2007. Lane wrote extensively in prison, and his publications included the three-page "White Genocide Manifesto," which was condensed into his "14 words" slogan: "We must secure the existence of our people and a future for White children."[32] The key points of Lane's mission statement are summarised by the White GeNOcide Project as:

(a) Anti-racist is a codeword for anti-White.
(b) Diversity is a codeword for White Genocide.
(c) It's not mixing the races (only the white race).[33]

Proponents of white genocide also refer to the legal apparatus to enforce respect and tolerance as "forced assimilation" and maintain that the combination of forced assimilation with mass immigration has created a situation in which the white race is victim to what Nicole Rafter calls a cultural genocide.[34] Many proponents of white genocide hold Jews as being responsible, although a few influential figures, such as Jared Taylor (editor of *American Renaissance*), include Jews as white and thus as fellow victims of genocide. White genocide is referred to as the "white genocide conspiracy theory" on Wikipedia, and the white genocide agenda is promoted by means of #whitegenocide on Twitter.

"Argentina: A Mirror of Your Future" is a feature article by Gustavo Semeria that was published by *American Renaissance* on 14 April 2017 and selected as one of the editor's recommendations for 2017—one of three in the "Correct History" category.[35] The article is subtitled "How Demographic Change Can Destroy a Country" and appears to be Semeria's only contribution to the magazine. He writes in a journalistic style, and the first paragraph serves as a lead:

> Argentina is a distant mirror that reflects what may be North America's future. My country is a small-scale laboratory of the effects of migration: A suitable migration policy can transform a nation for the good; a wrong one spoils it.[36]

The article is divided into four subtitled sections: "The Emergence of a Great Nation," "The Decline," "Segregation," and "Conclusion." The first introduces the Great Immigration (1880–1914), during which active recruitment by the Argentinian government produced a migration of six million people from Western Europe. This is followed by a discussion of the success of the country in the first three decades of the twentieth century—economically, culturally, and socially—which is emphasised by photographs of great works of architecture from the period. The second section proposes that the subsequent decline in prosperity, education, and security was the result of four factors: the Great Depression, the end of European immigration, the increase in urbanisation, and immigration from Paraguay, Bolivia, Peru, and Chile. The latter two factors involved the arrival of large numbers of "Mestizos and Amerindians" in Argentina's cities, a phenomenon that "White Argentina" ignored.[37] Immigration from South American countries continued throughout the twentieth century, and Semeria claims that it was only in the twenty-first century that some formal control and regulation was introduced. He provides a graph that shows the increasing proportion of foreigners in Argentina that are "not white" from 1980 to 2015.[38] He estimates that 40 percent of the current population is non-white and claims that the relation between this figure and the poor economic and social conditions of Argentina's cities is causal rather than correlational. Interestingly, however, the white supremacist history loses focus at this point, when Semeria states that, "Unlike the European influx, there has been no planning for recent immigration."[39] This is the second occasion on which the lack of planning is mentioned, which suggests that even within Semeria's narrative framework, the problems identified may be at least partly related to the failure of the authorities to manage (as opposed to prevent) the immigration.

In the third section, Semeria discusses the rise of the gated community in the latter half of the twentieth century, in response to the increase in immigration and (causally) commensurate increase in crime. He claims that there are now nearly one thousand gated communities in Argentina, covering hundreds of square miles and housing hundreds of thousands of people. He uses the example of the Nordelta Complex to show that some of these communities have evolved into self-sufficient, self-governing towns to become "real walled citadels."[40] The inhabitants of these citadels are almost all white, an inversion of the other type of secure domicile in Argentina—its prisons, which are almost all non-white. The object in Semeria's mirror image is revealed at this point: Argentinians (white Argentinians, who seem to be the only ones that matter) ignore racial divisions in society and are responsible for its present state because they have failed to take action against the destructive invasion by non-white immigrants in the past. "They refuse to see the connection between race and such things as poverty and crime. They repeat the mantra that improved education and welfare will solve all problems."[41] The conclusion attempts to shape the first three sections into the semblance of an argument for the causal relation between non-white immigration and national decline. In the final paragraph, Semeria reveals the reflection in the mirror image, addresses the (American) readers of *American Renaissance* directly, and issues his call to action:

> In both North and South America, Hispanics are pushing relentlessly towards the higher latitudes. You Americans still have a Hispanic population that is only 17 percent of the total, a figure we reached in the 1970s. Argentina is a mirror that shows what your country will be like when that figure reaches 40 percent.[42]

Semeria's article thus instantiates a more sophisticated version of Maan's victim master narrative. The narrative history begins at a neutral state: Argentina gaining independence from Spain in the early nineteenth century and establishing itself as a democracy in the middle of that century. This is followed by the rise to prosperity on the back of the European immigrants of the late nineteenth and early twentieth centuries. Prosperity is followed by national decline courtesy of the Hispanic immigrants, and the decline is exacerbated at the end of the twentieth century by the return of democracy to Argentina, which brings Semeria to the problematic present. He then abstracts the central theme of this narrative—the causal relation between Hispanic immigrants and economic, cultural, and social decline— and uses it as a scale (rather than a mirror) to predict American decline, actually suggesting that the percentage of the US Hispanic population is the single (or at least the single most important) factor in predicting the nation's future prosperity. So instead of a simple progression from paradise to para- dise lost to a call to action, Semeria produces a (linear) chronology on which Argentina is further ahead than America: decolonisation and democracy, paradise gained, paradise lost, and the current descent into multiracial hell. Semeria's narrative does not make explicit mention of white genocide, but it promotes the agenda of the White GeNOcide Project and issues an explicit call to take action against Hispanic immigrants: in America, paradise has (also) been lost, but—in contrast to Argentina—it can still be regained (i.e., *you American whites have not yet reached the crisis, but I have provided you with a good reason to act now*). This narrative, and the characterisation of Hispanic hordes "pushing relentlessly towards higher latitudes," no doubt has great resonance with most *American Renaissance* readers and with many of those in the Republican Party who support Donald Trump's as yet unreal- ised plan to build a border wall with Mexico. Again, it would be an exag- geration to describe Trump as being motivated by white genocide, but the controversial policies he has either introduced or endorsed since his inaug- uration—neatly summarised by the hashtags #MuslimBan, #HispanicPurge, and #massincarceration (of African Americans)—are implicitly complicit with the white genocide agenda.

37. CRUSADER

Within Salafi jihadism, the concept of the "crusader" serves a similar role to that of white genocide in white supremacism. The term is employed in the title of the World Islamic Front statement referred to by Maan and appears in the fifth paragraph of Osama bin Laden's *fatwa* of 1996 as the "Jewish- Crusaders alliance."[43] As noted by Maan, bin Laden was (among others) responsible for disseminating the view that the conflicts in the Middle East in the last decade of the twentieth century were part of a historical and global attack on Islam that should be resisted by jihad.[44] In their introduction to *Jihadism Transformed: Al-Qaeda and Islamic State's Global Battle of Ideas*, Simon Staffell and Akil Awan state that "the adversary in this 'war on Islam' is often blurred into the 'West' or the 'crusaders,' drawing on particular historical themes and collective memory."[45] The significance of "crusader" to the rationale for and justification of jihad is immediately evident in even the briefest look at the latest available issues of *Inspire* and *Dabiq*. The former is *Al-Qaeda* in the Arabian Peninsula's English-language online magazine, which was first published in June 2010 and most recently published in August 2017 (issue 17); the latter is the first of the IS's two English-language online magazines, first published in July 2014 and most recently published in July 2016 (issue 15). Issue 17 of *Inspire* is titled *Train Derail Operations*, and the contents pages are followed by an "Editor's Letter" that begins with: "In the midst of this great war between Muslims and the Crusaders, came the call from each party to confront one another."[46] Issue 15 of *Dabiq* is titled *Break the Cross*, and the foreword begins with a quote from the Qur'an and proceeds as follows:

> After the attacks in Orlando (USA), Dhaka (Bangladesh), Magnanville, Nice, and Normandy (France), and Würzburg and Ansbach (Germany) led to the martyrdom of twelve soldiers of the Caliphate and the deaths and injuries of more than six hundred Crusaders, one would expect the cross-worshipers and democratic pagans of the West to pause and contemplate the reasons behind the animosity and enmity held by Muslims for Westerners and even take heed and consider repentance by abandoning their infidelity and accepting Islam.[47]

The titles and opening sentences of each of the above magazines are indicative of their respective emphases in mobilising jihad. *Inspire* has more of a hard power focus, and eighteen of the forty-eight interior pages of issue 17 comprise detailed instructions on how to derail trains in the U.S. *Dabiq* has more of a soft power focus, on the battle of religious and philosophical ideals and ideas, with the "Operations" report comprising only six of the eighty interior pages of issue 15. With this is mind, it is not surprising that it was *Dabiq* rather than *Inspire* that dedicated a whole issue to the crusader concept: *The Failed Crusade* (issue 4, published in September 2014). The issue contains only four (of fifty-four) pages on "Military Operations," and most of the articles are aimed at either: (a) justifying the IS's existence and conduct, or (b) reassuring readers that the crusade against the Caliphate (a worldwide Muslim authority) will fail and that Rome will in fact be conquered by the Caliphate. Despite the distinct approaches, Haroro Ingram argues that both publications provide:

> a "competitive system of meaning" (i.e., an alternative perspective of the world compared to that presented by their opponents), that acts as a "lens" through which to shape their supporters' perceptions, polarize their support, and, ultimately, convince them to mobilize.[48]

Ingram's use of *system of meaning* and *lens* recalls the framework of exemplary narratives, and *Inspire* and *Dabiq* employ *crusader* as a conception of victimhood that underpins their shared master narrative. In section 35 I quoted Maan's commentary on Bush's inadvertent promotion of jihadism by immediately identifying (and associating) the War on Terror as (with the concept of) a crusade.[49] This error was compounded first by the use of *war* to describe the response to 9/11, and second by the use of *axis of evil* in preparation for the Iraq War. Where the former legitimises insurgents as enemy combatants rather than dangerous criminals, the latter provides further evidence for the victim master narrative (two of the three countries to which it refers are majority Muslim) and thus the justification of jihad.

Rumiyah ("Rome" in Arabic) is the IS's second English-language publication. The online magazine was first released in September 2016, and during September and October of 2016, issues of both *Dabiq* and *Rumiyah* were published. The latter appears to have replaced the former, and the change may have been motivated by military developments. Dabiq is a town on the Syrian side of the Syrian-Turkish border with special significance for IS and fell to them in August 2014 (a month after the first issue of *Dabiq* was published). The town was lost to Turkish-Syrian forces in October 2016 and the fact that it had been first gained and then lost served to draw attention to the IS's reversal of fortune (as opposed to Rome, which remains a conveniently distant ultimate objective).[50] *Rumiyah* was published on a monthly basis until its thirteenth issue, which is titled *Allah Cast Terror into Their Hearts* and was released in September 2017. The magazine follows the focus and style of *Dabiq* and issue 17 includes the article "The Hijrah of Umm Sulaym al-Muhajirah." *Hijrah* (also *hijra* or *hegira*) refers specifically to Muhammad's migration from Mecca to Medina in 622, from which the Muslim calendar is dated, and is understood more generally as a flight from persecution.[51] The article is presented as the autobiographical account of Umm Sulaym (a pseudonym that recalls one of Muhammad's earliest and most faithful female companions), an Australian woman who left home with her young children to join the IS in Syria at an undisclosed time in the recent past.[52] Although the article is written in a confessional rather than journalistic style, the opening paragraph serves as a lead, and the first sentence reads: "My hijrah to the Islamic State was a journey not unlike that undertaken by many others who sought to leave the lands of kufr and reside in the lands of tawhid."[53] A *kufr* (also *kafir*) is one who denies the truth or an unbeliever and *tawhid* is the foundation of the Muslim faith (belief in the indivisible oneness of God).[54] The article is divided into six subtitled sections: "The News of My Previous Husband's Shahadah [profession of faith]," "The Murtaddin [apostates] Are Exposed and the Mujahidin [jihadists] Remain True," "The First Steps on the Path of Hijrah," "Imprisoned by the Murtadd Turkish Forces," "From the

Hands of the Turkish Murtaddin to the Hands of Their Sahwah Allies," and "At Last We Reach Safety."

The narrative begins with Umm Sulaym and her children living in an undisclosed part of Australia. In December 2013 she receives a message from her husband (in either Syria or Iraq) confirming his allegiance to the IS and his commitment to fight against the "Sahwat," a term used variously to describe other Sunni, Shia, or secular opponents of the IS in Iraq and in Syria.[55] A month later she learns that her husband was killed in action against the Al-Tawhid Brigade, a jihadist group affiliated with the Muslim Brotherhood, a Pan-Islamic Sunni religious and political organisation. In the second section, Umm Sulaym discusses IS's desire to re-establish the Caliphate and her desire to join the movement with her children.[56] The third section details her plans to leave Australia without her parents' or in-laws' knowledge. The night before her scheduled departure, however, her family discovers her intentions, and her father (who is abroad) demands to meet her in Abu Dhabi (the first leg of her journey). On arriving at the airport, Umm Sulaym manages to evade her father, travels to Dubai, and then flies to Gaziantep in Turkey. Here she meets several others attempting to reach the IS, but they are betrayed and captured by a Turkish border patrol before they reach Syria. In the fourth section, Umm Sulaym and her fellow travellers pass first into the custody of the Turkish police and then Interpol, who intend to repatriate them. The section concludes with a change of heart by the authorities and the next describes their arrival in Syria, in Azaz, into Sahwat custody. A military commander agrees to send them to the IS, but he implores them to recommend a cessation of hostilities to the leadership. Umm Sulaym's response is:

> The events in Sham [the Levant] were considered a "fitnah" [distressful sedition] to some, but they were only a fitnah for those who were desperately trying to excuse themselves from joining the mujahidin, as it was unmistakably clear that the Islamic State was following the correct manhaj [methodology] and endeavored to re-establish the Khilafah [Caliphate] upon the prophetic methodology, and this ambition was interfering with the selfish and ulterior agendas of the Sahwat and their proprietors.[57]

In the final section, Umm Sulaym's group is handed over to the IS in Suluk, a small town on the border due north of Raqqa. If this is accurate, then her arrival was probably prior to June 2015, when Suluk fell to the Kurdish People's Protection Units.[58]

The narrative is of great interest for a variety of reasons, including its focus on the experience of a Muslim woman and a narrative framework that presents the Caliphate as a living paradise.[59] The central theme that unifies the representation is, however, the cowardice, ignominy, and worthlessness of *other Muslims*. Umm Sulaym repeatedly and vehemently expresses her disdain, contempt, and hatred for Muslims who do not support the IS, creating a Muslim out-group and identifying particular categories within this out-group as especially repugnant, namely: Sahwat jihadists, moderate Muslim scholars in Australia, and the Turkish authorities. So focused is her condemnation and scorn of the Muslim out-group that she has little to say about the unbeliever out-group, and her article appears to be a very poor example of the crusader concept at work—until the penultimate paragraph. The final paragraph is a short supplication, but the preceding one brings the narrative to the present, "where the Crusader armies have united in their quest to invade us, purely because we believe in and implement 'La ilaha illallah [There is no god but God].'"[60] *Crusader* is employed for the first time at precisely the point at which the article is revealed as a self-conscious victim master narrative, with the conception of the crusader forming the basis of that victimhood. The crusaders want to destroy the IS (purely) because the Caliphate is Muslim (i.e., all [true] Muslims are victims). Umm Sulaym then turns her attention to the crusaders, stating, "And let these Crusaders take heed, for just as the Khilafah is filled with men who love death more than the Crusaders love life, likewise are the women of the Islamic State."[61] This warning is particularly chilling in the context of the preceding three thousand words' worth of contempt for the Muslim out-group, producing a similar effect to a last-minute peripeteia. There is no reversal of fortune, but there is an intense reversal of focus, in which the prior absence of scorn for crusaders amplifies rather than reduces Umm Sulaym's hatred for the unbeliever outgroup (i.e., up to this point they have literally been beneath contempt). The explicit inclusion of the term in the concluding paragraph casts retrospective meaning on its previous absence and her message is clear: *I have shown you how much I hate my Muslim enemies, so imagine how much I hate my non-Muslim enemies (and how much I am prepared to sacrifice to destroy them)*. Umm Sulaym's autobiographical essay is a relatively straightforward instantiation of Maan's victim master narrative: there was once paradise in the Middle East (either Muhammad's *umma* or one of the three medieval caliphates), this was lost (as evinced by the contemporary situation), but it is in the process of being regained (by the IS). Both Umm Sulaym's story and her warning constitute a call to arms, with the former encouraging others to follow her lead and the latter providing reassurance that the Caliphate will be victorious against its enemies, foreign and domestic.

38. REDUCING VIOLENT EXTREMISM

The purpose of sections 36 and 37 was to explore the implications of Maan's initial identification and subsequent critique of the victim master narrative for narrative justice. Maan's deconstruction was achieved by means of a comparative analysis of two diametrically opposed extremist recruitment narratives. In order to apply Maan's method to the narrative justice thesis, I employed two exemplary narratives, following her lead in selecting one from the white supremacist *American Renaissance* and the other from the Muslim fundamentalist *Rumiyah*. With this diametric opposition in place, I chose the narratives on the basis of being: typical of their respective publications, published in 2017, and of a similar length. My analyses of Semeria's "Argentina: A Mirror of Your Future" and Umm Sulaym's "The Hijrah of Umm Sulaym al-Muhajirah" confirmed Maan's conclusion in revealing that both exemplary narratives instantiate the victim master narrative. Recall that narrative's structure from section 35:

(i) In the beginning, our people lived in utopia.
(ii) Then others arrived and took over.
(iii) This brings us to the present, where we have two choices.
(iv) We can either do nothing, in which case the situation will remain as it is now, or we can expel these others and restore the utopia in such a way that it is never threatened again.

In section 36 I claimed that Semeria's article provides the following variation on this structure: *instead of a simple progression from paradise to paradise lost to a call to action, Semeria produces a chronology on which Argentina is further ahead than America: decolonisation and democracy, paradise gained, paradise lost, and the current descent into multiracial hell.* In section 37 I claimed that Umm Sulaym's article provides a straightforward instantiation of the narrative structure: *there was once paradise in the Middle East (either Muhammad's umma or one of the three medieval caliphates); this was lost (as evinced by the contemporary situation), but it is in the process of being regained (by the Islamic State).*

Recall also from section 35 that the purpose and power of the victim master narrative is *getting the listener first to identify with victim status and then to blame himself for future victimization of other people unless he takes violent action.* Umm Sulaym establishes a subgroup of Muslims—Salafi jihadist—as her in-group, represents this in-group as being victimised by other Muslims and by non-Muslims, and demonstrates the need to defend the in-group by following her own example and joining the IS. Semeria divides his in-group into two geographically distinct subgroups—white Argentinians and white Americans—represents the former as living in a contemporary dystopia courtesy of the Hispanic out-group, and implores the latter to prevent suffering the same fate themselves. Maan argues that the victim master narrative is a call to global violence, however, and this might seem problematic in Semeria's case. Umm Sulaym's article is intended to recruit and maintain support for the IS, an organisation that the United Nations regards as constituting "a global and unprecedented threat to international peace and security."[62] In contrast, Semeria's article neither refers to a particular organisation nor proposes violence as a means of resisting multiracialism. In fact, *American Renaissance* does not publish violent propaganda at all, and its calls to action recommend donating, promoting the publication, attending conferences, and—most recently—the establishment of a white homeland by legal means.[63]

The absence of an explicit call to take up arms against Hispanics in Semeria's case (and non-whites in the case of *American Renaissance* more generally) does not preclude his article (and the publication) from issuing a call to global violence by more subtle means. Semeria is completely clear about both the extent of the dystopia in contemporary Argentina and its cause and is furthermore explicit in his appeal to his readers to avoid allowing the same to happen in America. So, while Semeria's position is explicitly consistent with Trump's immigration plans, it is implicitly consistent with violent action if legal measures are unsuccessful—on the basis of what has been established as being at stake (i.e., [white] America's economic, cultural, and social prosperity). *American Renaissance* is similarly complicit in promoting violence in that the publication is not only based on the desire to establish the superiority of the white race, but takes the violent crime committed by non-white Americans as one of its major themes. Taylor's most recent book, published in July 2017, is in fact titled *If We Do Nothing*, and both he and *American Renaissance* had their Twitter accounts suspended in December 2017 in consequence of contravening one or both of these policies:

(a) "Accounts that affiliate with organizations that use or promote violence against civilians to further their causes."[64]
(b) "Content that glorifies violence or the perpetrators of a violent act."[65]

Semeria's recommendation that white Americans take action against the relentless Hispanic hordes is as much a justification of racial violence as Umm Sulaym's recommendation that true Muslims join the IS. Semeria's call is simply one step removed from violent action and indeed the appeal to reason, attempt to provide empirical evidence for white supremacism, and refusal to subscribe to the various anti-Semitic global conspiracy theories provide *American Renaissance* with the opportunity for a broader readership than many other more reactionary far-right and ultra-conservative publications. The combination of a façade of rationality and objectivity with explicit promotion of the white genocide agenda makes the publication and its contributors more rather than less dangerous, dramatically increasing the potential of its influence and impact.

In addition to providing further evidence for Maan's victim master narrative claim, my analyses in sections 36 and 37 explained the significance of two concepts to Semeria and Umm Sulaym's respective narratives and to white supremacism and Muslim fundamentalism more generally. White genocide underpins the white supremacist victim master narrative and provides the conception of white victimhood upon which the global call to violence is based—to defend the white in-group against the non-white out-group that is attempting to destroy it. As noted above, Semeria's call to action is not an explicit call to violence, but it is an explicit reiteration of the idea that the white race requires protection and defence, and an explicit reiteration of Lane's "white genocide in fourteen words": *we must secure the existence of our people and a future for white children.* Crusader underpins the Muslim fundamentalist victim master narrative and provides the conception of Muslim victimhood upon which the global call to violence is based—to defend the Muslim in-group against the non-Muslim out-group that is attempting to destroy it. As noted above, Umm Sulaym's call to global violence identifies all those who are opposed to Salafi jihadism, including other Muslims, as her out-group. Maan argues that Stormfront and the World Islamic Front are both employing the same victim master narrative; my claim is that *American Renaissance* and *Rumiyah* employ the same core conception of victimhood (i.e., that *white genocide* and *crusader* are different aspects of the same concept).

The identity of *white genocide* and *crusader* is evident in my analysis of the role the respective concepts play in "Argentina: Mirror of Your Future" and "The Hijrah of Umm Sulaym al-Muhajirah": both establish a particular in-group as superior to and under threat from a particular out-group, whose destruction is required if the in-group is to survive.[66] Further evidence for this identity is found in the interchangeability of the language used to promote the white genocide and crusader agendas. In *American Renaissance*, white genocide motivates the need to prevent genocide by securing the future of the white race. In *Rumiyah*, crusader motivates the holy war required to defend Islam and launch a counter-crusade on Rome. *American Renaissance* might just as easily publish articles on a race war—and the sustained emphasis on non-white-perpetrated violent crime in the U.S. comes very close to this while retaining the appearance of non-violent respectability—and the need to defend the white race by launching a counter-crusade to expel the non-whites. Similarly, *Rumiyah* might just as easily publish articles on the need to prevent a Muslim genocide—were the IS not so opposed to other Muslim groups, they could cite compelling evidence, such as the current plight of the Rohingyas in Myanmar—and to secure the future of Islam. There is not only a single victim master narrative at work in white supremacism and Muslim fundamentalism, but a single conception of victimhood, which combines the desirability of the survival of the in-group (with its various superior qualities) and the likelihood of destruction by the out-group (with its vastly superior numbers) to justify resistance, defence, and attack. I shall call this core conception *deliverance*, employed in the sense in which the word combines the meaning of both salvation and liberation. White genocide and crusader are two instantiations of deliverance, and deliverance provides the conceptual core of the victim master narrative, which is instantiated by both white supremacists and Muslim fundamentalists.

One might well ask the question, *So what?* Why is it significant that *American Renaissance* and *Rumiyah* both make use of the victim master narrative and that this narrative has deliverance as its core concept? Maan does not explore this identity in *Narrative Strategies* because her deconstruction of terrorist recruitment narratives is employed in order to make a convincing case for a revision of soft power counterterror strategy—specifically, the need to place greater emphasis on alternative narratives and less on counternarratives. For her, the deconstruction is part of the argument for a new soft power approach rather than the actual approach itself. In contrast, I regard Maan's deconstruction of terrorist recruitment narratives and my demystification of the conceptual core of those narratives as an application of narrative justice (i.e., a way in which criminal inhumanity can be reduced by the cultivation of narrative sensibility). Narrative sensibility draws attention to the use of not only the same master narrative (victim), but the same concept underpinning that narrative (deliverance) by two diametrically opposed extremist organisations. The fact that two opposed ideologies are using the same narrative and the same core concept to justify violence can be used to undermine the recruitment narratives of both groups by means of the following line of reasoning. If the groups are opposed to one another, then they should be telling different stories, and members of one group would regard their own group's narrative as true and the other group's as false; but if both groups are telling the same story (and that story furthermore has the same core concept), then there are only two options: either the groups are not actually in opposition, or both stories are false. The groups clearly are in opposition, so both stories must be false.

The argument can be set out as follows:

(i) White supremacists and Muslim fundamentalists follow contradictory ideologies.

(ii) The ideologies of white supremacists and Muslim fundamentalists are based on the victim master narrative, which is in turn based on the concept of deliverance.

(iii) If ideologies are contradictory, they cannot both be true.

(iv) Therefore, either white supremacism and Muslim fundamentalism are not contradictory, or the victim master narrative and the concept of deliverance on which it is based are false.

(v) Therefore, the victim master narrative and the concept of deliverance on which it is based are false.

(i) is an uncontroversial premise: white supremacists elevate race above all else, and Muslim fundamentalists elevate religion above all else. Maan argues for the first part of (ii) in *Narrative Strategies*, and I argue for the second part above. (iii) is also uncontroversial; the ideologies cannot both be true, although they can both be false. (iv) follows from the first three premises, and (v) from the combination of (i) and (iv). If truth and falsity do not sit well with "master narrative" and "concept," then another way to articulate the conclusion is that the victim master narrative is fictional rather than factual.

Maan touches very briefly on the counterterror potential of the above argument in her discussion of the normalising function of master narratives, stating:

And once the notion of a "true" narrative is called into question and the normalizing function of narrative is brought out into light, individuals may feel less compelled to live as supporting characters in narratives told at their expense.[67]

She is actually sceptical of the truth of all narratives, and her position is reminiscent of the relationship that Worth proposes between narrative representation and the coherence model of truth, discussed in sections 8 and 22. Maan's observation nonetheless accords with my appropriation of master narratives and core concepts into narrative justice: narrative sensibility reveals the identity of the white supremacist and Muslim fundamentalist recruitment narratives and, as such, calls their truth or basis in fact into question, which in turn reduces the potential influence of the courses of action they prescribe. It is only when doubt is cast on the accuracy of these narratives that they will cease to be regarded as legitimate and, in consequence, lose at least some of their power to motivate violence. If this seems implausible, consider the profound, widespread, and lasting impact of James George Frazer's *The Golden Bough: A Study in Comparative Religion*, first published in 1890. Frazer's representation of Christianity as one of several religions that was based on the primitive cult of the dying and revived god dissolved its uniqueness and contributed to the increase in scepticism at the end of the nineteenth century.[68] His work cast doubt on Christianity as the one true faith in a similar manner to that in which Karl Marx, Charles Darwin, and Sigmund Freud cast doubt on accepted conceptions of social, biological, and psychological reality, respectively. Regardless of the strength or weakness of Maan's argument for alternative narratives as preferable to counternarratives, her deconstruction of terrorist recruitment narratives can itself serve as the basis of a soft power counterterror strategy. The comparison of two exemplary narratives demonstrates that narrative sensibility is an important tool in calling extremism into question (i.e., exemplary narratives can undermine criminal inhumanity).

39. CODA: METHODOLOGY?

In section 38, I compared my analyses of two exemplary narratives in order to develop a third example of the narrative justice thesis in practice, which involved the appropriation and development of Maan's work on master narratives. In this section, I want to make another comparative analysis, broadening my scope from the sections within this chapter to the final three chapters of the monograph in order to determine whether a methodology has emerged for applying theory to practice in narrative justice. Although the denotation of *methodology* is neither particularly intricate nor particularly abstruse, it is frequently used incorrectly, most often as a synonym for *method*. Methodology does involve method, but it has two other components: theory and rationale. Theory refers to the theoretical assumptions upon which the research is based and the context within which the research is undertaken. A rationale is an exposition of the principles employed and of their implication for the method or methods selected. Finally, the method is the combination of techniques and procedures used to gather and analyse data for the research. If one puts these three components together, one has:

> *Methodology*: a theory of research, set of principles, and system of methods regulating a particular inquiry or a discipline more generally.

The assumptions of narrative justice were established in chapter 1, and an argument was presented for the thesis in chapters 3, 4, and 5. The most significant of these, given the context of theory to practice, are that the following claims apply to all exemplary narratives, regardless of the extent to which they are fictional:

(a) Every story has a moral, but that moral may be virtuous, vicious, or somewhere in between.

(b) Stories can provide genuine knowledge just by being stories.

The question is now whether a set of principles and systematic method can be extracted from the practices employed in chapters 7, 8, and 9.

In chapter 7, I demonstrated how an exemplary narrative can be employed to reduce criminal inhumanity by providing an evaluation of responsibility for criminal inhumanity, answering the question of what, if anything, the posthumous accusations of collaboration with the Third Reich revealed Paul de Man to have done wrong. In chapter 8, I demonstrated how an exemplary narrative can be employed to reduce criminal inhumanity by affording an understanding of the psychology of inhumanity, solving the evaluative problem of the apparent conflict of aesthetic and ethical value in the narrative representation of torturers in South Africa under apartheid. In this chapter, I have demonstrated how a pair of exemplary narratives can be employed to reduce criminal inhumanity by undermining extremist recruitment strategies, identifying white supremacist and Muslim fundamentalist conceptions of victimhood as identical. In each case, the analysis of one or more exemplary narratives—the cultivation of narrative sensibility—has presented an opportunity for the reduction of criminal inhumanity. This potential reduction is on the basis of explaining the responsibility for and psychology of crimes against humanity (chapters 7 and 8, respectively) and the recruitment strategies that motivate both lone wolf and organised terrorism (this chapter). I argued for the relation between explanation and reduction in chapter 5, and this relation can be considered as one of the principles I have employed in my inquiry:

(i) Explanations of crime have crime reduction potential in virtue of developing understanding of the causes of crime.

The understanding occurs in virtue of the phenomenological ethical knowledge conveyed by one or more of the exemplary narratives employed—for example, the phenomenological ethical knowledge from *Mother Night* places one in a better position to judge the actions of de Man; the phenomenological ethical knowledge from *In the Heart of the Whore* reveals the aesthetic failure of *Waiting for the Barbarians*; and the similarity of the phenomenological ethical knowledge provided by "Argentina: A Mirror of Your Future" and "The Hijrah of Umm Sulaym al-Muhajirah" undermines their respective claims to truth. I have not employed an example of lucid phenomenological ethical knowledge having a practical application, but it is nonetheless part of the principles of narrative justice such that the second and third are:

(ii) Stories convey phenomenological ethical knowledge in virtue of their narrativity.

(iii) Some stories convey lucid phenomenological ethical knowledge in virtue of their narrativity.

A reflection on the actual method employed in my arguments for each of the above three applications of narrative justice reveals not only the comparative analysis of two exemplary narratives in each case, but the exploitation of the relationship between documentary and fiction within narrative representation. In chapter 7 I employed two biographies, one of a real person and one of a fictional character, in order to establish the former's responsibility for collaboration in crimes against humanity. In chapter 8 I employed two narratives concerned with totalitarian oppression, one fictional and one documentary, in order to understand how an exemplary narrative can succeed in exploring the psychology of a torturer while simultaneously condemning his or her actions. In this chapter, I employ a comparison of two ostensibly documentary narratives, an article and an essay, to illustrate the fictional basis of both. Focusing on fact and fiction, one could set out this relationship as follows:

(A) The use of a fictional narrative to illuminate a real person's character.
(B) The use of a documentary narrative to illuminate a novel's weakness.
(C) The comparison of two documentary narratives to reveal their fictional basis.

(A) and (B) involve the comparison of a work of fiction with a work of documentary in order to illuminate both the fiction and the reality. (C) involves the comparison of two documentaries as fictions. The comparison of fiction and documentary or of two documentaries as fiction yields insight into criminal inhumanity, and this insight has the potential to reduce crimes against humanity and terrorism (i.e., the comparative analysis of documentary and fictional narratives has the potential to reduce criminal inhumanity). I think that (A) to (C) clearly constitutes a method, and my main purpose in this section is to draw attention to it as being the method by which the narrative justice thesis is put to practical use. This method—the careful selection, analysis, and comparison of documentary and fictional narratives for the purposes of disclosure, demystification, and deconstruction—is worth reproducing, even if it is pursued from the point of view of a perspective that is not underpinned by narrative justice. As to whether (i) to (iii) are sufficient to constitute a set of principles that connect narrative justice theory to the method and thus create a new or alternative methodology, I am neither especially concerned nor in the best position to judge. I am content to claim that chapters 7, 8, and 9 have established a method and that this method is both original and useful.

The question of methodology and/or method brings me back to my introduction in chapter 1, where I characterised narrative justice as both a thesis of aesthetic education and part of the narrative turn within criminology. In their editorial of a special issue of *Crime, Media, Culture: An International Journal* on narrative criminology, Sveinung Sandberg and Thomas Ugelvik note that the narrative criminology framework has been applied to a wide variety of crimes, including those that fall into the category of criminal inhumanity, such as terrorism, genocide, and resistance to radicalisation.[69] Narrative justice is an example of narrative criminology because of its focus on stories as stories rather than stories as true or false. Lois Presser identifies this approach as distinctive of narrative criminology in her contribution to the *Crime, Media, Culture* special issue:

> Hence the second and principal difference between narrative criminology and other views on narrative within criminology: narrative criminology takes a constitutive view of stories, against the prevailing representational view. . . . Narrative criminologists are interested in what stories *do*—specifically, how they affect crime and other harm—and not principally in what they *reveal*. For narrative criminologists, subjectivity, which is always forged discursively, is *the* analytic focal point.[70]

Within this framework, narrative justice is distinguished by the uses to which it puts fictional narratives. With the exception of Sarah Colvin's "Why Should Criminology Care about Literary Fiction?," narrative criminology has thus far largely ignored fiction and the relationship between fiction and documentary. Colvin's research draws on Shadd Maruna's work in *Making Good* and examines the effect of literary fiction on offender rehabilitation in prison and probation programmes.[71] As noted in section 8, Sarah Worth is concerned with literacy in prisons, and she further maintains that literature programmes are beneficial in developing the moral imagination of offenders.[72]

Worth and I both emphasise the ethical value of narrative, and my final point is about narrative justice as gesturing toward a bridge between philosophy and criminology. In an age where neoliberalism has taken root in almost every aspect of public and private life, philosophy is in danger of being characterised as what Jock Young calls *grand theory* and caricatures as a *theorodactyl* in *The Criminological Imagination*:

> Let us envisage this academic creature as another dinosaur like our old friend the datasaur, my metaphor for abstracted empiricism, that we met at the beginning of this book. It was you will recall a creature with a little brain wandering from dataset to dataset, grant to grant; it had a small head yet a huge gut for processing survey material; it was always on the move but it was strangely without direction of purpose. Grand theory nowadays evokes another creature,

a theorodactyl, with a domed head and huge wings soaring high above reality in an endless quest for a fashionable perch, gliding from theory to theory, detected from below only by the trail of references it leaves behind, mouthing near incomprehensible sentences with a hint of a French accent and yet strangely like the datasaur, unsure of where it is going and what it is there for.[73]

Narrative justice provides a reason for the theorodactyl to keep close to the earth, maintain its source of sustenance, and avoid fashionable perches. It is similarly to be hoped that the discipline of criminology, concerned with the explanation and reduction of crime, will benefit from a new philosophical perspective that combines analysis with interpretation without seeking a return to the classicism of Cesare Beccaria and Jeremy Bentham or the neo-classicism of Derek Cornish, Ronald Clarke, and Marcus Felson. As Richard Rorty pointed out in his famous article on Derrida, there are, after all, at least "two ways of thinking about various things."[74]

NOTES

1. Alex P. Schmid, "Al-Qaeda's 'Single Narrative' and Attempts to Develop Counter-Narratives: The State of Knowledge," *ICCT Research Paper*, International Centre for Counter-Terrorism—The Hague, January 2014: 4–5. Available at: https://www.icct.nl/download/file/Schmid-Al-Qaeda%27s-Single-Narrative-and-Attempts-to-Develop-Counter-Narratives-January-2014.pdf.

2. Institute for Strategic Dialogue and RAN Centre of Excellence, "Counter Narratives and Alternative Narratives," *RAN Issue Paper*, 1 October 2015: 4. Available at: https://ec.europa.eu/home-affairs/sites/homeaffairs/files/what-we-do/networks/radicalisation_awareness_network/ran-papers/docs/issue_paper_cn_oct2015_en.pdf.

3. ISD and RAN, "Counter Narratives and Alternative Narratives," 4.

4. ISD and RAN, "Counter Narratives and Alternative Narratives," 4.

5. Ajit Maan, *Counter-Terrorism: Narrative Strategies* (Lanham, MD: University Press of America, 2015), 5.

6. Maan, *Narrative Strategies*, 9.

7. Maan, *Narrative Strategies*, 11.

8. Maan, *Narrative Strategies*, 16.

9. Maan, *Narrative Strategies*, 17.

10. Maan, *Narrative Strategies*, 20.

11. I want to be clear that *non-white* is a white supremacist term, but I employ it here and elsewhere in this chapter because it clearly and concisely describes the *other* to which white supremacists believe they are opposed.

12. Maan, *Narrative Strategies*, 28.

13. Maan, *Narrative Strategies*, 29.

14. Maan, *Narrative Strategies*, 36.

15. Maan, *Narrative Strategies*, 39.

16. Maan, *Narrative Strategies*, 40.

17. George W. Bush, "Remarks by the President upon Arrival," *The White House: President George W. Bush*, 16 September 2001. Available at: https://georgewbush-whitehouse.archives.gov/news/releases/2001/09/20010916-2.html.

18. Maan, *Narrative Strategies*, 33.

19. Maan, *Narrative Strategies*, 70.

20. Maan, *Narrative Strategies*, 3.

21. Maan, *Narrative Strategies*, 71.

22. Maan, *Narrative Strategies*, 73.

23. Maan, *Narrative Strategies*, 66.

24. Maan, *Narrative Strategies*, 19, 20.

25. Dr. Ford, "Introduction to Stormfront," *Stormfront.org*, 5 July 2013. Available at: https://www.stormfront.org/forum/t538924/. Although listing *American Renaissance*, Black and his team note that it (erroneously) includes Jews as white, whereas Jews are (in fact) the main problem facing the white race.

26. Ramón Spaaij, "The Enigma of Lone Wolf Terrorism: An Assessment," *Studies in Conflict and Terrorism* 33 (2010): 856.

27. BBC News, "Timeline: How Norway's Terror Attacks Unfolded," 12 April 2012. Available at: http://www.bbc.co.uk/news/world-europe-14260297; Tessa Berenson, "Everything We Know about the Charleston Shooting," *Time*, 18 June 2015. Available at: http://time.com/3926112/charleston-shooting-latest/.

28. Matthew Taylor, "Breivik Sent 'Manifesto' to 250 UK Contacts Hours before Norway Killings," *The Guardian*, 26 July 2011. Available at: https://www.theguardian.com/world/2011/jul/26/breivik-manifesto-email-uk-contacts; Rob Crilly and Raf Sanchez, "Dylann Roof: The Charleston Shooter's Racist Manifesto," *The Telegraph*, 20 June 2015. Available at: http://www.telegraph.co.uk/news/worldnews/northamerica/usa/11688675/Dylann-Roof-The-Charleston-killers-racist-manifesto.html.

29. Dylann Roof, "rtf88," *New York Times*, 13 December 2016. Available at: https://www.nytimes.com/interactive/2016/12/13/universal/document-Dylann-Roof-manifesto.html; Anders Behring Breivik, "2083. A European Declaration of Independence," *The Washington Post*, 25 July 2011: 96. Available at: https://www.washingtonpost.com/world/anders-behring-breivik-oslo-terror-suspect-detailed-attack-planning-in-diary/2011/07/25/gIQAPiiHZI_story.html?utm_term=.89069f74ffd5.

30. William Luther Pierce (as Andrew Macdonald), *The Turner Diaries* (Hillsboro, WV: National Vanguard Books, 1978).

31. J. M. Berger, "Alt History: How a Self-Published, Racist Novel Changed White Nationalism and Inspired Decades of Violence," *The Atlantic*, 16 September 2016. Available at: https://www.theatlantic.com/politics/archive/2016/09/how-the-turner-diaries-changed-white-nationalism/500039/.

32. See: Southern Poverty Law Center, "David Lane," no date. Available at: https://www.splcenter.org/fighting-hate/extremist-files/individual/david-lane; Der Brüder Schweigen Archives and David Eden Lane's Pyramid Prophecy, "White

Genocide Manifesto," no date, accessed 19 February 2018. Available at: https://www.davidlane1488.com/whitegenocide.html.

33. White GeNOcide Project, "Terminology & Education," 2017, accessed 22 December 2017. Available at: http://whitegenocideproject.com/terminology/.

34. White GeNOcide Project, "About White Genocide," 2017, accessed 22 December 2017. Available at: http://whitegenocideproject.com/about-white-genocide/.

35. *American Renaissance* Staff, "The Best of *American Renaissance* in 2017," *American Renaissance*, 31 December 2017. Available at: https://www.amren.com/commentary/2017/12/best-american-renaissance-2017/.

36. Gustavo Semeria, "Argentina: A Mirror of Your Future: How Demographic Change Can Destroy a Country," *American Renaissance*, 14 April 2017. Available at: https://www.amren.com/features/2017/04/argentina-a-mirror-of-your-future-buenos-aires-latin-america/.

37. Semeria, "Mirror of Your Future."

38. Semeria, "Mirror of Your Future."

39. Semeria, "Mirror of Your Future."

40. Semeria, "Mirror of Your Future."

41. Semeria, "Mirror of Your Future."

42. Semeria, "Mirror of Your Future."

43. Osama bin Laden, "Declaration of Jihad against the Americans Occupying the Land of the Two Holiest Sites," *Combating Terrorism Center at West Point*, no date. Available at: https://ctc.usma.edu/posts/declaration-of-jihad-against-the-americans-occupying-the-land-of-the-two-holiest-sites-english-translation-2. Or, the "Zionist-Crusaders alliance," depending on the translation employed.

44. Shiraz Maher, *Salafi-Jihadism: The History of an Idea* (London: C. Hurst & Co., 2016), 42–46.

45. Simon Staffell and Akil Awan, "Introduction," in *Jihadism Transformed: Al-Qaeda and Islamic State's Global Battle of Ideas*, ed. S. Staffell and A. Awan (London: C. Hurst & Co., 2016), 8.

46. Yahya Ibrahim, "Editor's Letter," *Inspire 17: Train Derail Operations* (2017): 3. Available at: http://jihadology.net/2016/07/31/new-issue-of-the-islamic-states-magazine-dabiq-15/.

47. Anonymous, "Foreword," *Dabiq 15: Break the Cross* (2016): 4. Available at: https://azelin.files.wordpress.com/2016/07/the-islamic-state-e2809cdacc84biq-magazine-1522.pdf.

48. Haroro J. Ingram, "An Analysis of *Inspire* and *Dabiq*: Lessons from AQAP and Islamic State's Propaganda War," *Studies in Conflict and Terrorism* 40 (2017): 358.

49. Maan, *Narrative Strategies*, 66.

50. Kareem Shaheen, "Turkish-Backed Syrian Rebels Recapture Town of Dabiq from Isis," *The Guardian*, 16 October 2016. Available at: https://www.theguardian.com/world/2016/oct/16/turkish-opposition-fighters-syria-dabiq-islamic-state.

51. Fred M. Donner, *Muhammad and the Believers: At the Origins of Islam* (Cambridge, MA: Harvard University Press, 2012 [2010]), 85–87.

52. See: Kathryn M. Kueny, *Conceiving Identities: Maternity in Medieval Muslim Discourse and Practice* (New York: SUNY Press, 2014 [2013]), 141–44.

53. Anonymous, "The Hijrah of Umm Sulaym al-Muhajirah," *Rumiyah* 13 (9 September 2017): 30. Available at: https://azelin.files.wordpress.com/2017/09/rome-magazine-13.pdf.

54. Donner, *Muhammad and the Believers*, 57–59. See also: Shahah Ahmed, *What Is Islam? The Importance of Being Islamic* (Princeton, NJ: Princeton University Press, 2016), 135–40.

55. Anonymous, "The Hijrah," 31.

56. The Islamic State of Iraq and the Levant (ISIL, also ISIS) changed its named to Islamic State and announced that the caliphate had been restored on 29 June 2014. See: Adam Withnall, "Iraq Crisis: Isis Declares Its Territories a New Islamic State with 'Restoration of Caliphate' in Middle East," *The Independent*, 30 June 2014. Available at: http://www.independent.co.uk/news/world/middle-east/isis-declares-new-islamic-state-in-middle-east-with-abu-bakr-al-baghdadi-as-emir-removing-iraq-and-9571374.html.

57. Anonymous, "The Hijrah," 35.

58. Wladimir van Wilgenburg, "Analysis: Can Syrian Kurds Maintain Momentum after IS Defeat in Tal Abyad?" *Middle East Eye*, 15 June 2015. Available at: http://www.middleeasteye.net/news/analysis-can-syrian-kurds-maintain-momentum-after-defeat-tal-abyad-345059446.

59. For more on the latter point and its significance to the Islamic State's recruitment, see: Charlie Winter, "Apocalypse, Later: A Longitudinal Study of the Islamic State Brand," *Critical Studies in Media Communication* 35 (2018): 103–21.

60. Anonymous, "The Hijrah," 35.

61. Anonymous, "The Hijrah," 35.

62. United Nations, "Security Council 'Unequivocally' Condemns ISIL Terrorist Attacks, Unanimously Adopting Text That Determines Extremist Group Poses 'Unprecedented' Threat," *Meetings Coverage and Press Releases*, 20 November 2015. Available at: https://www.un.org/press/en/2015/sc12132.doc.htm.

63. See: New Century Foundation, "Activist's Corner," *American Renaissance*, 2018. Available at: https://www.amren.com/about/activists/; Southern Poverty Law Center, "American Renaissance," no date. Available at: https://www.splcenter.org/fighting-hate/extremist-files/group/american-renaissance.

64. Twitter Safety, "Enforcing New Rules to Reduce Hateful Conduct and Abusive Behavior," *Twitter Blog*, 18 December 2017. Available at: https://blog.twitter.com/official/en_us/topics/company/2017/safetypoliciesdec2017.html. See also: Ryan Lenz, "Twitter Begins Long-Awaited Crackdown on Hate Groups and Extremist Rhetoric," Southern Poverty Law Center *Hatewatch*, 18 December 2017. Available at: https://www.splcenter.org/hatewatch/2017/12/18/twitter-begins-long-awaited-crackdown-hate-groups-and-extremist-rhetoric.

65. Twitter Safety, "Enforcing New Rules."

66. I do not employ identity in the strict philosophical sense of indiscernible identicals but in the sense of being different instantiations of the same concept (i.e., in the same way that Maan has shown the identity of the Stormfront and World Islamic Front recruitment narratives).

67. Maan, *Narrative Strategies*, 29.

68. John B. Vickery, *The Literary Impact of "The Golden Bough"* (Princeton, NJ: Princeton University Press, 2015 (1973), 13–28.

69. Sveinung Sandberg and Thomas Ugelvik, "The Past, Present, and Future of Narrative Criminology: A Review and an Invitation," *Crime, Media, Culture: An International Journal* 12 (2016): 131–32.

70. Lois Presser, "Criminology and the Narrative Turn," *Crime, Media, Culture: An International Journal* 12 (2016): 139. The first difference is narrative criminology's focus on narrative form.

71. See: Sarah Colvin, "Why Should Criminology Care about Literary Fiction? Literature, Life Narratives and Telling Untellable Stories," *Punishment & Society* 17 (2015): 211–29.

72. Worth, *Defense of Reading*, 23–27.

73. Jock Young, *The Criminological Imagination* (Cambridge: Polity Press, 2011), 218.

74. Richard Rorty, "Philosophy as a Kind of Writing: An Essay on Derrida," *New Literary History* 10 (1978): 143.

Bibliography

Agnew, Robert. 1992. Foundation for a General Strain Theory of Crime and Delinquency. *Criminology* 30: 47–87.

———. 2001. Building on the Foundation of General Strain Theory: Specifying the Types of Strain Most Likely to Lead to Crime and Delinquency. *Journal of Research in Crime and Delinquency* 38: 319–61.

———. 2005. *Pressured into Crime: An Overview of General Strain Theory.* New York: Oxford University Press.

Ahmed, Shahab. 2016. *What Is Islam? The Importance of Being Islamic.* Princeton, NJ: Princeton University Press.

American Psychological Association. 2015. *Resolution on Violent Video Games* (August). Available at: http://www.apa.org/about/policy/violent-video-games.aspx.

American Renaissance Staff. 2017. The Best of *American Renaissance* in 2017. *American Renaissance* (31 December). Available at: https://www.amren.com/commentary/2017/12/best-american-renaissance-2017/.

Amis, Martin. 2001. *The War against Cliché: Essays and Reviews, 1971–2000.* London: Jonathan Cape.

Anderson, Craig A., Shibuya, Akiko, Ihori, Nobuko, Swing, Edward L., Bushman, Brad J., Sakamoto, Akira, Rothstein, Hannah R., and Saleem, Muniba. 2010. Violent Video Game Effects on Aggression, Empathy, and Prosocial Behavior in Eastern and Western Countries: A Meta-Analytic Review. *Psychological Bulletin* 136: 151–73.

Anonymous. 2016. Foreword. *Dabiq 15: Break the Cross*: 4–7. Available at: https://azelin.files.wordpress.com/2016/07/the-islamic-state-e2809cdacc84biq-magazine-1522.pdf.

———. 2017. The Hijrah of Umm Sulaym al-Muhajirah. *Rumiyah* 13 (9 September): 30–35. Available at: https://azelin.files.wordpress.com/2017/09/rome-magazine-13.pdf.

Apostolidès, Jean-Marie. 1989. On Paul de Man's War. *Critical Inquiry* 15: 765–66.

Aristotle. 2004. *Poetics*. Translated by P. Murray and T. S. Dorsch. In P. Murray, ed., *Classical Literary Criticism*, 57–97. London: Penguin.

Arnold, Matthew. 1925 [1880]. The Study of Poetry. In *Essays in Criticism: Second Series*, 1–55. London: Macmillan.

Attridge, Derek. 2004. *J. M. Coetzee and the Ethics of Reading: Literature in the Event*. Chicago: University of Chicago Press.

———. 2004. *The Singularity of Literature*. New York: Routledge.

Bal, P. Matthijs, and Veltkamp, Martjin. 2013. How Does Fiction Reading Influence Empathy? An Experimental Investigation on the Role of Emotional Transportation. *PLoS ONE* 8: 1–12. DOI:10.1371/journal.pone.0055341.

Barish, Evelyn. 2014. *The Double Life of Paul de Man*. New York: Liveright.

Battersby, John. 1997. Admitting White Guilt. *The World Today* 53: 23–25.

BBC News. 2012. Timeline: How Norway's Terror Attacks Unfolded (12 April). Available at: http://www.bbc.co.uk/news/world-europe-14260297.

Beiser, Frederick. 2005. *Schiller as Philosopher: A Re-Examination*. New York: Syracuse University.

Berenson, Tessa. 2015. Everything We Know about the Charleston Shooting. *Time* (18 June). Available at: http://time.com/3926112/charleston-shooting-latest/.

Berger, J. M. 2016. Alt History: How a Self-Published, Racist Novel Changed White Nationalism and Inspired Decades of Violence. *The Atlantic* (16 September). Available at: https://www.theatlantic.com/politics/archive/2016/09/how-the-turner-diaries-changed-white-nationalism/500039/.

Berns, Gregory S., Blaine, Kristina, Prietula, Michael J., and Pye, Brandon E. 2013. Short- and Long-Term Effects of a Novel on Connectivity in the Brain. *Brain Connectivity* 3: 590–600.

Bernstein, John Andrew. 1977. Shaftesbury's Identification of the Good with the Beautiful. *Eighteenth-Century Studies* 10: 304–25.

bin Laden, Osama. no date. Declaration of Jihad against the Americans Occupying the Land of the Two Holiest Sites. *Combating Terrorism Center at West Point*. Available at: https://ctc.usma.edu/posts/declaration-of-jihad-against-the-americans-occupying-the-land-of-the-two-holiest-sites-english-translation-2.

Bold, Christine. 2012. *Using Narrative in Research*. London: SAGE.

Booth, Wayne. 1988. *The Company We Keep: An Ethics of Fiction*. Berkeley: University of California.

Boulenger, Véronique, Hauk, Olaf, and Pulvermüller, Friedmann. 2009. Grasping Ideas with the Motor System: Semantic Somatotopy in Idiom Comprehension. *Cerebral Cortex* 19: 1905–14.

Breivik, Anders Behring. 2011. 2083: A European Declaration of Independence. *Washington Post* (25 July). Available at: https://www.washingtonpost.com/world/anders-behring-breivik-oslo-terror-suspect-detailed-attack-planning-in-diary/2011/07/25/gIQAPiiHZI_story.html?utm_term=.89069f74ffd5.

Brooks, Peter. 1992 [1984]. *Reading for the Plot: Design and Intention in Narrative*. Cambridge, MA: Harvard University Press.

Bruer, Lawrence R. 1989. *Sanity Plea: Schizophrenia In the Novels of Kurt Vonnegut*. Tuscaloosa: University of Alabama Press.

Burri, Alex. 2009 [2007]. Art and the View from Nowhere. In J. Gibson, W. Huerner, and L. Pocci, eds., *A Sense of the World: Essays on Fiction, Narrative, and Knowledge*, 308–17. London: Routledge.

Bush, George W. 2001. Remarks by the President upon Arrival. *The White House: President George W. Bush* (16 September). Available at: https://georgewbush-whitehouse.archives.gov/news/releases/2001/09/20010916-2.html.

Carroll, Noël. 1996. Moderate Moralism. *British Journal of Aesthetics* 36: 223–38.

———. 1998. Art, Narrative, and Moral Understanding. In J. Levinson, ed., *Aesthetics and Ethics: Essays at the Intersection*, 126–160. Cambridge: Cambridge University Press.

———. 2001. On the Narrative Connection. In N. Carroll, *Beyond Aesthetics: Philosophical Essays*, 118–33. New York: Cambridge University Press.

———. 2012 [2010]. *Art in Three Dimensions*. Oxford: Oxford University Press.

———. 2013. *Minerva's Night Out: Philosophy, Pop Culture, and Moving Pictures*. Malden, MA: Wiley-Blackwell.

———. 2017. Architecture, Art, and Moderate Moralism. *The Nordic Journal of Aesthetics* 25 (February). Available at: http://dx.doi.org/10.7146/nja.v25i52.25618.

Clandinin, D. Jean, and Connelly, F. Michael. 2004. *Narrative Inquiry: Experience and Story in Qualitative Research*. New York: Jossey-Bass.

Coetzee, J. M. 1974. *Dusklands*. Johannesburg: Ravan Press.

———. *Waiting for the Barbarians*. London: Penguin.

———. 1986. Into the Dark Chamber: The Novelist and South Africa. *New York Times* (12 January). Available at: http://www.nytimes.com/books/97/11/02/home/coetzee-chamber.html.

———. 2004 [2003]. *Elizabeth Costello: Eight Lessons*. London: Vintage.

Cohen, Ted. 1982. Why Beauty Is a Symbol of Morality. In T. Cohen and P. Guyer, eds., *Essays in Kant's Aesthetics*, 221–36. Chicago: University of Chicago Press.

Collini, Stefan. 2017. *Speaking of Universities*. London: Verso.

Colvin, Sarah. 2015. Why Should Criminology Care about Literary Fiction? Literature, Life Narratives and Telling Untellable Stories. *Punishment & Society* 17: 211–29.

Crilly, Rob, and Sanchez, Raf. 2015. Dylann Roof: The Charleston Shooter's Racist Manifesto. *The Telegraph* (20 June). Available at: http://www.telegraph.co.uk/news/worldnews/northamerica/usa/11688675/Dylann-Roof-The-Charleston-killers-racist-manifesto.html.

Currie, Gregory. 2010. *Narratives & Narrators: A Philosophy of Stories*. Oxford: Oxford University Press.

———. 2011. Literature and the Psychology Lab. *The Times Literary Supplement* (21 August). Available at: https://www.the-tls.co.uk/articles/public/literature-and-the-psychology-lab/.

———. 2013. Does Great Literature Make Us Better? *The New York Times Opinionator* (1 June). Available at: https://opinionator.blogs.nytimes.com/2013/06/01/does-great-literature-make-us-better/.

———. 2016. Does Fiction Make Us Less Empathic? *Teorama XXXV*: 47–68.

de Man, Paul. 1988. *Wartime Journalism, 1939–43*. Lincoln: University of Nebraska Press.

Der Brüder Schweigen Archives and David Eden Lane's Pyramid Prophecy. No date. White Genocide Manifesto. Accessed 19 February 2018. Available at: https://www.davidlane1488.com/whitegenocide.html.

Derrida, Jacques. 1988. Like the Sound of the Sea Deep within a Shell: Paul de Man's War. *Critical Inquiry* 14: 590–652.

———. 1989. Biodegradables Seven Diary Fragments. *Critical Inquiry* 15: 812–73.

———. 1992. From *Psyche*. In D. Attridge, ed., *Acts of Literature*, 310–43. New York: Routledge.

———. 1997 [1967/1976]. *Of Grammatology*. Translated by G. C. Spivak. Baltimore: Johns Hopkins University Press.

———. 2001 [1967/1978]. *Writing and Difference*. Translated by A. Bass. Abingdon: Routledge.

———. 2001. On Forgiveness. In J. Derrida, *On Cosmopolitanism and Forgiveness*, 25–60. Translated by M. Dooley and M. Hughes. London: Routledge.

———. 2007 [2003]. Abraham, the Other. Translated by G. Anidjar. In B. Berg, J. Cohen, and R. Zagury-Orly, eds., *Judeites: Questions for Jacques Derrida*, 1–35. New York: Fordham University Press.

———. 2008 [1992]. *The Gift of Death*. In J. Derrida, *The Gift of Death (2nd ed.) and Literature in Secret*, 1–116. Translated by D. Wills. Chicago: University of Chicago Press.

Devereaux, Mary. 1998. Beauty and Evil: The Case of Leni Riefenstahl's *Triumph of the Will*. In J. Levinson, ed., *Aesthetics and Ethics: Essays at the Intersection*, 227–56. Cambridge: Cambridge University Press.

Dill, Karen E., and Dill, Jody C. 1998. Video Game Violence: A Review of the Empirical Literature. *Aggression and Violent Behavior* 3: 407–28.

Donner, Fred M. 2012 [2010]. *Muhammad and the Believers: At the Origins of Islam*. Cambridge, MA: Harvard University Press.

Dr. Ford [pseudonym]. 2013. Introduction to Stormfront. *Stormfront.org* (5 July). Available at: https://www.stormfront.org/forum/t538924/.

Eaton, A.W. 2003. Where Ethics and Aesthetics Meet: Titian's *Rape of Europa*. *Hypatia* 18: 159–88.

———. 2007. A Sensible Antiporn Feminism. *Ethics* 117: 674–715.

Elson, Malte, and Ferguson, Christopher J. 2014. Twenty-Five Years of Research on Violence in Digital Games and Aggression: Empirical Evidence, Perspectives, and a Debate Gone Astray. *European Psychologist* 19: 33–46.

Evans, Brad. 2016. When Law Is Not Justice. *New York Times* (13 July). Available at: https://www.nytimes.com/2016/07/13/opinion/when-law-is-not-justice.html.

Evans, Gavin. 2013. Dirk Coetzee: Death Squad Commander Who Helped Expose Apartheid's Killing Machine. *The Independent* (12 March). Available at: http://www.independent.co.uk/news/obituaries/dirk-coetzee-death-squad-commander-who-helped-expose-apartheids-killing-machine-8530136.html.

Fabb, Nigel. 2009. Why Is Verse Poetry? *PN Review* 189: 52–57.

Falla, Frank. 1968 [1967]. *The Silent War: The Inside Story of the Channel Islands under the Nazi Jackboot*. London: New English Library.

Felman, Shoshana. 1989. Paul de Man's Silence. *Critical Inquiry* 15: 704–44.

Ferguson, Christopher J. 2014. Scholars' Open Statement to the APA Task Force on Violent Media (Delivered to the APA Task Force, 9/26/13) (5 August). Available at: http://www.christopherjferguson.com/APA%20Task%20Force%20Comment1. pdf.

Fessenbecker, Patrick. 2013. In Defense of Paraphrase. *New Literary History* 44: 117–39.

Fong, Katrina, Mullin, Justin B., and Mar, Raymond A. 2013. What You Read Matters: The Role of Fiction Genre in Predicting Interpersonal Sensitivity. *Psychology of Aesthetics, Creativity, and the Arts* 7: 370–76.

———. 2015. How Exposure to Literary Genres Relates to Attitudes Toward Gender Roles and Sexual Behavior. *Psychology of Aesthetics, Creativity, and the Arts* 9: 274–85.

Foucault, Michel. 2005 [1966]. *The Order of Things: An Archaeology of the Human Sciences*. Translated by A. Sheridan. London: Routledge.

Frank, Jason, 2007. Walt Whitman: Aesthetic Democracy and the Poetry of the People. *The Review of Politics* 69, 402–30.

Frazer, James George. 1890. *The Golden Bough: A Study in Comparative Religion. Volume I*. London: Macmillan & Co.

Freeman, Mark. 2013. Foreword. In S. Cobb, *Speaking of Violence: The Politics and Poetics of Narrative in Conflict Resolution*, vii–xi. New York: Oxford University Press.

Freese, Peter. 2012. The Critical Reception of Kurt Vonnegut. *Literature Compass* 9/1: 1–14.

Froom, Phil. 2012. Fred Koenig: A SS Grenadier from Chicago USA. *Axis History* (22 July). Available at: http://www.axishistory.com/axis-nations/germany-a-austria/waffen-ss/124-germany-waffen-ss/germany-waffen-ss-other/6182-fred-koenig-a-ss-grenadier-from-chicago-usa.

Futter, Mike. 2015. More Than 200 Psychology Scholars Speak Out Against APA Video Game Aggression Task Force. *Game Informer* (14 August). Available at: http://www.gameinformer.com/b/news/archive/2015/08/14/more-than-200-psychology-scholars-speak-out-against-apa-video-game-aggression-task-force. aspx.

Gairola, Rahul K. 2012. Occupy Education: An Interview with Gayatri Chakravorty Spivak. *Politics and Culture* (25 September). Available at: https://politicsandculture. org/2012/09/25/occupy-education-an-interview-with-gayatri-chakravorty-spivak/.

Gaskin, Richard. 2013. *Language, Truth, and Literature: A Defence of Literary Humanism*. Oxford: Oxford University Press.

Gaut, Berys. 1998. The Ethical Criticism of Art. In J. Levinson, ed., *Aesthetics and Ethics: Essays at the Intersection*, 182–203. Cambridge: Cambridge University Press.

———. 2007. *Art, Emotion and Ethics*. Oxford: Oxford University Press.

———. 2011. Telling Stories: Narration, Emotion, and Insight in *Memento*. In N. Carroll and J. Gibson, eds., *Narrative, Emotion, and Insight*, 23–44. University Park: Pennsylvania State University Press.

———. 2015. Elegy in L.A.: *Blade Runner*, Empathy and Death. In A. Coplan and D. Davies, eds., *Blade Runner (Philosophers on Film)*, 31–45. New York: Routledge.

Genette, Gérard. 1980 [1972]. *Narrative Discourse: An Essay in Method*. Translated by J. E. Lewin. Ithaca, NY: Cornell University Press.

Geras, Norman. 2015. *Crimes Against Humanity: Birth of a Concept*. Manchester: Manchester University Press.

Gibson, John. 2007. *Fiction and the Weave of Life*. Oxford: Oxford University Press.

———. 2008. Cognitivism and the Arts. *Philosophy Compass* 3: 573–89.

———. 2011. The Question of Poetic Meaning. *Nonsite* 4 (1 December). Available at: http://nonsite.org/article/the-question-of-poetic-meaning.

Gobodo-Madikizela, Pumla. 2006. *A Human Being Died That Night: Forgiving Apartheid's Chief Killer*. London: Portobello.

Goldie, Peter. 2012. *The Mess Inside: Narrative, Emotion, and the Mind*. Oxford: Oxford University Press.

Graham, Lucy Valerie. 2012. *State of Peril: Race and Rape in South African Literature*. New York: Oxford University Press.

Guyer, Paul. 1990. Feeling and Freedom: Kant on Aesthetics and Morality. *The Journal of Aesthetics and Art Criticism* 48: 137–46.

Hare, R. M. 1981. *Moral Thinking: Its Levels, Method and Point*. Oxford: Clarendon.

Harpham, Geoffrey Galt. 1999. *Shadows of Ethics: Criticism and the Just Society*. Durham, NC: Duke University Press.

Hogg, Russell. 2007. Criminology, Crime and Politics Before and After 9/11. *The Australian and New Zealand Journal of Criminology* 40: 83–105.

Hollander, Ethan J. 2013. The Banality of Goodness: Collaboration and Compromise in the Rescue of Denmark's Jews. *Journal of Jewish Identities* 6: 41–66.

Hume, David. 1888 [1740]. *A Treatise of Human Nature*. Edited by L. A. Selby-Bigge. Oxford: Clarendon.

Hyvärinen, Matti. 2010. Revisiting the Narrative Turns. *Life Writing* 7: 69–82.

Ibrahim, Yahya. 2017. "Editor's Letter." *Inspire 17: Train Derail Operations*, 3. Available at: http://jihadology.net/2016/07/31/new-issue-of-the-islamic-states-magazine-dabiq-15/.

Ingram, Haroro J. 2017. An Analysis of *Inspire* and *Dabiq*: Lessons from AQAP and Islamic State's Propaganda War. *Studies in Conflict and Terrorism* 40: 357–75.

Ingrao, Christian. 2011. *The SS Dirlewanger Brigade: The History of the Black Hunters*. Translated by P. Green. New York: Skyhorse Publishing.

Institute for Strategic Dialogue & RAN Centre of Excellence. 2015. Counter Narratives and Alternative Narratives. *RAN Issue Paper* (1 October): 1–15. Available at: https://ec.europa.eu/home-affairs/sites/homeaffairs/files/what-we-do/networks/radicalisation_awareness_network/ran-papers/docs/issue_paper_cn_oct2015_en.pdf.

International Committee of the Red Cross. 1949. *Convention (I) for the Amelioration of the Condition of the Wounded and Sick in Armed Forces in the Field*. Available at: https://ihl-databases.icrc.org/applic/ihl/ihl.nsf/ART/365-570005?OpenDocument.

International Criminal Court. 1998. Rome Statute for the International Criminal Court, Art. 7. Available at: http://legal.un.org/icc/statute/99_corr/cstatute.htm.

International Military Tribunal. 1945. *Nuremberg Trial Proceedings Vol. 1: Charter of the International Military Tribunal*. Yale Law School. The Avalon Project. Available at: http://avalon.law.yale.edu/imt/imtconst.asp.

Internet Movie Database (IMDb). 2018. *Blade Runner* (1982)—Alternate Versions. Available at: http://www.imdb.com/title/tt0083658/alternateversions.

Jamosky, Edward, and Klinkowitz, Jerome. 1988. Kurt Vonnegut's Three *Mother Nights*. *Modern Fiction Studies* 34: 216–20.

Johnson, Dan R., Huffman, Brandie L., and Jasper, Danny M. 2014. Changing Race Boundary Perception by Reading Narrative Fiction. *Basic and Applied Social Psychology* 36: 83–90.

Johnson, Dan R., Jasper, Daniel M., Griffin, Sallie, and Huffman, Brandie L. 2013. Reading Narrative Fiction Reduces Arab-Muslim Prejudice and Offers a Safe Haven from Intergroup Anxiety. *Social Cognition* 31: 578–98.

Jorgensen-Earp, Cheryl R. 2013. *Discourse and Defiance under Nazi Occupation: Guernsey, Channel Islands, 1940–1945*. East Lansing: Michigan State University Press.

Kania, Andrew. 2009. Scene Tables. In A. Kania, ed., *Memento (Philosophers on Film)*, 13–22. Abingdon: Routledge.

Kant, Immanuel. 2001 [1790]. *Critique of the Power of Judgment*. Translated by P. Guyer and E. Matthews. Cambridge: Cambridge University Press.

———. 2007 [1781]. *Critique of Pure Reason*. Translated by N. K. Smith. Basingstoke: Palgrave Macmillan.

Kermode, Frank. 1989. Paul de Man's Abyss. *London Review of Books* 11 (16 March): 3–7. Available at: http://www.lrb.co.uk/v11/n06/frank-kermode/paul-de-mans-abyss#.

Kertzer, Jonathan. 2010. *Poetic Justice and Legal Fictions*. Cambridge: Cambridge University Press.

Kidd, David Comer, and Castano, Emanuele. 2013. Reading Literary Fiction Improves Theory of Mind. *Science* 342: 377–80.

———. 2016. Panero et al. (2016): Failure to Replicate Methods Caused the Failure to Replicate Results. *Journal of Personality and Social Psychology* 112: e1–e4.

Kleinman, Zoe. 2015. Do Video Games Make People Violent? *BBC News* (17 August). Available at: http://www.bbc.co.uk/news/technology-33960075.

Kueny, Kathryn M. 2014 [2013]. *Conceiving Identities: Maternity in Medieval Muslim Discourse and Practice*. New York: SUNY Press.

Lamarque, Peter. 2009. Poetry and Abstract Thought. *Midwest Studies in Philosophy* XXXIII: 37–52.

———. 2014. *The Opacity of Narrative*. London: Rowman & Littlefield International.

Legal Information Institute. No date. 18 U.S. Code § 2331—Definitions. Cornell Law School. Available at: https://www.law.cornell.edu/uscode/text/18/2331.

———. No date. 22 U.S. Code § 2656f—Annual Country Reports on Terrorism. Cornell Law School. Available at: https://www.law.cornell.edu/uscode/text/22/2656f.

Lehman, David. 1992 [1991]. *Signs of the Times: Deconstruction and the Fall of Paul de Man*. New York: Poseidon.

———. 1992. Paul de Man: The Plot Thickens. *New York Times* (24 May). Available at: http://www.nytimes.com/1992/05/24/books/paul-de-man-the-plot-thickens.html?pagewanted=all&src=pm.

Lemkin, Raphael. 1944. *Axis Rule in Occupied Europe: Laws of Occupation, Analysis of Government, Proposals for Redress*. Washington, DC: Carnegie Endowment for International Peace.

Lenz, Ryan. 2017. Twitter Begins Long-Awaited Crackdown on Hate Groups and Extremist Rhetoric. Southern Poverty Law Center *Hatewatch* (18 December). Available at: https://www.splcenter.org/hatewatch/2017/12/18/twitter-begins-long-awaited-crackdown-hate-groups-and-extremist-rhetoric.

Levinas, Emmanuel. 1985 [1982]. *Ethics and Infinity: Conversations with Philippe Nemo*. Translated by R. A. Cohen. Pittsburgh, PA: Duquesne University Press.

———. 2007 [1961]. *Totality and Infinity: An Essay on Exteriority*. Translated by A. Lingus. Pittsburgh, PA: Duquesne University Press.

Maan, Ajit. 2015. *Counter-Terrorism: Narrative Strategies*. Lanham, MD: University Press of America.

Maclean, French L. 1998. *The Cruel Hunters: SS-Sonderkommando Dirlewanger Hitler's Most Notorious Anti-Partisan Unit*. Atglen, PA: Schiffer Military History.

Macleod, Christopher. 2010. Towards a Philosophical Account of Crimes Against Humanity. *The European Journal of International Law* 21: 281–302.

Maher, Shiraz. 2016. *Salafi-Jihadism: The History of an Idea*. London: C. Hurst & Co.

Mar, Raymond. 2004. The Neuropsychology of Narrative: Story Comprehension, Story Production and Their Interrelation. *Neuropsychologia* 42: 1414–34.

Mar, Raymond A., Oatley, Keith, Hirsh, Jacob, dela Paz, Jennifer, and Peterson, Jordan B. 2006. Bookworms versus Nerds: Exposure to Fiction versus Non-Fiction, Divergent Associations with Social Ability, and the Simulation of Fictional Social Worlds. *Journal of Research in Personality* 40: 694–712.

Mason, Robert, and Just, Marcel Adam. 2006. Neuroimaging Contributions to the Understanding of Discourse Processes. In M. J. Traxler and M. A. Gernsbacher, eds., *Handbook of Psycholinguistics*, 765–79. Amsterdam: Elsevier.

Matravers, Derek. 2014. *Fiction and Narrative*. Oxford: Oxford University Press.

McClintock, Anne, and Nixon, Rob. 1986. No Names Apart: The Separation of Word and History in Derrida's "Le Dernier Mot du Racisme." *Critical Inquiry* 13: 140–54.

McGinn, Colin. 1997. *Ethics, Evil, and Fiction*. Oxford: Oxford University Press.

McGregor, Rafe. 2012. The Problem of Cinematic Imagination. *Contemporary Aesthetics* 10. Available at: http://www.contempaesthetics.org/newvolume/pages/article.php?articleID=629.

———. 2014. Cinematic Philosophy: Experiential Affirmation in *Memento*. *The Journal of Aesthetics and Art Criticism* 72: 57–66.

———. 2014. A Critique of the Value Interaction Debate. *British Journal of Aesthetics* 54: 449–66.

———. 2016. *The Value of Literature*. London: Rowman & Littlefield International.

———. @rafemcgregor. 12 August.

———. 2018. Blindness and Double Vision in *Richard III*: Zamir on Shakespeare on Moral Philosophy. In C. Bourne, and E. Caddick Bourne, eds., *The Routledge Companion to Shakespeare and Philosophy*. London: Routledge.

McIntyre, J. J., Teevan Jr., J. J., and Hartnagel, T. 1972. Television Violence and Deviant Behaviour. In G. A. Comstock and E. A. Rubinstein, eds., *Television and Social Behavior 3: Television and Adolescent Aggressiveness*, 383–435. Washington, DC: U.S. Government Printing Office.

Mellet, E., Bricogne, S., Crivello, F., Mazoyer, B., Denis, M., and Tzourio-Mazoyer, N. 2002. Neural Basis of Mental Scanning of a Topographic Representation Built from a Text. *Cerebral Cortex* 12: 1322–30.

Menand, Louis. 2014. The De Man Case: Does a Critic's Past Explain His Criticism? *The New Yorker* (24 March). Available at: http://www.newyorker.com/arts/critics/atlarge/2014/03/24/140324crat_atlarge_menand?currentPage=all.

Merrill, Robert. 1990. Kurt Vonnegut as a German-American. In P. Freese, ed., *Germany and German Thought in American Literature and Cultural Criticism*, 230–43. Essen: Blaue Eule.

Minor, W. William. 1975. Political Crime, Political Justice, and Political Prisoners. *Criminology* 12: 385–98.

Mischler, Elliot G. 1986. *Research Interviewing: Context and Narrative*. Cambridge, MA: Harvard University Press.

Morse, Donald E. 2003. *The Novels of Kurt Vonnegut: Imagining Being an American*. Westport, CT: Praeger.

New Century Foundation. 2018. Activist's Corner. *American Renaissance*. Available at: https://www.amren.com/about/activists.

Nussbaum, Martha. 1990. *Love's Knowledge: Essays on Philosophy and Literature*. New York: Oxford University Press

———. 1995. *Poetic Justice: The Literary Imagination and Public Life*. Boston: Beacon Press.

Oliver, Kelly. 2013. *Technologies of Life and Death: From Cloning to Capital Punishment*. New York: Fordham University Press.

Panero, Maria Eugenia, Weisberg, Deena Skolnick, Black, Jessica, Goldstein, Thalia R., Barnes, Jennifer L., Brownell, Hiram, and Winner, Ellen. 2016. Does Reading a Single Passage of Literary Fiction Really Improve Theory of Mind? An Attempt at Replication. *Journal of Personality and Social Psychology* 111: e46–e54.

———. 2017. No Support for the Claim That Literary Fiction Uniquely and Immediately Improves Theory of Mind: A Reply to Kidd and Castano's Commentary on Panero et al. 2016. *Journal of Personality and Social Psychology* 112: e5–e8.

Pauw, Jacques. 1992. *In the Heart of the Whore: The Story of Apartheid's Death Squads*. Johannesburg: Southern Book Publishers.

———. 2006. *Dances with Devils: A Journalist's Search for Truth*. Cape Town: Struik.

Pawlak, Patryk. 2015. Understanding Definitions of Terrorism. European Parliamentary Research Service, PE 571.320 (November). Available at: http://www.europarl.europa.eu/RegData/etudes/ATAG/2015/571320/EPRS_ATA%282015%29571320_EN.pdf.

Polkinghorne, Donald E. 1988. *Narrative Knowing and the Human Sciences*. Albany, NY: State University of New York Press.

Presser, Lois. 2009. The Narratives of Offenders. *Theoretical Criminology* 13 (2009): 177–200.

———. 2016. Criminology and the Narrative Turn. *Crime, Media, Culture: An International Journal* 12: 137–51.

Presser, Lois, and Sandberg, Sveinung. 2015. Introduction: What Is the Story? In L. Presser and S. Sandberg, eds., *Narrative Criminology: Understanding Stories of Crime*, 1–20. New York: New York University Press.

Rabaka, Reiland. 2016. *The Negritude Movement: W. E. B. Du Bois, Leon Damas, Aime Cesaire, Leopold Senghor, Frantz Fanon, and the Evolution of an Insurgent Idea*. Lanham, MD: Rowman & Littlefield.

Rafaty, Ryan. 2014. Who Will Educate the Educators? An Interview with Gayatri Spivak. *King's Review* (24 April). Available at: http://kingsreview.co.uk/articles/who-will-educate-the-educators-an-interview-with-gayatri-spivak/.

Rafter, Nicole. 2016. *The Crime of All Crimes: Toward a Criminology of Genocide*. New York: New York University Press.

Renzo, Massimo. 2012. Crimes against Humanity and the Limits of International Criminal Law. *Law and Philosophy* 31: 443–76.

Ribeiro, Anna Christina. 2009. Toward a Philosophy of Poetry. *Midwest Studies in Philosophy XXXIII*: 61–77.

Ricoeur, Paul. 1980. Narrative Time. *Critical Inquiry* 7: 169–90.

Riessman, Catherine Kohler. 2002. Analysis of Personal Narratives. In J. F. Gubrium and J. A. Holstein, eds., *Handbook of Interview Research: Context and Method*, 695–710. Thousand Oaks, CA: SAGE.

———. 2008. *Narrative Methods in the Human Sciences*. New York: SAGE.

Roof, Dylann. 2016. rtf88. *New York Times* (13 December). Available at: https://www.nytimes.com/interactive/2016/12/13/universal/document-Dylann-Roof-manifesto.html.

Rorty, Richard. 1978. Philosophy as a Kind of Writing: An Essay on Derrida. *New Literary History* 10: 141–60.

Rosenberg, Tina. 1997. A South African Killer Goes Free. *New York Times* (11 August). Available at: http://www.nytimes.com/1997/08/11/opinion/a-south-african-killer-goes-free.html.

Ross, Jeffrey Ian. 2014. Political Crime. In W. G. Jennings, ed., *The Encyclopedia of Crime and Punishment*, 983–89. Chichester: Wiley-Blackwell.

Ryle, Gilbert. 1971. The Thinking of Thoughts: What Is "Le Penseur" Doing? In *Volume II: Collected Essays 1929–1969*, 480–96. London: Hutchinson & Co.

Rymer, Tomas. 1678. *The Tragedies of the Last Age Consider'd and Examind by the Practice of the Ancients, and by the Common Sense of All Ages*. London: Richard

Tonson, University of Oxford Text Archive. Available at: http://tei.it.ox.ac.uk/tcp/Texts-HTML/free/A58/A58024.html.

Sandberg, Sveinung, and Ugelvik, Thomas. 2016. The Past, Present, and Future of Narrative Criminology: A Review and an Invitation. *Crime, Media, Culture: An International Journal* 12: 129–36.

Sarbin, Theodore R. 1986. *Narrative Psychology: The Storied Nature of Human Conduct.* New York: Praeger.

Schellekens, Elisabeth. 2007. *Aesthetics and Morality.* London: Continuum.

Schiller, Friedrich. 1967 [1794]. *On the Aesthetic Education of Man: In a Series of Letters.* Translated by E. M. Wilkinson and L. A. Willoughby. London: Oxford University Press.

Schmid, Alex P. 2014. Al-Qaeda's "Single Narrative" and Attempts to Develop Counter-Narratives: The State of Knowledge. *ICCT Research Paper*, International Centre for Counter-Terrorism—The Hague (January): 1–38. Available at: https://www.icct.nl/download/file/Schmid-Al-Qaeda%27s-Single-Narrative-and-Attempts-to-Develop-Counter-Narratives-January-2014.pdf.

Semeria, Gustavo. 2017. Argentina: A Mirror of Your Future: How Demographic Change Can Destroy a Country. *American Renaissance* (14 April). Available at: https://www.amren.com/features/2017/04/argentina-a-mirror-of-your-future-buenos-aires-latin-america/.

Shaftesbury, Third Earl of (Anthony Ashley-Cooper). 2001 [1714]. *Characteristicks of Men, Manners, Opinions, Times, Volume I.* Indianapolis, IN: Liberty Fund.

———. 2001 [1714]. *Characteristicks of Men, Manners, Opinions, Times, Volume II.* Indianapolis, IN: Liberty Fund.

———. 2001 [1714]. *Characteristicks of Men, Manners, Opinions, Times, Volume III.* Indianapolis, IN: Liberty Fund.

Shaheen, Kareem. 2016. Turkish-Backed Syrian Rebels Recapture Town of Dabiq from ISIS. *The Guardian* (16 October). Available at: https://www.theguardian.com/world/2016/oct/16/turkish-opposition-fighters-syria-dabiq-islamic-state.

Shakespeare, William. 2001 [1604]. *Hamlet.* London: Penguin.

———. 2005 [1592–1593]. *Richard III.* London: Penguin.

Smith, David. 2015. South African Death Squad Leader Eugene de Kock to Be Freed from Jail. *The Guardian* (January 30). Available at: http://www.theguardian.com/world/2015/jan/30/south-africa-eugene-de-kock-released-prime-evil.

Southern Poverty Law Center. No date. David Lane. Available at: https://www.splcenter.org/fighting-hate/extremist-files/individual/david-lane.

———. No date. *American Renaissance.* Available at: https://www.splcenter.org/fighting-hate/extremist-files/group/american-renaissance.

Spaaij, Ramón. 2010. The Enigma of Lone Wolf Terrorism: An Assessment. *Studies in Conflict and Terrorism* 33: 854–70.

Spivak, Gayatri Chakravorty. 1988. Can the Subaltern Speak? In C. Nelson and L. Grossberg, eds., *Marxism and the Interpretation of Culture*, 271–313. Urbana: University of Illinois.

———. 1993. *Outside in the Teaching Machine.* New York: Routledge.

———. 1999. *A Critique of Postcolonial Reason: Toward a History of the Vanishing Present*. Cambridge, MA: Harvard University Press.

———. 2003. *Death of a Discipline*. New York: Colombia University Press.

———. 2010. *Nationalism and the Imagination*. Chicago: Chicago University Press.

———. 2013 [2012]. *An Aesthetic Education in the Era of Globalization*. Cambridge, MA: Harvard University Press.

Squire, Corinne, Andrews, Molly, and Tamboukou, Maria. 2013. Introduction: What Is Narrative Research? In M. Andrews, C. Squire, and M. Tamboukou, eds., *Doing Narrative Research*, 2nd ed., 1–26. London: SAGE.

Staffell, Simon, and Awan, Akil. Introduction. In S. Staffell and A. Awan, eds., *Jihadism Transformed: Al-Qaeda and Islamic State's Global Battle of Ideas*, 1–20. London: C. Hurst & Co.

Tauber, Zvi. 2006. Aesthetic Education for Morality: Schiller and Kant. *The Journal of Aesthetic Education* 40: 22–47.

Taylor, Matthew. 2011. Breivik Sent "Manifesto" to 250 UK Contacts Hours before Norway Killings. *The Guardian* (26 July). Available at: https://www.theguardian.com/world/2011/jul/26/breivik-manifesto-email-uk-contacts.

Thomson-Jones, Katherine. 2005. Inseparable Insight: Reconciling Cognitivism and Formalism in Aesthetics. *The Journal of Aesthetics and Art Criticism* 63: 375–84.

Todorov, Tzvetan. 1977. *The Poetics of Prose*. Translated by R. Howard. Oxford: Blackwell.

Tunnell, Kenneth D. 1993. Political Crime and Pedagogy: A Content Analysis of Criminology and Criminal Justice Texts. *Journal of Criminal Justice Education* 4: 101–14.

Turner, Barry. 2010. *Outpost of Occupation: How the Channel Islands Survived Nazi Rule 1940–45*. London: Aurum.

Twitter Safety. 2017. Enforcing New Rules to Reduce Hateful Conduct and Abusive Behavior. *Twitter Blog* (18 December). Available at: https://blog.twitter.com/official/en_us/topics/company/2017/safetypoliciesdec2017.html.

United Kingdom. 2000. Terrorism Act 2000. Available at: http://www.legislation.gov.uk/ukpga/2000/11/schedule/7.

United Nations. 1948. General Assembly Resolution 260 (9 December). Available at: http://www.ohchr.org/EN/ProfessionalInterest/Pages/CrimeOfGenocide.aspx.

———. 1996. Ad Hoc Committee established by General Assembly resolution 51/210 of 17 December 1996. Last modified 16 February 2017. Available at: http://legal.un.org/committees/terrorism/.

———. 2015. Security Council "Unequivocally" Condemns ISIL Terrorist Attacks, Unanimously Adopting Text That Determines Extremist Group Poses "Unprecedented" Threat. *Meetings Coverage and Press Releases* (20 November). Available at: https://www.un.org/press/en/2015/sc12132.doc.htm.

Van Wilgenburg, Wladimir. 2015. Analysis: Can Syrian Kurds Maintain Momentum after IS Defeat in Tal Abyad? *Middle East Eye* (15 June). Available at: http://www.middleeasteye.net/news/analysis-can-syrian-kurds-maintain-momentum-after-defeat-tal-abyad-345059446.

Van Zanten Gallagher, Susan. 1988. Torture and the Novel: J. M. Coetzee's *Waiting for the Barbarians*. *Contemporary Literature* 29: 277–85.

Vickery, John B. 1973. *The Literary Impact of "The Golden Bough."* Princeton, NJ: Princeton University Press.

Vonnegut Jr., Kurt. 1979 [1961]. *Mother Night*. St. Albans: Triad/Panther.

Walsh, Dorothy. 1969. *Literature and Knowledge*. Middletown, CT: Wesleyan University Press.

Weale, Adrian. 1994. *Renegades: Hitler's Englishmen*. London: Weidenfeld & Nicolson.

White GeNOcide Project. 2017. About White Genocide. Accessed 22 December 2017. Available at: http://whitegenocideproject.com/about-white-genocide/.

———. 2017. Terminology & Education. Accessed 22 December 2017. Available at: http://whitegenocideproject.com/terminology/.

White, Hayden. 1980. The Value of Narrativity in the Representation of Reality. *Critical Inquiry* 7: 5–27.

———. 1987. The Problem of Style in Realistic Representation: Marx and Flaubert. In B. Lang, ed., *The Concept of Style*, 279–98. Ithaca, NY: Cornell University Press.

Wilson, Catherine. 1983. Literature and Knowledge. *Philosophy* 58: 489–96.

Winter, Charlie. 2018. Apocalypse, Later: A Longitudinal Study of the Islamic State Brand. *Critical Studies in Media Communication* 35: 103–21.

Winter, Gordon. 1981. *Inside BOSS: South Africa's Secret Police*. Harmondsworth: Penguin.

Withnall, Adam. 2014. Iraq Crisis: ISIS Declares Its Territories a New Islamic State with "Restoration of Caliphate" in Middle East. *The Independent* (30 June). Available at: http://www.independent.co.uk/news/world/middle-east/isis-declares-new-islamic-state-in-middle-east-with-abu-bakr-al-baghdadi-as-emir-removing-iraq-and-9571374.html.

Worth, Sarah E. 2017. *In Defense of Reading*. London: Rowman & Littlefield International.

Xu, Jiang, Kemeny, Stefan, Park, Grace, Frattali, Carol, and Braun, Allen. 2005. Language in Context: Emergent Features of World, Sentence and Narrative Comprehension. *Neuroimage* 25: 1002–15.

Young, Jock. 2011. *The Criminological Imagination*. Cambridge: Polity Press.

Zamir, Tzachi. 2007. *Double Vision: Moral Philosophy and Shakespearean Drama*. Princeton, NJ: Princeton University Press.

Zwaan, Rolf. 1994. Effect of Genre Expectations on Text Comprehension. *Journal of Experimental Psychology: Learning, Memory, and Cognition* 20: 920–33.

Index

About the Author

Rafe McGregor is senior lecturer in criminology at Edge Hill University. He specialises in narrative representation, crimes against humanity, and terrorism. He is the author of *The Value of Literature*, two novels, and more than 250 journal articles, review essays, and short stories. He can be found online at @rafemcgregor.

Lightning Source UK Ltd.
Milton Keynes UK
UKHW040622301218
334646UK00001B/61/P